Salsa and Its Transnational Moves

Salsa and Its Transnational Moves

Sheenagh Pietrobruno

LEXINGTON BOOKS

A division of
ROWMAN & LITTLEFIELD PUBLISHERS, INC.
Lanham • Boulder • New York • Toronto • Oxford

LEXINGTON BOOKS

A division of Rowman & Littlefield Publishers, Inc.
A wholly owned subsidiary of The Rowman & Littlefield Publishing Group, Inc.
4501 Forbes Boulevard, Suite 200
Lanham, MD 20706

PO Box 317
Oxford
OX2 9RU, UK

British Library Cataloguing in Publication Information Available

Library of Congress Cataloging-in-Publication Data

Pietrobruno, Sheenagh, date.
  Salsa and its transnational moves / Sheenagh Pietrobruno.
    p. cm.
  Includes bibliographical references.
  ISBN-13: 978-0-7391-1053-5 (cloth : alk. paper)
  ISBN-10: 0-7391-1053-5 (cloth : alk. paper)
  ISBN-13: 978-0-7391-1468-1 (pbk. : alk. paper)
  ISBN-10: 0-7391-1468-9 (pbk. : alk. paper)
  1. Salsa (Dance)—Social aspects—Québec (Province)—Montréal. 2. Salsa (Dance)—
Cross-cultural studies—Québec (Province)—Montréal. I. Title.
GV1796.S245P54 2006
793.33—dc22   2005028209

Printed in the United States of America

♾™ The paper used in this publication meets the minimum requirements of
American National Standard for Information Sciences—Permanence of Paper for
Printed Library Materials, ANSI/NISO Z39.48-1992.

For my family

Contents

Acknowledgments

I am very grateful to many people for their contributions and advice during the writing of this book. First, I would like to thank all the interviewees and informants who gave their time to speak to me of their involvement in the Montreal salsa scene. I would like specifically to acknowledge dancers Maria Ordonez and Charles Kanzi for imparting to me their vision of salsa. I also greatly appreciate the comments and feedback that I received from dance scholars whom I met during my attendance at annual conferences of the Congress on Research in Dance. In particular, my thanks go to Joan Burroughs, Julie Malnig, and Iro Valaskakis Tembeck.

I want to express my gratitude to my dissertation supervisor, Will Straw, at McGill University: many of the ideas in this book were first developed there. Furthermore, I would also like to thank Will Straw for providing comments on drafts of various chapters in this book. I would like to acknowledge my gratitude to Helen Thomas, with whom I worked as a postdoctoral researcher at Goldsmiths College, University of London: various of the book's key ideas were further developed through this research. I am also very grateful to the following people for their encouragement and support: Brigido Galvan, Jocelyn Guilbault, Sheryl Hamilton, Jeder Janotti, Keir Keightley, Brian Massumi, Andra McCartney, Grant McCracken, and Norman Urquía.

An earlier version of the book's conclusion was presented at a symposium at Goldsmiths College sponsored by the Centre on the Body and Performance. Chapter 3 is a revised version of an article previously published in the journal *Revista mexicana de estudios canadienses*. I would like to thank the

Asocacíon Mexicana de Estudios Sobre Canada as well as Graciela Martínez-Zalce for permitting a version of this article to be included here.

I am indebted to acquisitions editors Rob Carley and Katie Funk at Rowman and Littlefield for their faith in this project. I would further like to acknowledge my production editor, Lea Gift. I am also grateful to Robert Lewis for copyediting and to Sarah McKee for proofreading. Thanks are due to my friends in Montreal, Vancouver, and London, UK, as well as my students at the Institut de recherche Robert-Sauvé en anté et sècurité du travail in Montreal for their invaluable support during the writing of this book.

Lastly, I would like to express my deep gratitude to my parents, especially for introducing me to dance so many years ago, as well as to my sisters, Anna and Ileana, for being my first dance partners.

Introduction
Toward the Global

global (ization)

Salsa embodies regional and national crossings. Its history was forged as the roots of contemporary salsa migrated from Cuba to numerous sites in the Americas during the twentieth century. Various people from within Latin America as well as America itself, such as Cubans, Puerto Ricans, Venezuelans, Panamanians, Colombians, and New Yorkers, consequently claim salsa as part of their cultural heritage. This diversity of "origins" is not unanimously embraced by aficionados, musicians, dancers, and theorists but has led to continuous debates in both scholarly and popular contexts[1] concerning its rightful "owner." From its development in parts of the Caribbean and Latin America as well as in New York, this expressive art of the Americas has spread throughout the world since the 1980s.

Salsa dance and music become part of the cultural landscapes of cities primarily through migration and mediated technology. Places, according to Anthony Giddens, are becoming increasingly "phantasmagoric" as they are permeated and forged by social and cultural factors that have been transplanted into local environments rather than developed organically within them. Locations blur the real and imagined by rendering familiar that which has come from afar (Giddens, 1990: 18, 140). Salsa enters Western urban spaces in various ways: the migration of people from certain nations in Latin America and the Caribbean; the rising travel to Latin countries by Westerners, often leading to their concomitant seeking and supporting Latin cultural forms in their home nations and cities; and the temporary visits of foreign students from

I love it

1

cities and nations where salsa is heritage. Salsa music and dance can be further accessed through Latin music videos distributed on cable television networks. Community, university, and commercial radio stations often disseminate salsa through select programming. The circulation of salsa products, namely CDs and videos, provides further access to those outside key salsa centers. Since the late 1990s, the Internet has increasingly served as a means to distribute information, knowledge, and products related to salsa music and dance (see conclusion).

Even though this rising global distribution disconnects salsa from its ties to specific geographic locations, this dance and music remain anchored to cultural identity. In contemporary contexts, salsa dance can become an expression of an individual's cultural heritage in various salsa centers in the Americas, such as New York, Cali, Caracas, or Havana, as well as beyond these key sites. Latin culture can be found dispersed throughout cities in North America where people of Latin descent have migrated: as people move from pivotal centers, salsa travels to new locations through the bodies, minds, and memories of its dancers. This dance and music complex can become an expression of cultural heritage for a given individual not necessarily as a result of her or his geographic location or national identity but rather through how the dance is acquired and maintained. ⟵ Nice.

Salsa shares a key characteristic of folk dance: folk cultures thrive and transform through collective artistry. Robert Farris Thompson's elegant description of "folk" dance as "art without artists, moves without masters" (Thompson, 2002: 342) captures the essence of this tradition. The development of the *casino*, the Cuban version of salsa, for instance, has been anonymous (Balbuena, 2003: 43); individual dancers are not credited with the creation of an art form arising from the performances of unacknowledged dancers in lived circumstances. Dances deemed part of "high" art, such as ballet, evolve through the artistic work of individual chorographers and dancers (Thompson, 2002: 342).[2] When a dance such as salsa is part of an individual's heritage, it is typically learned without formal instruction within lived contexts such as family or community settings. The salsa that is danced in families and by communities is intergenerational and therefore performed equally by children and adults.

Today, salsa is an urban genre that has developed from both folk and elite dances (see chapter 1). Folk dance is typically defined as a rustic traditional genre. Being a transnational urban dance performed in numerous cities, salsa is not a rural practice linked to a single tradition. In contemporary cultural studies discourse, salsa is more commonly described as a popular dance. The use of the term "popular" varies. "Popular" could be understood in a general way as "widely liked." It could also denote that which is not part of the middle or upper classes (Chasteen, 2004: xi). Once denigrated for its low-class origins, salsa has been incorporated into the lifestyles of the middle classes in both Latin America and beyond since the 1980s. Salsa is a popular genre through its historical connection to the working classes, yet this link does not entirely reflect its current worldwide class affiliations. My use of the term "popular dance" to describe salsa refers instead to an art form that thrives and evolves through collective practices within the context of lived circumstances. Generally, a popular dance is not performed on stage but takes place in lived dance events. An absolute division between performance and popular genres cannot, of course, be firmly established. Contemporary salsa, for instance, becomes a theatrical performance in club dance competitions. Furthermore, popular dancers often incorporate moves that they have observed on stage or in films into their everyday dancing.

The global commercialization of salsa promotes this dance as a highly sexualized and youthful adult pastime enjoyed primarily by heterosexual couples in the nighttime economy of clubs and music venues. Sexuality sells salsa and draws people to clubs and dance lessons dispersed throughout the world. Images of salsa highlight its currency as a titillating spectacle, overshadowing the artistic, cultural, political, or historical value that it may embody for certain people of Latin descent who regard it as heritage. Dance has often been a marker of identity for Latin Americans and people of the Caribbean. Ramiro Guerra, the Cuban choreographer and dance scholar elucidates, for instance, how performing dances in organizations called *cabildos* in Cuba, *candombes* in Argentina and Uruguay, and *confrarías* (*cofradías*) in Brazil became a means for people of African descent in the Americas to preserve and communicate their heritage amid the threat of cultural annihilation from the onslaught of slavery (Guerra, 1993: 93). The potency of dance to impart cultural tradition continues within contemporary realities of diaspora: according to Lisa Sánchez González, dancing to salsa music has been a way for Puerto Ricans living in the United States to maintain their culture and identity (Sánchez González, 1999: 244–45).

Research has stressed the expressive role of dance in relation to cultural groups (Aschenbrenner, 1981; McRobbie, 1984; Hazzard-Gordon, 1985; Desmond, 1993–1994; Cowan, 1990). This book extends an understanding of popular dance as an embodiment of a given culture, group, or people into an analysis of the commodification and commercialization of movement. A key concern of this work is therefore the tension between the status of dance as a bodily expression of identity and its function as a cultural commodity within the economic life of modern-day cities. Unlike music, which can be recorded and commercially distributed in the form of a CD, dance is less easily transformed into a product. Nonetheless, the refashioning of popular dance forms from a cultural practice into a selection of moves "bought" and "sold" as dance lessons transforms this cultural heritage into a commodity.

The impact of commodification on lived cultural expression offers a specific understanding of dance amid the myriad ways that this corporeal practice has been conceptualized. Interpretations of dance vary: it is viewed as a nonverbal form of communication (Hanna, 1979a), a kind of language (Hanna, 1987: 228; Williams, 1978; Kaeppler, 1978: 48), a form of socialization (Spencer, 1985: 8–11), a sexual expression (Hanna, 1988; McRobbie, 1984; Gotfrit, 1991), an art form (Thomas, 1995), a means of political resistance (Browning, 1995; Hazzard-Gordon, 1985; Aschenbrenner, 1981), an escape from everyday routine (Spencer, 1985: 28; McRobbie, 1984), and an expression of inner emotions (Brinson, 1985). Researchers from a variety of disciplinary vantage points and historical times have often come up with similar interpretations of the nature of dance. For example, Herbert Spencer's nineteenth-century anthropological observation that dance serves to release pent up emotions (Spencer, 1985: 4) is echoed in contemporary analyses of club dancing. The documentary *Check Your Body at the Door*, directed and produced by dance historian Sally Sommer, portrays various fast-moving New York club dance styles and reveals how dance provides a vehicle for emotive expression by facilitating the experience of emotional highs (Sommer, 1996).

From both historical and contemporary perspectives, very little work has been conducted on the commodification of Latin and Caribbean dance through instruction. A rare instance can be found in *Los bailes y el teatro de los negros en el folklore de Cuba*, in which Fernando Ortiz mentions the effects of the "dance teacher" on dances in Cuba and other areas of the Caribbean. According to Ortiz, dances from Havana and various regions in the Caribbean were becoming deformed and marred as they were being taught to tourists in academies on the islands and in the United States. Teachers, for instance, were popularizing Cuban forms within the United States, such as the conga and the rumba. Instruction was destroying Caribbean dance since this heritage must be altered in accordance with the movement culture of the clients. He writes, "But so as the musicians in the North 'adjust' African-derived dance music to the taste of their consumers, so in the schools, the exotic dances are adulterated to easily fit into the dance routines of their clients" (Ortiz, 1951: 258, my translation).[3] Ortiz's observations illustrate how formal instruction as a means to commercialize Caribbean dance is not a new phenomenon of contemporary entertainment industries of the late twentieth and early twenty-first centuries. Instead, the practice of "selling" Cuban dances in the form of dance lessons to Western audiences dates back to the early decades of the twentieth century.

The teaching of European dance, according to John Charles Chasteen, has a long history in Latin America. One of the earliest known instructors from Europe was a Spaniard called "Ortiz the Musician" who taught dance in Mexico City as early as 1519 (Chasteen, 2004: 117). During the colonial period, dance masters taught international elite styles from Europe, such as the minuet, the *contredanse*, the waltz, and the polka, in urban centers in Latin America. While initially providing lessons only to the rich in their homes, masters in nineteenth-century Havana also began to give studio classes to those who were not able to afford private lessons (117–18). Affluent whites were not the only ones who performed European dances: black people of means who could afford to emulate upper-class dance fashions performed styles from Europe. Chasteen notes the example of a formal ball among affluent black people in the 1840s in which dancers performed quadrilles and waltzes while paying serious attention to European formality and etiquette (131). Moreover, in Havana during the 1800s the majority of the city's dance masters were of African descent (118).

The black dances of Cuba, maintained and preserved in the neo-African nations or in *cabildos* representing distinct ethnic groups, were rarely performed by whites. Instead, whites observed these dances only at public events featuring the dancing of African nations, such as the black Day of Kings celebration, which was abolished with the end of slavery in 1887 (Chasteen, 2004: 108, 112). Whites learned the African body movements, which were perpetuated by the dance practices of the neo-African nations, only after African-derived corporeal moves seeped into the choreographic structure of European social dances. This process created dance forms such as the *danzón* of the late 1800s, an ancestor of contemporary salsa (112). Descendants of the *danzón*, such as the twentieth-century son and mambo, are regarded as a part of Cuban dance culture that blends European and African forms. These two popular forms, also precursors of salsa, enjoyed crazes in North America: the son in the 1920s and the mambo in the 1950s. In versions that differed from their "original" Cuban renditions, the mambo and the son have been incorporated into the formal instruction of the British- and American-derived ballroom dance tradition (Buckman, 1978: 199–200) (see chapter 3).

Formal instruction of popular dance commodifies practices that once "originated" in lived contexts. Nonetheless, referring to dance as a commodity seems problematic. Dance differs from other popular cultural practices, such as reading romance novels or comic books, watching soap operas or blockbuster

[handwritten margin note at top: "for me so does listening to music etc – I see her point, but I'm not totally convinced!!"]

movies, and listening to music or buying CDs, since it requires that participants reproduce the cultural "artifact" through active engagement. Fernando Ortiz intimates as much when he alludes to how the actual dance culture that the foreign consumer brings to the context of Cuban dance instruction transforms the very performance of the Caribbean culture that is being "consumed" (Ortiz, 1951: 258). If the dancer is the one producing the cultural commodity that she or he is "buying" in the form of dance lessons, does it make sense then to refer to dance instruction as a commodity?

[handwritten margin note: "Good Q"]

This focus on cultural commodities draws from the "culture-of-production" approach within social analysis, which deals with the interlocking institutions and practices involved in the production, consumption, and distribution of cultural products (Aggar, 1992: 13). The culture-of-production analysis ultimately deals with the production of objects that are distributed by cultural industries, not really with culture as such (Mukerji and Schudson, 1991a: 33). Since popular dance does not readily translate into a cultural object, it cannot be easily taken up within this mode of theorizing. Chandra Mukerji and Michael Schudson define cultural products as "'nonmaterial' goods directed at a public of consumers, for whom they generally serve an aesthetic or expressive, rather than clearly utilitarian function" (Mukerji and Schudson, 1991b: 215). Dance could, perhaps, fit into their definition—particularly regarding the nonutilitarian aspect of a cultural product—if it were not for their notion of the cultural industry, which is an integral part of their understanding of cultural products. As they say, "The term 'cultural organization' refers here only to profit-seeking firms producing cultural products for national distribution" (315). Bernard Miège describes three types of cultural commodities: reproducible products that do not require culture workers in their production, such as visual and recording equipment; reproducible products that do require these workers, such as books, records, and videos; and semi-reproducible products, such as "craft work, certain types of performance, audiovisual productions for training or information distribution purposes and art prints" (Miège, 1989: 26).

[handwritten margin note: "?"]

Miège's characterization of a cultural commodity as a semi-reproducible product offers tools for theorizing dance within the culture-of-production method. Dance is a semi-reproducible product in the sense that this practice is a type of performance. Yet popular dance is not a traditional performance, in which there is clear division between the spectators and the performers. Dance is both a "spectacle" in which dancing bodies are "read" as signs and an intersubjective process that enables dance to function as a site of experience for the dancers (Cowan, 1990: 24). People can be both active and passive participants in a dance event. Dancing in a particular setting, such as a club, they can participate by observing the dances of others or by dancing

[handwritten margin note: "nice theory"]

themselves, which in turn transforms their bodies into a spectacle subject to the gazes of dancers and onlookers.

Dance requires the active involvement of the bodies and minds of individuals and groups within a lived context. Thus it cannot be frozen into a cultural commodity that can be easily distributed and consumed. Nevertheless, dance does influence the distribution and consumption of records, music videos, performances, and concerts. Research on dance and musical practices needs to include elements of the culture-of-production in order to capture how people experience and practice dance within contemporary urban life. The globalization of culture and migration patterns has altered urban local dance and music scenes to such an extent that it has become difficult to speak of any cultural practice as indigenous to a particular city (Straw, 1991: 370). Knowledge of dance and music is often perpetuated through the circulation and distribution of cultural commodities at the local and international levels. The distribution of dance through the "dance lesson" most notably transforms dance into a cultural commodity. Nonetheless, since the dancer must corporeally reproduce the "object" that she or he is either buying or selling through commercial dance instruction, the human body is not separate from the object being consumed or produced. This elaboration of how a practice as intangible as dance can become commodified reinterprets the meaning of the commodity itself. As Marx postulated in his early writings, the commodity as the object of labour is external to the body of the worker in the capitalist economy and exists outside of himself, alien and independent of his being (Marx, 1844: 78). The "labour" of both the producer of the dance (the instructor) and the consumer (the client/customer/student) corporeally creates and reproduces the "commodity" that is being sold and bought. (Comprising creativity, artistry, and pleasure, the work involved in the commodification of salsa stands in contrast to the Marxian vision of labour as alienated toil, yet for many working in dance industries, teaching salsa is still a means of earning a living.)

Salsa moves become "products" distributed and consumed in the dance instruction offered at studios, clubs, and cultural institutions in cities throughout the world. Casting popular dance as a commodity is surprising for two reasons. In its very essence, movement is an elusive expression that cannot be bound within the parameters of a concrete product. A dance, such as salsa, that has developed in a lived context remains anchored to a cultural heritage and therefore cannot be totally appropriated or seamlessly imitated, steps that are necessary to transform it into a marketable commodity. Salsa dancing slips between two opposing spheres: it is simultaneously a "product" that is bought and sold and a practice that escapes commodification.

The transformation of dances, thriving as part of lived communal cultural life, into a set of movements and patterns "bought" and "sold" in the form of dance lessons could be viewed as displacements to modernity from the realm of the traditional. Modernity is in fact a highly general concept that relates to a broad range of economic, social, and political phenomena (Therborn, 1995: 126). Its generality emerges in Anthony Giddens's definition of the term, which he describes as "modes of social life or organisation which emerged in Europe from about the seventeenth century onwards and which subsequently became more or less worldwide in their influence" (Giddens, 1990: 1). With modernity, key institutions emerged: capitalism, industrialism, urbanism, the nation-state, and mass communication (Tomlinson, 1999: 33). Roland Robertson notes that the idea of modernity often implies a general uniformity of institutions as well as central temporal and historical conditions. Nonetheless, there is an emerging acknowledgement that modernity has evolved differently in particular areas (Robertson, 1995: 27). Göran Therborn locates three regions outside of Europe where modernity developed relatively separately (Therborn, 1995: 133). Modernity emerged in the New Worlds, for instance, as a result of the genocide of the indigenous peoples and transcontinental migration (132).

The transmutation of lived popular dance into a commodity moves practices initially embedded within communal life into the realm of capitalism. The advent of capitalism has played a key role in the dislocation of social and cultural life from the traditional sphere. According to Giddens, capitalism is fundamentally extremely mobile because of the interconnection that is set up between the competitive economic enterprise and the widespread mechanisms of commodification. The capitalist economy from both within and outside the nation-state is essentially volatile and unsettled. All economic reproduction in capitalism is, in the Marxian understanding, "expanded reproduction" because the economic order is unable to stay in a basic stable equilibrium, which had been the situation of most traditional systems (Giddens, 1990: 61).

Nonetheless, we must be careful about drawing too stark distinctions between the modern and the traditional. Within contemporary social and cultural contexts, the traditional is often interlaced with the modern. The continuities between these two spheres lead Giddens to conclude that it is questionable whether broad divisions between the modern and the traditional can be firmly established (Giddens, 1991: 4). Many have argued that the traditional and modern are so interconnected that it is not possible to provide general attributes that distinguish between these two conditions (Giddens, 1990: 36). James Clifford, for instance, claims that modernity, from its earliest moments, actually created the traditional as a concept in order to provide a point of contrast with itself (Clifford, 1988).

However, Giddens does provide an understanding of the traditional that distinguishes it from modernity. Tradition is engaged with maintenance of the past (Giddens, 1994: 62). In traditional cultures, the past is valued and symbols and practices are revered because they convey the experiences of previous generations. Traditions deal with the time-space organization of the community, which configures practices and experiences within the continuity of past, present, and future (Giddens, 1991: 37). The realm of tradition is also grounded in specific sites of origin or key central locations (Giddens, 1994: 80). Not completely unchanging, it has to be reinvented by the new generations that inherit it. Traditional societies do not defy change as such but rather produce a context in which time-space differentiation is so minimal that change is prevented from assuming a meaningful form (Giddens, 1991: 37). The dynamism of modernity is a result of the separation of time and space produced by modern institutions (16).

As understood by Giddens, the character of reflexivity within modernity influences the role that tradition plays in modern circumstances. Reflexivity produces a situation in which thought and action are continuously refracted back upon the other, each in constant interrelation (Giddens, 1991: 38). Traditions are maintained in modern societies not because of an allegiance to the past but if they can be defended in accordance with the knowledge of the time (38). In referring to the existence of tradition in modernity, Giddens states, "For justified tradition is tradition in sham clothing and receives its identity only from the reflexivity of the modern" (38). The traditional is not a specific set of beliefs and practices but refers to the organization of beliefs and practices within relations of time. In contrast to the modern perspective, the "past" and the "future" are not separate entities that stand distinct from the "continuous present" in the traditional sphere (Giddens, 1990: 105). Modernity in fact envisions the present as the beginning of the future rather than as an embodiment of the past. With modernity, the future is discovered as a realm to strive for and construct (Therborn, 1995: 126). The traditional's inseparability of the past and the future from the present suggests that it exhibits a sense of timelessness. At the same time, Giddens points out that traditions are not inherently static. He writes, "Traditions have an organic character: they develop and mature, or weaken and 'die'" (Giddens, 1994: 62–63).

Even though traditions do change, there lies an assumption within the notion of tradition itself that traditional beliefs or practices will resist change (Giddens, 1994: 62). In a discussion of the analogy between vernacular and tradition in contemporary contexts, Gwendolyn Wright argues that both the vernacular and traditional have been erroneously perceived as evocations of a timelessness that are beyond social strife and commercialization (Wright, 1998: 475). A vernacular, the indigenous language of a specific people or nation, is a local oral dialect used to speak about the concrete concerns of daily life. The domain of the vernacular is the street and home (477). Dances that stem from the lived culture of a people are also referred to as vernacular. Katrina Hazzard-Gordon, for instance, refers to the communal dances of African Americans developed in relative isolation from white society as "Afro-American vernacular" (Hazzard-Gordon, 1985: 428). Since the eighteenth century, Western culture has identified the traditional or the vernacular within two seemingly immutable spaces located outside the modern city: the European and North American folk culture and the "exotic" cultures, peoples, and lands that were being colonized. Implicit in the timelessness of the traditional is its primitive quality (Wright, 1998: 475).

The traditional dances of non-Western peoples have been regarded as primitive. Western scholars have often characterized the dances of specific groups outside of the European-based cultures as monolithic wholes, such as the "African dance" and the "American Indian dance" (Kealiinohomoku, 1983: 535). Terms such as "untechnical, without artistry, disorganized and frenzied, orgiastic, natural, timeless, unfettered, instinctive, ecstatic and underdeveloped" project the primitive stereotype onto these dances (535). Reacting to how theorists have depicted the dances of "exotic" "primitive" peoples, Joann Kealiinohomoku states that she cannot identify the dance practices of one group that would fit their description. Using her actual field research on the Hopi, she describes how their dances have changed over time, are choreographed, and do not bring about states of ecstasy or exaltation (538–39). Kealiinohomoku's work illustrates how concluding that traditional cultures are timeless and unchanging may be misleading.

The claim that formal instruction transposes dance from the traditional to the modern establishes these two conditions as distinct. Nonetheless, it has been shown that possible misconceptions concerning the traditional, notably its timeless quality, may be made in order to perhaps artificially distinguish it from the modern. Despite the pitfalls inherent in setting up a distinction between modernity and the traditional, I would like to hold on to the idea that the dance lesson moves popular lived Latin dance into the realm of commercialization and hence modernity. It is in this very narrowly defined perspective that I situate this displacement from the traditional to the modern in popular dance practices. In contemporary contexts, both the modern and the traditional can coexist. For instance, certain people of Latin descent for whom salsa is part of their heritage may, upon migration, cultivate a salsa dance culture within their host city or nation. This culture becomes an expression of a past cultural affiliation dislodged from its fixed site of "origin." When sustained through communal and family life within the new host city or nation, salsa dance becomes a kind of traditional culture maintained within circumstances of diaspora. Nonetheless, dancing to salsa becomes tradition within the context of modernity: how salsa is accessed within community settings in host nations or cities is not only based on memories of past communal experiences, but also accessed through commodification and the media. Salsa dance and music, for instance, reach communities beyond their "indigenous" locations through the dissemination of Latin music videos on cable television, through the commercial distribution of music recordings, and through radio and television broadcasting. At the same time, the dance culture that develops and thrives within communal and family settings in salsa centers may also have been influenced by commerce and media. Mediated and commercial processes disrupt the link of traditional cultures to community, memory, and origin. In illustrating how cultures and traditions were no longer continuous in the twentieth century, James Clifford writes, "Everywhere individuals and groups improvise local performances from (re)collected pasts, drawing on foreign media, symbols and languages" (Clifford, 1988: 14). √ · true.

Alterity emerged as a consequence of modernity (Friedman, 1994: 241). According to Jonathan Friedman, identity had previously been comprehended as holistic, the subject being included in the larger field of structural forces that constituted selfhood. With modernity, the subject is severed from larger structures. This separation occurred in Europe in the eighteenth century with the breakdown of European aristocratic hierarchies (240). In anthropological inquiries from the 1960s, prior to the practice approach of the 1980s (Cowan, 1990), dances of non-Western peoples had been largely analyzed as a premodern practice in the sense that they contributed to a holistic conception of society. The work of anthropologist Joann Kealiinohomoku, for instance, deals with how specific dance practices connect to an understanding of a society in its entirety. Kealiinohomoku's research is based on holistic inquiry, which according to George Marcus and Michael M.J. Fischer is intended to represent a culture as fully as possible by viewing cultural practices in context and making connections between elements of the culture (Marcus and Fischer, 1986: 22). As Judith Lynne Hanna states, "Assuming the interaction of elements in a culture and the interconnectedness of social phenomena, holism is an effort to consider what people say, what they actually do, and how both fit into the broader context of a group's history, ecology, social organization and cultural life" (Hanna, 1987: 227-28). Because particular practices are regarded as relating to the total social structure, there is a functionalist component in holistic enquiry; nevertheless, it "does not assume total interrelatedness nor relationships of equal importance" (Hanna, 1979b: 19). Holistic enquiries are based within symbolic or interpretivist anthropology, whose general premises are that cultural practices produce meaning and that specific cultural practices connect to an understanding of society in its entirety.

The article "Cultural Change: Functional and Dysfunctional Expressions of Dance" by Joann Kealiinohomoku (1979a) illustrates the holistic approach to dance research. Kealiinohomoku elaborates how dance practices in Bali and Hawaii developed differently as a result of each region's contact with a new cultural force. Although she is concerned with how cultures change and adapt when their context is altered, the basic precepts underlying her position reflect interpretative anthropology. Kealiinohomku uses the term "affective culture" to refer to "cultural manifestations that implicitly and explicitly reflect the values of a given group of people through consciously devised means that arouse emotional responses and that strongly reinforce group identity" (Kealiinohomoku, 1979a: 47). Because this notion of culture encompasses both the performance and material production of arts and rites, which are often linked to other types of behaviour, such as religious and political practices, affective behaviour has the potential to be all encompassing. Therefore, affective culture not only reflects a society, but also actually affects it. If dance mirrors a society, any change in the society will be reflected in a change in the dance (47–48).

Holistic interpretations of culture find resonance in contemporary attitudes toward dance, linking dance to tradition. The social cohesiveness that underlies holistic analyses of practices connects them to the traditional realm. According to Giddens, in anthropological inquiries the idea of tradition, particularly the repetition of a given practice, has often been fused with cohesiveness (Giddens, 1994: 62). The view that a cultural practice, such as dance, reinforces and expresses the social order can be situated within symbolic or interpretivist anthropology. This branch of anthropology has been criticized for its functionalist assumption that a given social practice maintains the society as a whole. This reasoning cannot take into account cultural practices, such as salsa dancing, which occur in a multicultural milieu and are influenced by the global flow of people, commodities, and media. The anthropological method has been typically applied to small, supposedly isolated, homogeneous societies, an inherent limitation that precludes my employing symbolic anthropology concepts uncritically. Nonetheless, the idea that the identity of a people is embodied in salsa still carries weight and influences how this dance is perceived in contemporary circumstances. The contention that a cultural form such as salsa can express a collective identity echoes holistic interpretations of culture, which link a particular practice to a whole society or a people. The notion of tradition further resonates in the linking of cultural practice to an entire people or group. It is in the ways that salsa has come to represent Latin culture for some people of Latin origin that I maintain that this dance is anchored to the realm of tradition despite its entanglement within modern processes of commodification and commercialization.

Contemporary anthropological perspectives generally do not define culture as a reflection of society as a whole (Appadurai, 1996: 12; Friedman, 1994: 74). Arjun Appadurai, for instance, states that "culture is not usefully regarded as substance but is better regarded as a dimension of phenomena, a dimension that attends to situated and embodied difference" (Appadurai, 1996: 12–13). In alluding to symbolic anthropology's emphasis on holistic understandings of society, I do not wish to put forward an idea of culture based on cohesion. Instead, I illustrate how an understanding of salsa as an embodiment of Latin culture, a perspective that many salsa dance practitioners and aficionados hold, finds a certain resonance with holism. The practice approach that emerged in the 1980s directed anthropological research toward a political focus since it views culture not as a reflection of society as a whole but as a site of difference. Reacting against structuralism, this perspective claims that system or structure does not completely determine human behaviour and focuses on the interconnection between structure and agency, holding both as necessary complements (Ortner, 1984: 146). This approach illustrates how human actions and feelings are constrained, formed, and defined by culture, which reproduces asymmetrical relations of power (159). The practice approach incorporates theorists outside of anthropology, such as Anthony Giddens and Raymond Williams, as well as Pierre Bourdieu, whose research intersects with anthropology and sociology. Pierre Bourdieu, for instance, elucidates how power imbalances between classes, as well as genders, physically imprint the bodies of individuals to such an extent that they embody the system (Bourdieu, 1977: 89). Jane Cowan's ethnographic work on the dance culture of Sohos, Greece, situated within the practice approach, reveals how asymmetrical relations of power between men and women mark this dance space (Cowan, 1990: 6).

In the 1970s and 1980s, analyses from the Birmingham school on youth and working-class culture echoed the theoretical frame of practice anthropology, wherein culture is viewed as a struggle over meaning. This account of culture counters the functionalist stance, which emphasizes the normative and unifying elements of cultural practices. Employing Antonio Gramsci's concept of hegemony, research in cultural studies argues that it is predominantly through the ways that subcultures subvert the prevailing meanings of certain practices and symbols that these groups manage to resist the imposition of the reigning discourse's regimes of meaning. From this work, I retain the key premises that culture is a site of struggle over meaning and that the cultural terrain in which the production of salsa unfolds is a site of difference. In Montreal, for instance, instructors with diverse origins seek to distinguish themselves from others by appealing to issues of legitimacy and authenticity, making claims on the basis of ethnicity, cultural heritage, and gender. These instructors argue over who has a more legitimate "right" to teach salsa and who teaches a "truer" or more comprehensive version of the dance (see chapter 3).

Culture is not a fixed product such as a text, code, paradigm, essence, or substance of which we attempt to take hold but, as Jonathan Friedman states, "a relatively instable product of the practice of meaning" (Friedman, 1994: 74). Texts, codes, paradigms, essences, and substances are merely abstractions from lived productions and practices (103). An understanding of culture as inextricably linked to lived creation and circumstances and hence as potentially always in flux needs to be kept in mind when drawing links between dance and identity. The ability to dance has often been accredited to groups broadly defined by a specific race or ethnicity. This can lead to the erroneous assumption that all the people falling within an identity category share a given dance ability. Dance is often regarded as an essential trait of a people. The tendency to essentialize dance in terms of particular ethnic or racial identities can be overcome through a conceptualization that does not envision this cultural practice as a fixed essence, substance, or text that exists outside of the lived circumstances of the dancer. Dance is produced through actual performances that can change and evolve as a dance heritage is acquired and maintained and possibly expanded to incorporate outside forms.

Observing the dance practices of diverse people has led me to the conclusion that an individual grows up in a specific dance or movement culture. This culture may not always be circumscribed by such identity categories as ethnicity, race, class, sexual orientation, or gender. For instance, during my ethnographic research in salsa dance schools in Montreal, I noticed that Montrealers of Haitian descent, learning salsa for the first time, often pick up the hip movement of the dance effortlessly. The salsa hip movement stems from African Caribbean movement patterns and consequently includes Haitian dance vernacular. These Montrealers who can move their hips with the fluid undulations that salsa requires have grown up in dance cultures in which this motion is part of their movement heritage. It is not because of their racial and ethnic backgrounds that they can move their hips in what appears to be a "natural" manner: a Montrealer of Haitian descent who did not grow up learning any African Caribbean influenced dances or dances from certain African American genres would not pick up the hip movements in salsa as easily. The dancing ability of people of Latin and Caribbean origin is commonly regarded as a skill that is "in the blood." This popular misconception conceals how this dance ability is an acquired knowledge that develops from growing up in a specific movement culture. The moves that comprise an individual's dance culture can, of course, be expanded or even altered as she or he adopts and integrates other ways of moving the body.

Culture, identity, and commercialization underlie this book's analysis, which focuses on the commodification of an expressive practice. I suggest that salsa dance movements, representing the cultures of the Latin diaspora, have become commodities that are marketed and "consumed" in multicultural cities throughout the globe. Furthermore, this work investigates the interconnection between global factors and the commodification of culture in local circumstances. I provide a case study, based on a detailed ethnography of cultural institutions in Montreal, examining the influence that the transnational migration of people and the global exchange of various forms of media have on the development of a particular local scene. These factors influence the particular movement culture selected for marketing and distribution by cultural institutions. This commercialization of practices, in turn, engenders points of division and cooperation among diverse cultures, ethnicities, races, and both sexes involved in this specific dance industry as well as within communities in Montreal.

I broach this analysis of salsa dance from within the context of one of its recent sites on the globe, providing a unique example of how the commodification of salsa and its link to a cultural heritage unfold within a specific place. Nonetheless, many of the factors that characterize local expressions have global dimensions, creating a dialectic between the local and global (Tomlinson, 1999: 16). This interconnection finds resonance in Anthony Giddens's definition, which states that, "Globalization can thus be defined as the intensification of worldwide social relations which link distant localities in such a way that local happenings are shaped by events occurring many miles away and vice versa" (Giddens, 1990: 64). An understanding of global processes stemming from literary studies and the Birmingham-based cultural sociology regards cultural globalization as the rising worldwide interrelations, exchanges, and flows of people, images, and commodities (Friedman, 1994: 95). This conceptualization of cultural globalization, as an empirical condition of worldwide interchange, finds resonance in a great deal of work conducted in the social sciences and humanities. John Tomlinson, for instance, refers to these empirical circumstances of worldwide interconnection within the modern world as "complex connectivity." He also envisions globalization as how goods, people, knowledge, images, and beliefs move across regional, national, and territorial boundaries (Tomlinson, 1999: 2). The notion of connectivity leads to a rise in "global-spatial proximity" (3) or to "time-space compression," as referred to by David Harvey (1989), which continues to make globalization possible by shortening distances between parts of the world through a dramatic reduction in the time that it takes to cross them either physically by air travel or representationally through the dissemination of mediated information (Tomlinson, 1999: 3). Neutral technological development, according to Jonathan Friedman, is not the only galvanizing force behind time-space compression; rather, processes of capitalist accumulation—that is, the particular social pattern of the strategies that structure the world economy—play into this ongoing condensing of the world (Friedman, 1994: 196). Moreover, Giddens argues that modernity (which includes the institutions of mass communication and capitalism) unleashes social relations from the confines of face-to-face interactions, the domain of premodern societies, enabling the stretching across time and space that is an essential force behind globalization (Giddens, 1990: 16–17).

Collective deployments of the imagination as well as a sense of global consciousness have been combined with the conditions of exchange and compression. For instance, Roland Robertson claims that "Globalization as a concept refers both to the compression of the world and the intensification of consciousness of the world as a whole" (Robertson, 1992: 8). Citing Frank Lechner in the forthcoming *Encyclopedia of Social Theory*, George Ritzer proposes a working definition of globalization as "the worldwide diffusion of practices, expansion of relations across continents, organization of social life on a global scale, and growth of a shared global consciousness" (Lechner, quoted in Ritzer, 2004: 72). Arjun Appadurai explores how the forces that enable globalization—media and migration—have a dual effect on the imagination, which in turn creates imagined selves and imagined worlds (Appadurai, 1996: 3). As a result of technological changes that have taken place over the past century, the imagination within recent decades has become in Appadurai's vision "a collective social fact" (5). The imagination has moved from the sphere of art, myth, and ritual to the everyday mental work of people (4). When the imagination is collective, it can lead to action. Just as it forged ideas of neighborhood and nationhood (Anderson, 1983), the imagination mobilized through memory and desire can forge diasporic affiliations that span regional and national boundaries (Appadurai, 1996: 5). Appadurai emphasizes the role of the imagination in globalization processes through the link that he establishes between this collective force and the creation of diasporic and transnational connections within the global arena. Rather than following the critics of mass culture of the Frankfurt school in claiming that the imagination will be thwarted by commoditization and industrial capitalism (6), he argues that the consumption of mass media throughout the world has the possibility to mobilize the imagination creatively.

Opinions vary regarding whether the empirical condition of global exchange creating cultural flows is a new or old phenomenon. Jonathan Friedman argues that compression of the world through global interconnections is an ongoing process that dates back centuries (Friedman, 1994: 195). Beginning in the seventeenth century, the slave trade, for instance, led to a massive enforced dislocation of Africans and brought people of both European and African backgrounds together in the New World (195), creating contacts between these two groups. The contemporary situation of globalization is only distinguished, according to Friedman, in the ways that the natures of these flows are identified: those who have the power and authority to analyze and identify the nature of the contemporary situation regard these exchanges as mixtures of cultures of diverse origins (210). Cultural mixture and movements of people and commodities are not new, but they have not always been envisioned and fathomed as a mix of cultures (245). Nonetheless, Arjun Appadurai would argue that the contemporary situation of global exchange is distinct. Only since the 1970s have media and mass migration become extensively globalized on such a widespread transnational scale (Appadurai, 1996: 9).

This book examines how some Montrealers of Latin descent connect to the Latin diaspora upon migration through their participation in a salsa culture within the new context of a Canadian city. Dancing and listening to salsa for certain Montrealers of Latin descent may not have been a part of their heritage in their countries of origin. Many Montrealers of Latin descent who have migrated to this city from nations in Latin America and the Caribbean adopt salsa as part of their cultural heritage only after arriving in Canada, connecting, through salsa, to a transnational Latin identity that crosses the Americas (see chapter 2). The collective formation of cultural diaspora around a practice that was both acquired within and outside of the host nation finds resonance in the role that Appadurai claims for the imagination in the creation of diaspora. Through engagement in expressive practices, imaginations are collectively mobilized, enabling individuals to connect to a cultural diaspora dispersed throughout the Americas.

Identity affiliations that extend beyond the nation-state, specifically cultural diaspora, come into play in the dissemination of salsa within a specific context. Other primordial affinities that had been absorbed within the boundaries of the nation-state, such as ethnicity, "race," gender, local community, and language, emerge in the evolution of this dance and music within a Canadian context. The development of various identity affiliations, although expressed in a unique way in the city, is a process that is shared within the global arena (Friedman, 1994: 100–101). This creation of new identities—diasporic and primordial connections—has been credited to the decline of a homogenizing modern identity, typically centered around national identity, which is being challenged by mass migration fueled by the decentralization of wealth in the modern world system (234). This decentralization is created through multinationalization, capital export, and the creation of new industrial spheres intended to augment the wealth at the center. This rise in prosperity has rendered production at the center too expensive compared to production on the underdeveloped perimeters. Decentralization is how the capitalist system deals with the issue of competition, redirecting production to areas of the world that are more financially beneficial in terms of labor costs and taxes (243). Capital's pursuit of more beneficial prospects on the periphery has led to an increased disorganization in the global sphere that has brought about mass migration (233). Since the 1980s mass migration within the context of the decentralization of wealth has led to a decline of hegemony at the center and to a waning of homogenizing modern identity. Thus mass migrations under such circumstances have brought about a flourishing of identities (244).

At the same time that salsa dancing in Montreal proclaims a Latin identity extending beyond the boundaries of Quebec and Canada, this practice thrives in a multicultural context: the Montreal salsa scene comprises diverse individuals who promote, teach, and dance salsa. Although multiculturalism is one of the defining traits of Canadian cities, multicultural-based identities have become a transnational phenomenon (Friedman, 1994: 252). The concern with multiculturalism within North America and Europe is, according to Arjun Appadurai, a sign of the inability of states to discourage their minority populations from connecting to identity affiliations other than that of the nation. This tendency has brought an end to a public sphere that can be characterized as only national in scope (Appadurai, 1996: 22). Nations have consequently fragmented, leading to policies stressing multiculturalism as opposed to the former tendency toward assimilation (Friedman, 1994: 245, 252).

The decline of modernist identity has led to a tendency to yearn for what has been lost. Within the global arena, this desire to reclaim the past often finds expression in the intensification of national identities (Friedman, 1994: 90). Globalization, therefore, can lead to both the eroding and strengthening of the national. The formation of identity affiliations in Montreal's salsa scene are not necessarily nationalistic in scope but rather extend beyond the Canadian border or specific national Latin American identities to embrace the Latin diaspora that spans the Americas. Nonetheless, sentiments of nostalgia, which are not necessarily motivated by a desire to return to a nationalist identity, emerge within the dissemination of salsa in Montreal. Through engagement in this practice, Montrealers of Latin descent recuperate aspects of the past that may at times be only recollections of an imagined past. According to Arjun Appadurai, nostalgia without memory, especially in the area of entertainment and leisure, is a product of global cultural flows (Appadurai, 1996: 30). For instance, as previously mentioned, many of the Montrealers of Latin descent who both teach and dance salsa learned to dance to its rhythms for the first time in Montreal. Others start listening to music in Spanish only after their arrival in the city. The desire to adopt salsa as a cultural practice within the contemporary context of a Canadian city can be viewed as a means to recuperate what has been lost through migration: a connection to Spanish-language culture (see chapter 2). Through their engagement in salsa, these Montrealers embody a cultural affiliation that many people of non-Latin descent may believe is tied to their previous experiences in Latin America or the Caribbean—even though this "heritage" has been acquired on Canadian soil. Certain Montrealers of Latin descent either learn or teach a Latin dance that is not a key part of the cultural fabric of their country of origin partly because of salsa's commercial status as a transnational marker of Latin identity distributed through the media (see chapter 2). Appadurai points out that as the past heritage of diverse groups becomes increasingly exhibited in national and transnational spectacles, culture has extended from Pierre Bourdieu's notion of habitus, based on the tacit reproduction of practices and disposition, to one in which individuals choose the culture that they want to adopt (Appadurai, 1996: 44).

The wish to return to a past imagined as more ordered might also underlie salsa's global appeal. For many Montrealers, for instance, who were never raised with salsa rhythms, engaging in this dance marks a return to prefeminist gendered relations, in which the roles of the sexes are clearly delineated and hierarchized: the male dancer leads, and the female follows. As a result of structural changes in society and the strivings of the feminist movement, contemporary strides have been made to attain gender equality in society as well as to develop a consciousness that seeks to question and challenge imbalances between the sexes. Nonetheless, salsa unabashedly embodies gender hierarchies that characterize the traditional roles of men and women in prefeminist times. In the geographically prescribed and rule-governed spaces of clubs, schools, and venues, dancers can corporally experience (and find pleasure in) masculine dominance and female submission (see chapter 5). The highly fluid nature of global change in the contemporary phase of globalization since the twentieth century has, according to Roland Robertson, nourished the nostalgic tendency for more certain and stable forms of "world order" (Robertson, 1992: 162). This desire for security, as mentioned above, can lead to a rise in nationalist sentiments to counter what may be perceived as the "chaos" of transnational fusions and mixtures. This longing for stability in the global arena can also find expression in micropractices of leisure and entertainment such as salsa dance.

The complex connectivity of globalization transforms the culture of local spaces by weakening the links of culture to place, a phenomenon known today as deterritorialization (Tomlinson, 1999: 106), which draws from a concept initially put forward by Gilles Deleuze and Felix Guattari (Deleuze and Guattari, 1987). Salsa in Montreal could be viewed as an example of the cultural experience of deterritorialization: this dance, which is obviously not "indigenous" to the city or to the country, has become, through migration and the media, a part of Montreal and countless cities around the world. The concept of deterritorialization assumes that prior to globalization a well-defined connection between culture and place existed. The belief that cultures endured that were not influenced by outside forces is for many a myth (Tomlinson, 1999: 128–29). For Franz Boas, the founder of cultural relativism in anthropology, all cultures were impure, combined with imports from outside contacts (Friedman, 1994: 75). Arjun Appadurai questions whether there could have once existed a people who were completely sheltered from any foreign connection: the "native" as pure and isolated is a creation of the Western imagination (Appadurai, 1992: 37–38). Despite claims made that deterritorialization does not necessarily refer to a new phenomenon arising from contemporary circumstances of globalization, Tomlinson wishes to salvage the term, claiming that it represents a distinct disconnection between culture and location that is characteristic of the modern era. The time-space distanciation[4] created through globalization and the institutions of modernity has enabled a greater gap between culture and location than was possible in premodern societies (Tomlinson, 1999: 130). Salsa dance elicits debate about whether deterritorialization is a relevant concept applicable to the current global cultural experience. Although the relatively recent performances of salsa in Western cities such as Montreal can be viewed as deterritorialized culture, even in its "birthplaces," salsa has always been deterritorialized: the history of salsa involves such intricate transnational connections that it is difficult to pinpoint its "original" location (see chapter 1). The boundaries between "indigenous" and "deterritorialized" culture become highly porous when referring to cultural forms such as salsa that do not have a clearly defined source.

The process of deterritorialization leads to cultural hybridization. If culture is dislodged from location through rising cultural transfers in the global arena, then it becomes possible for cultural forms to intermingle and create new hybrid forms. In a hybrid, two or more elements from diverse cultures or areas of the world are combined (Ritzer, 2004: 78). For instance, in the eighteenth century the *contredanse*, a French country dance originally from England, arrived in Cuba after the Haitian revolution in 1791 via the migrations of French colonial families fleeing the uprising. The enslaved Haitians of African origin brought to Cuba by the French colonials eventually altered the rhythm of the *contredanse* by adding an African-derived rhythmic structure to a European-derived dance (see chapter 1). The transformation of the *contredanse* into the Cuban genre known as the *contradanza criolla* illustrates not only how dislodging cultures from their original location can produce hybrid forms, but also how contemporary salsa, which is derived from the *contredanza criolla*, in addition to various Cuban "creolized" dances, is also a hybrid genre born from the circulation of diverse cultures.

The concept of hybridization seems to capture what is occurring at the level of practice: once uprooted from its original location, either through migration or mediated technology, a particular culture can fuse with other forms, producing a new genre. Nonetheless, if all "original" and "indigenous" cultures have been influenced by outside forces, no cultures that are pure can exist. Culture, at its core, is always in flux and dynamic. The actual condition of culture approximates what Pnina Werbner, applying Bakhtin's work on linguistic hybridization to culture and society, envisions as "organic, unconscious hybridity," in which all cultures develop through "unreflective borrowings, mimetic appropriations, exchanges and inventions" (Werbner, 1997: 4–5; Tomlinson, 1999: 144). The evolution of all languages, according to Bakhtin, engendered processes of "unintentional, unconscious hybridization (Bakhtin, 1981: 358). In addition to hybridization, creolization has been put forward to describe the mixing of cultures. Creolization has been applied primarily to colonial "others."[5] Jonathan Friedman notes how many culture productions, such as the English language, are actually creole in the sense that they derive from a blend of origins, yet they have never been conceptualized in this manner. Every culture in the world, according to Friedman, is creolized to the extent that each is derived from mixed origins (Friedman, 1994: 100). The decision to identify a particular practice as creole has stemmed from specific actors, often situated at centers of power, who have been able to determine whether a tradition was part of a "pure" or "creolized" heritage, a process that has been tied with their own self-identification (210). All cultures are in a sense hybrid (or creole). Implicit in the notion of hybridity is the myth of cultural purity since the cultures being fused or mixed are more often than not construed as bounded original traditions. Given the potential hybridization of all cultural forms, the decisions to link a given cultural form to a particular origin is probably more a social act than a cultural fact (210). What's the diff - find out!

If all cultures are intrinsically hybridized, the concept of hybridization itself and the concomitant notion of cultural purity on which the creation of hybrids depends should both seemingly be dismantled. Yet hybridization lingers in the contemporary analyses of the globalization of culture. Jan Nederveen Pieterse argues that the concept of hybridization can be retained as a critique of essentialism, demonstrating the mixed nature of all cultural forms (Nederveen Pieterse, 1995: 64). This book incorporates hybridization in both historical and contemporary analyses while taking into account that the cultures being merged are not in themselves bounded. In a detailed account of its historical roots, salsa is presented as a dance and music complex that has combined diverse traditions based in Europe, Africa, America, and the Caribbean (see chapter 1). The commodification of salsa within the contemporary dance scene in Montreal further entails the mixing of dance aesthetics based in European and African traditions (see chapters 1 and 3).

The claim that salsa combines African and European forms seems to posit these two traditions as distinct and bounded expressions. Nonetheless, both the European and African influences upon which Cuban dance culture is built were necessarily already mixed. For instance, the Spanish culture in Cuba had previously been influenced by African cultural traditions. The hip movement of Spanish dance stemming from various Spanish cultures, such as Andalucian, Canarios, Castellanos, Asturianos, Gallegos, and Catalanes, came from the Moorish invasion (A.D. 711), which brought North African culture into Spain (Daniel, 2002: 31). This Spanish-derived hip movement became a part of Cuban dance prior to the incorporation of more pronounced hip movement that would enter Cuba later than the period of Spanish rule beginning in 1511 through the African cultures of the sub-Saharan (31). The African influences in the dances of Cuba, which became most pronounced from 1800 to the 1860s, resulted from numerous ethnic groups being brought forcefully as enslaved people from Africa to the island. Besides the African influences in Cuba that emerged in the *tumba francesca* (see chapter 1), four expansive groups of distinct African dance cultures developed as a result of the amalgamation of hundreds of African ethnic groups

(Daniel, 2002: 33; Ortiz, 1951). These four dance and music traditions are often referred to as *kongo, arará, carabalí,* and *yoruba* (Daniel, 2002: 33). The history of Cuban dance, from whence salsa stems, reveals that countless traditions, none of them necessarily pure cultural productions, have fashioned its contemporary expression (see chapter 1).

Conceptual problems arise in linking the roots of contemporary salsa to cultural traditions defined by such expansive affiliations as African or European. The use of the terms "African culture" and "European culture" appears to posit these two extensive cultural terrains as pure, bounded, and unitary when they are in fact intrinsically diverse and influenced by cultures outside of their boundaries. Nonetheless, I maintain these distinctions while simultaneously considering their interconnection to examine the political implications involved in the interaction of cultural forms that are deemed to be either African or European in origin. For instance, during various eras the African influence in Latin music and dance has been either denigrated or ignored (see chapter 1). The metaphors that are used to describe processes of hybridization, such as cultural mixture and fusion as well as the biologically based hybrid, imply cultural combining that draws equally from the initial sources (Tomlinson, 1999: 145). Nonetheless, more often than not hegemonic forces seep into processes of hybridization (146). Relations of power are consequently at play in the fusing of European- and African-derived aesthetics and forms in contemporary dance scenes as well as within salsa's historical evolution in the Americas (see chapter 1).

Roland Robertson's work provides insight into how uniformity and difference intersect within the global arena. This dual tendency is based on global connectivity, which is transforming the world into a single social and cultural setting (Robertson, 1992: 6). Nonetheless, Robertson does not position this global unicity in the simplistic formulation of a world culture. He envisions this unicity as an intricate social and phenomenological situation or, in his words, the "global-human condition," in which different orders of human life are brought together. He identifies four such orders: individual human beings, national societies, the world system of societies, and the overarching collectivity of humankind (27). For Robertson, globalization becomes the rising interconnection between these orders of human life. Thus conceiving of the world as a singular space changes these aspects of life, as they are progressively placed against and compelled to consider one another (Tomlinson, 1999: 11). Within Robertson's paradigm of unicity, social and cultural difference may become intensified even while it is being identified in connection to the world in its entirety (Robertson, 1995: 40). Robertson's model maintains the wholeness implicit within globalization while dealing with the empirical complicatedness of a world that manifests concurrent tendencies toward differentiation (Tomlinson, 1999: 12). As connectivity extends to local spaces, it alters local lived realities, but at the same time connectivity binds the lives, cultures, and experiences of specific locales within a singular global sphere (12).

The issue of whether global change increases homogeneity, heterogeneity, or both simultaneously is linked to the relationship between the local and global. According to George Ritzer, a dominance of the local would give rise to heterogeneity, whereas a predominance of the global would bring about homogeneity (Ritzer, 2004: 73). The global and the local are not distinct but interconnect in circumstances in which either the global or local preside, yielding respectively either cultural uniformity or diversity. For Robertson, the interconnection between the global and the local arises because that which is referred to as the local is often in essence contained within the global (Robertson, 1995: 35). Robertson has put forward the term *glocalization*, whose use has become widespread in contemporary globalization research. This concept deals with the interrelation between the global and local. Although Robertson is concerned with both the processes of homogeneity and heterogeneity, his research stresses the importance of the glocal and the consequent phenomenon of heterogeneity (Ritzer, 2004: 73). Glocalization, according to George Ritzer, can be defined in cultural terms as the interrelationship of the global and local leading to unique expressions and consequences in diverse geographic locations (73).

From one vantage point, this book illustrates how the dissemination of salsa in Montreal is an example of glocalization. Salsa dance has become a global expressive art through commercial and mediated processes, yet its performance in specific localities can yield distinct renditions and interpretations. Montrealers of both Latin and non-Latin descent, for instance, have absorbed this global practice into their cultural repertoire within the context of a multicultural Canadian city. The way salsa has developed in Montreal is unique to the city. This distinctiveness arises in the types of styles that circulate, the development of a Montreal style, and the creation of hybrid forms. The distinct mix of populations—both of Latin and non-Latin descent—involved in its performance and promotion in the city further contributes to the creation of a particular salsa scene. Through a detailed ethnography of the Montreal scene, this book illuminates how the absorption of a global practice within a local site gives rise to unique expressions (see chapters 3 and 5). Nonetheless, the development of a local salsa scene is not unique to Montreal but is a phenomenon that characterizes cities throughout the world where salsa is popular. Therefore, as Robertson asserts, the local is not counterposed to the global but included within it (Robertson, 1995: 35).

In contrast to the notion of glocalization, George Ritzer offers the counterperspective of *grobalization*, which he defines as the imperialistic aims of nations, corporations, and organizations and their concomitant desire and need to prevail within numerous geographic sites (Ritzer, 2004: 73). Ritzer envisions grobalization as the transnational intensification and extension of homogeneous codes and practices (75). Grobalization is a highly modern stance that stresses the rising international capacity of capitalist organizations and modern states to heighten their control and influence throughout the world (74). Cultural imperialism underlies the global move toward homogeneity, which takes shape through the dominance of American culture, the West, or core countries (75). The circulation of commodities and mediated technology are viewed as key agents enabling the homogeneity of practices (77). The homogenization thesis claims that globalization renders culture uniform because it is forced to adhere to a standardized consumer culture (Tomlinson, 1999: 6). Homogeneity and uniformity are consequently largely fueled by capitalism: profits are maximized by industries, firms, and corporations if the products distributed and marketed are tapered to their most rudimentary, basic components (Ritzer, 2004: 90). Hence the forces of grobalization render the world, in Ritzer's words, "more capitalistic, Americanized, rationalized, codified and restricted" (80). Ritzer extends the terrain of grobalization from means of consumption, such as franchises, shopping malls, mega-malls, superstores, and Internet sites, to the cultural terrain. He illustrates, for instance, how core elements of national cinemas are being altered so that they can be distributed in America. He cites the case of Chinese cinema, in which leading directors such as Zhang Yimo and Chen Kaige are making films that accentuate the exotic in Chinese culture so that they can be sold more successfully to Western audiences (86).

Instructors in salsa schools in Montreal and other cities throughout the globe often incorporate aesthetics and movement patterns derived from ballroom dance because they are more accessible to their clients, who are generally not well versed in African-derived movement patterns that characterize salsa thriving in lived circumstances. This absorption of the ballroom tradition in salsa schools enables instructors to more successfully "sell" the dance to Western clients (see chapter 3). The impact of ballroom on the commodification of salsa in local sites illustrates how grobalization and hence cultural imperialism extends to popular Latin dance cultures.

Ballroom dance is a tradition that stems from white American and British dance culture. Today it is an industry that sells dances in schools located in

North America, Europe, Japan, Singapore, the Philippines, South Africa, Australia, and elsewhere across the globe. As previously noted, this heritage appropriated and modified various Latin dances from Cuba in the first half of the twentieth century in terms of its aesthetics and corporeal ideals. Latin dances, thriving within actual lived circumstances, were also transformed into marketable products: these dances were reduced to a set of fixed codes and practices that in turn enabled them to be taught in schools as well as performed in competitions in basically the same way throughout the world. This codification of Latin dance in terms of rules and regulations governing performance also rendered these dances more restrictive and uniform than their counterparts born and evolving in real-life contexts. The transformation of Cuban dances within the ballroom tradition could be viewed as a form of grobalization: Caribbean dance culture based in lived realities was channelled into the capitalist economy, rendered more restrictive, codified at the level of movement vernacular, and refigured in terms of American and British culture. Contemporary salsa instruction, which therefore integrates elements of the ballroom tradition, creates performances that are more codified, standardized, and Westernized than versions thriving in lived Latin milieux. Although the Latin dances within ballroom do promote cultural homogeneity, the dances' standards within this tradition are not pure but derived from mixed origins, namely the fusion of European and Latin American dance. Jan Nederveen Pieterse cautions against viewing homogenization as absolutely distinct from heterogeneity when he asserts that "many of the standards exported by the West and its cultural industries themselves turn out to be of culturally mixed character if we examine their cultural lineages" (Nederveen Pieterse, 1995: 53).

Rather than determining whether globalization engenders either cultural homogenization or diversity, this book illustrates, through an analysis of the Montreal scene, how both tendencies are occurring simultaneously. Jonathan Friedman maintains that globalization provokes a dialectic between homogeneity and heterogeneity (Friedman, 1994: 210). While claiming that the debate of whether globalization leads to homogenization or heterogenization needs to be surpassed, Robertson asserts that both tendencies have become a part of life in the world of the late twentieth century (Robertson, 1995: 27). In roughly the last five years, salsa dance instruction has moved from lived spaces, such as schools, clubs, and music venues, to the virtual sphere of the Internet. The concluding chapter elucidates how this online dissemination can also potentially elicit a concurrent diversification and uniformity of forms.

To understand the effects exerted by globalization on the salsa that is danced, taught, and promoted in the city, I have conducted a detailed ethnography informed by both historical and theoretical research. Despite a key direction of this ethnography being the dissemination of this transnational practice within a local context, this book illustrates how the development of this specific dance culture is linked to effects of globalization, such as migration, the formation of diaspora, hybridization, and the mixing of populations. A section of my ethnographic work comprises in-depth interviews with dance instructors in the city, which were designed to obtain information that would allow me to develop two central concerns. First, I wanted to find out if a discourse of authenticity and origins is connected to the selling of salsa dancing in terms of the actual movements taught. Second, I wanted to explore whether the relationship between men and women that is created in the actual teaching of the dance connects to how salsa is commodified as an expression of Latin culture. Given the transnational "origins" of salsa, dance instructors have different opinions of what constitutes an "authentic" rendition of the dance. They also have disparate standpoints concerning the nature of the gender dynamics that are embodied in the dance and the consequences of this gendered relation. As salsa crosses cultural and ethnic boundaries within local dance schools situated within a multicultural city, this gender dynamic takes on various forms in both the teaching and the marketing of this dance. In interpreting my ethnographic findings and the texts of my interviews, I am not, in fact, too concerned with which instructor provides a truer or more realistic portrait of the Montreal urban scene. Rather, I bring the response of various instructors into contact with each other to reveal how each of their viewpoints creates the salsa story—that is, creates a dialogue within the salsa dance world. I am more interested in how the dynamics of this dialogue have the potential to produce or dismantle hierarchies based on distinctions of gender, ethnicity, race, and culture within the realm of discourse and practice than with presenting a "genuine" description of this dance world. *excellent*

This enquiry into the Montreal dance scene combines the notion of transgression with the commodification of culture. This book draws from the idea that cultural practices can transgress hegemonic structures while addressing how cultural commodification intersects with the way that culture becomes a meaningful and potentially transgressive activity. Dancing is not framed only as a cultural commodity because this perspective does not take into account how a given dance or musical culture often thrives partly in order to express the identity of a given group. Salsa dancing has political implications for those who are involved in the practice. Many Montrealers of Latin descent, for instance, assert their heritage by adopting salsa dancing and music within the Canadian context. An analytical approach that focuses purely on the circulation of salsa as a cultural commodity risks erasing the political aspect of this dance and music complex. Furthermore, this analysis of salsa does not simply focus on how the connections that are embodied in the salsa dance field construct or break down hierarchies between societal groups—in other words, how a cultural practice can reinforce or transgress dominant structures—because, in the case of salsa, a notion of transgression and resistance must be viewed through the filter of commodification.

The approach that I take in my analysis of Montreal's salsa scene has been significantly inspired by the Birmingham school of cultural studies, yet this theoretical perspective is not sufficient for an adequate understanding of how salsa develops in specific localities such as Montreal. The idea that subcultures subvert predominant discourses and practices was highly innovative at the time of its inception (Hebdige, 1979). The concept of resistance has since become so widespread in cultural analysis that the notion of transgression has lost its political efficacy. As a great deal of work has been done on how cultural practices resist dominance, almost any cultural practice has come to be perceived as transgressive. Notions of resistance persist in my work even though the central focus is not on those ways in which salsa contains transgressive potential.

Although obviously not indigenous to the cultural panorama of Montreal, salsa is at the same time not entirely a "foreign" practice. The study of foreign cultures in anthropology partly influenced the focus on the "other" in cultural studies, beginning with the analysis of the working class of the 1950s (During, 1993: 4). Since the 1980s attention has also been turning to diasporic communities in the West. The "other" is constructed taking into account outside influences. A particular culture cannot be explored solely in terms of its national or communal identity because the forces of globalization blur the boundaries dividing nations and influence local culture. My decision to research the salsa scene in Montreal can be seen as a part of the intellectual trend within cultural studies to explore an "other" from within the boundaries of a Western nation rather than finding it in a faraway land as ethnographers have previously done. Just as theorists influenced by poststructuralism have argued that the "other" studied by ethnographers could never have been entirely isolated from the outside world, the Montreal salsa dance scene is not completely an "other" culture. Since people from diverse backgrounds, including those of the predominant cultures, participate in the production and consumption of salsa dancing, this practice stands both inside and outside mainstream cultural practices in the city. Salsa in Montreal illustrates how the flow of ideas, practices, and cultures from migrant non-Western populations affect and alter dominant societies and regions of the world.

Notes

1. For an example of a scholarly work, see Sánchez González 1999. For an example in a popular context, see the discussion forum on the To Salsa website (http://www.tosalsa.com/welcome.html).

2. Robert Farris Thompson puts both "folk" and "high" in italics when used in reference to dance forms in order to denote that both have artistic merit even though only dances such as ballet have been regarded as "high" art and consequently deemed worthy of being included in the domain of art history (Thompson, 2002: 342).

3. Pero así como los músicos en el Norte "ajustan" la bailable música afroide a los gustos de sus consumidores, así en la escuelas adulteran los bailes exóticos para adecuarlos fácilmente a las rutinas de sus clients.

4. Time-space differentiation can be defined as the "stretching of social relations in time and space" (Jessop, 2005). According to Anthony Giddens, modern society is marked by processes that reorganize time and space. This reorganization unleashes social relations from their connection to specific locations, reconstituting them across expansive time-space distances (Giddens, 1991: 2).

5. "Creolization" has been used differently in various contexts. In the Caribbean and North America, the term signifies the combination of African and European traditions. In Latin America the Spanish word *criollo* originally denoted people of European descent born in the Iberian New World (Nederveen Pieterse, 1995: 54).

6. According to Robertson, the term *glocalize* was seemingly developed in Japan from the word *dochakuka*, meaning "global localization," as a marketing term to address Japan's concern with and success in the global economy while taking into account the problem of the interconnection between the local and the global (Robertson, 1992: 173–74).

CHAPTER ONE

~

Beyond Caribbean Roots

Salsa dancing often conjures up images of frivolity and sexuality, especially in the minds of those who have never danced the salsa steps. Moving to the salsa rhythms can indeed be sexy as well as sensual, fun, creative, innovative, or artistic depending on the dancing context. But alongside the sexuality, pleasure, and joy commonly associated with dance, salsa also engenders the political consequences of different cultures interacting. Historical and contemporary struggles are inscribed in dance and, consequently, in dancing bodies. The conflicts that arose as a result of interactions between African and European ethnic groups are embedded in the Cuban music and dances the *danzón* and the *son*, precursors of contemporary salsa. Although salsa dancers may not always be aware of the history imprinted in their gestures, the movements remain manifestations of earlier strife. New tensions emerge in the transplantation of salsa dancing to Montreal.

Struggle is embedded in the evolution of salsa. Contemporary salsa is rooted in the African slave trade that scarred Cuba for centuries. From 1518 until the abolishment of slavery in 1886, enslaved Africans were brought to Cuba (Angeloro, 1992: 301; Daniel, 1995: 17). New York composers, musicians, and dancers, key players in the beginnings of salsa's story in the first half of the twentieth century were primarily from working-class Puerto Rican, Cuban, and African American backgrounds. Life in the United States for people of color was harsh, as they endured bleak conditions, particularly racial segregation. During the birth of modern salsa, in the late 1960s and 1970s, this musical expression was a vehicle to articulate the oppression of the Puerto Rican diaspora. Salsa also spoke to working-class people in Latin American cities, who faced oppressive conditions as a result of prejudice and poverty. Although salsa has lost much of its political aspect today, traces of conflict emerge in contemporary expressions. This focus on salsa in a present-day context addresses the points of division and cooperation between different ethnicities and racial groups as well as between men and women as they unfold in the cultural commodification of salsa dancing in Montreal. To broach this contemporary situation, I must first look back at the history of this dance and music complex. Salsa's history is continuously reinvoked in the ways that diverse groups and individuals come into contact with one another in Montreal's dance and music scene as well as in locations throughout the globe.

The corporeal traits of contemporary salsa reflect the meeting of two traditions—European and African. This fusion was not based on a joyful contact between two heritages, as stereotyped images of dances of the New World often convey, but was rooted in European brutality and inhumanity toward Africans. African and European forms have, nonetheless, joined to fashion contemporay salsa. European-derived elements of the dance can be found, for instance, in the upright bodily stance that maintains a straight back. This posture was first brought to Cuba by Spaniards from southern Spain through a dance culture that uses an extended and uplifted upper body (Daniel, 2002: 31). The couple formation in which the male and female dancer touch one another is also part of the European legacy (43). A key African-derived element is the isolation of various body parts, particularly the separate moves of hips that roll, swing, and shake (Hamilton Crowell, Jr., 2002: 18). This fusing of the cultures of two continents reflects the history of Cuba, where salsa is rooted. A great number of Europeans, primarily from Spain and the Canary Islands, settled in Cuba during the centuries of Spanish domination (1511–1898). A number of factors also nurtured a thriving culture based on African traditions. Enslaved people of African background were more easily able to buy their freedom in Cuba than they were in the United States and nations in the Caribbean under British rule. In the early eighteenth century, large numbers of freed Africans lived in urban centers in Cuba, facilitating the creation of new forms of African-derived culture. Whereas the transplantion of enslaved Africans had lessened considerably by the 1800s in the United States and British-dominated Caribbean nations, the majority of enslaved peoples were brought to Cuba between 1800 and the 1860s. With their enslavement, large numbers of Africans endured severe and violent conditions. Yet their oppression enabled new music and dance traditions from Africa to enrich the Cuban culture (Manuel, 1995: 20).

Varied influences mark contemporary salsa, but its roots can be traced back primarily to the Cuban dance and music complexes of the rumba, *danzón*, and *son*. Salsa has also evolved from the mambo and the *chachachá* (Robbins, 1989). The history of salsa combines both music and dance given the interconnection between its two expressive forms. Salsa is a dance and music complex, meaning that its musical and corporeal expressions in actual circumstances are inextricably intertwined: only at the level of theory can the music and dance be separated. The terms for salsa's predecessors, the rumba, *danzón*, and *son*, also refer both to musical forms and to dances.

Because this chapter provides a chronological history of the roots of salsa, it tends toward a rigid portrayal of the dance evolution. Yet dances are continuously evolving and changing, assuming new names and forms. Many of the dance forms from which salsa originated are identified by the decades when they were popular. Dances in lived practice are not always performed within finite time periods: they often have neither definite beginnings nor endings. Once their popularity wanes, they may not necessarily disappear altogether. Traces of a dance may remain well beyond its fashionable era. For instance, the *danzón*, which was popular in Cuba from the 1880s through the 1920s, is still performed today in parts of Latin America, most notably Mexico.

The first of salsa's predecessors, rumba, an Afro-Cuban secular music and dance genre, evokes African musical patterns and contains neither European melodic influences nor chordal instruments. The rumba was developed by diverse people from West and Central Africa who were brought over as slaves to Cuba. The nineteenth century was marked by increased urbanization in Cuba and by the eventual abolition of slavery in 1887. During this century, blacks in towns and cities were given the right to form societies, called *cabildos*, composed of distinct "nations" or African ethnic groups, such as *congos*, *yoruba*, *mandingas*, *lucumíes*, *ararás*, and *carabalí* (Martínez Furé, 1974: 87). Of these African ethnicities, the Kongo[1] tradition has had the strongest and longest impact in Cuba (Daniel, 2002: 34). The *cabildos* became organizations that fostered mutual support as well as religious and cultural activities. They also offered a venue to preserve the sacred and secular traditions of diverse African groups, particularly the ancient traditional dances, which the onslaught of slavery had tried to obliterate through a brutal process of deculturation (Guerra, 1993: 93). At the beginning, the ethnic groups remained distinct, and each heritage developed and performed its own particular dances and music as well as other practices (Daniel, 2002: 24).

In the secular activities of these societies, different ethnicities eventually blended to produce syncretic music and dance genres, which included the rumba. The rumba was therefore born in the *cabildos*. The term "rumba" not only described a type of music and dance but also designated an informal fiesta or gathering among blacks (Crook, 1992: 31–42). This dance and music complex developed in the early nineteenth century in primarily African communities or in areas where dark-skinned Africans resided near the ports of Matanzas and Havana. The dance and music of rumba emphasize rhythm. Both the dancer and musician also engage in extensive improvisation sequences. Since the dance is highly complex, immersion in the culture is required if one is to obtain a real understanding of its choreographic and rhythmic elements (Daniel, 2002: 47).

Despite its intricacy and virtuosity, the rumba was denigrated by white upper-class Cubans as a practice of a low and inferior culture primarily because of its African Cuban roots (Crook, 1992: 34). Commenting on how it was viewed at the time of its development, Larry Crook writes, "For the white upper class, the rumba was little more than a barbarian expression of an inferior and primitive culture and was intimately tied to such things as drinking, rowdy and licentious behaviour, and crime" (33). Since 1959 the rumba has been transformed into the national dance of Cuba in an attempt to realize some of Fidel Castro's revolutionary goals, such as the eradication of racial distinctions and a celebration of the African presence within Cuban society and culture (Daniel, 1995). Since the revolution Cuban audiences have been exposed to both the history and performance of rumba. According to Yvonne Daniel, this popularization of African-derived dance and music complexes has lessened the "shame" that for centuries was associated with the actual gestures and rhythms of these practices, specifically the exhibition of the dancing body isolating the hips with the back bent forward to the beats of complex drumming (Daniel, 2002: 51).

The revolutionary government capitalized on rumba's link to African roots and brought it into the cultural foreground as an example of Cuba's renewed identity as an Afro-Latin nation. This image of Cuba as a nation marked by African heritage was put forward to Cubans and the world, creating a contrast with its past unrealistic portrayal as a Euro-American nation. Before the nineteenth century, Cuba's identity had been more predominantly Euro-American (Daniel, 2002: 50–51), as the greatest number of people of African descent were brought by force to Cuba after 1800. Despite the promotion of an African-centered image of Cuba, the African-derived dance culture in Cuba may still be denigrated even under Communism. In light of comments made by David Calzado (1994), Robin Moore reveals how Communist Party officials do not necessarily hold African-derived Cuban dance music in high esteem, often referring to it as vulgar, crude, and low-class. Nonetheless, given its popularity, dance music is promoted and supported, according to Moore, as a means to reward those who support the government (Moore, 2002: 56).

Salsa has links with the various versions of the rumba. Under the heading of rumba, there are a number of forms: the *guaguancó*, *yambú*, and *columbia*. The first two dances are performed by a single couple, whereas the *columbia* is historically a male competitive dance. Today young women also perform the complex footwork of the *columbia*. The tempos of the three types vary: the *yambú* is slow, the *guaguancó* is faster, and the *columbia* is the fastest (Daniel, 2002: 40). These three dances are similar in that they are essentially subtle variations of a particular assemblage of instrumentation and choreography (Hamilton Crowell, Jr., 2002: 14). Incorporating highly creative and improvisational stylization, the dancers interpret the rhythm of the clave, one of the two sticks (or claves) that beat out the rhythm. The term "clave" also refers to the organizing rhythmic structure that is characteristic of Cuban music. In the first two versions of the rumba, the male-female couple dances alone in a circle, adopting a bodily stance that consists of lowering the knees and bending forward as much as possible. The man enacts a chase of the woman in both the *yambú* and *guaguancó* (Daniel, 2002: 49). In the *guaguancó*, the male dancer excecutes gestures, termed in the contemporary context *el vacunao*, that involve a pelvic thrust derived from the Kongo tradition. In response to the male advances, the female dancer hides and protects herself (49).

The developments of the rumba complex are centuries old. The *guaguancó* and the other styles descended from social dances popular in Cuba before the nineteenth century. Researchers of Cuban music associate the rumba with dances such as the *yuka* and *makuta*, which were performed by enslaved people from the Congo and by their descendants (Santos Gracia and Armas Rigal, 2002: 51), and argue that rumba derives particularly from these forms. The *yuka*, for instance, exhibits the rolling hips and pelvis derived from the Congo-Angola tradition (Hamilton Crowell, Jr., 2002: 15). Cuban dance, like other dances of the Americas, has inherited hip and pelvic movements that have been linked with the dance culture of the African peoples from the Congo (Stearns and Stearns, 1968: 14).

The rumba is both an uncomplicated and intricate dance. It is simple because at its core is a basic step consisting of the rumba dancer stepping to the side with the right foot and then bringing the feet together before repeating this move on the left with consequent alternations (Daniel, 2002: 49-50). The rumba is complex because the body movements are so varied and layered. According to Yvonne Daniel, it is a dance that is extremely difficult to describe with words. Nonetheless, she does provide the following depiction: "Suffice to say, the objective of rumba dances is to augment, decorate, and ornament the rhythmic pattern or clave, in absolute time but with the utmost of syncopation, and with the use of any and every body part that can move, especially the hips" (49).

Although the link between salsa and rumba emerges in all three forms, Nathaniel Hamilton Crowell, Jr., uses the *guanguancó* as an example of style in order to demonstrate this connection. In showing how salsa has emerged in part from the rumba, this chapter's depiction of the rumba integrates Hamilton Crowell, Jr.'s, illustration of the choreographic links between the *guaguancó* and salsa.

The rhythm of the *guaguancó* is straight, with accents on the 1 and 3. The time signature is 4/4, with an eighth note before the 1, which is a grace note. In the basic step of the rumba, the feet face forward. The dancer stands with her feet shoulder width apart. The knees are slightly bent. The arms should be bent enough that they are at the height of the dancer's chest. At each note, the dancer performs a corresponding step. The basic step, which is similar to that of salsa, consists of stepping from one side to another, a movement that is alternated (Hamilton Crowell, Jr., 2002: 14).

Because men and women do not dance together in the rumba, there is a feature of the choreography that is unique to the male dancers. The male choreography consists of an isolation of the ball of the foot at the grace note and the first beat, the 1, of the four-beat time signature. This separation of the toe and the heel orginates with the Congolese tradition (Hamilton Crowell, Jr., 2002: 16-17). The male dancers also isolate the hip at the 1 (14).

Salsa has therefore preserved much of the *guaguancó*'s version of the rumba as well as the rumba in general. This comes through in salsa's straight rhythm. It has a 4/4 time signature, with rhythmic accents on the 1 and 3. When the Puerto Ricans adapted the rumba, changing it into salsa, they altered the grace note from an eighth note to a sixteenth note. The salsa and rumba dances share common traits. First, the basic step of each dance is similar. Rumba and salsa dancers essentially step out to one side and then to the other. Second, salsa has inherited the isolation of the foot, which is a movement pattern reserved for only the male rumba dancer. This foot pattern has been maintained in a less complex form in salsa and entails the dancers placing the ball of the foot for the first and third notes of the four-beat rhythmic phrasing. Third, salsa perpetuates the hip isolations of rumba. The salsa dancer swings her or his hip to the left and then to the right with the first and third beats of the music in a way that is parallel to the hip swinging movement of the rumba (Hamilton Crowell, Jr., 2002: 14-15).

The rumba's musical spectrum includes only claves (or sticks), drums, shakers, and human voices. The clave as an organizing rhythm exists in salsa as either a *son* clave or a rumba clave. The *son* clave is the following: "one, two, three/ one, two//one, two, three/ one, two//" (Daniel, 2002: 47). The rumba clave alters the *son* clave in the following way: "one, two ___ three/ one, two// one, two ___ three/ one, two//" (47). The rumba clave has a half-beat more than the *son* clave. A connection lies between the rumba and the *son* in that Cuban composers integrated rumba forms into *son*-based music (50).

Unlike the Cuban rumba, with its predominant link to African-derived expressive arts, the mambo and the *son* both emerged from a more pronounced blend of African and European cultures. The *son* as well as the Cuban contemporary dance the *casino*, known internationally as Cuban salsa, can be traced back to the *contredanse* (referred to in Spanish as the *contradanza*), which originated in England and Normandy (Balbuena, 2003: 24). Although initially rooted in England, the *contredanse* migrated to other countries, such as France, Holland, and Spain. It was the most popular in France and hence is often referred to as the French *contredanse* (Balbuena, 2003: 24; Leymaire, 1995). The *contredanse* arrived in Cuba through various European channels. It was introduced by Spain, which imposed its colonial customs and practices on this Caribbean island. It also arrived via England after the British captured Havana in 1762 during the Seven Years War (1756–63). Lastly, it came via France as a result of the migrations of Franco-Haitians (black and white colonials) to the Oriente Province of Cuba during the period of the Haitian revolution in 1791 (Balbuena, 2003: 25; León, 1974: 7). French colonials left Haiti either before or during the Haitian revolution; others came to Cuba to escape the United States' rule of French Louisiana (1803) and New Orleans (Daniel, 2002: 31; León, 1974: 8).

French colonial families, some of whom came with their slaves, introduced an aristocratic dance culture to Cuba patterned after court dancing in Europe (Daniel, 1995: 38). These French court dances, which had also previously been brought by the Spanish, included the *contredanse, los quadrilles,* and *los minuetes* (the quadrilles and minuets). Unlike the Spanish, who favoured the *zapateo*, a southern Andalucian dance tradition, over the court dances, the French settlers chose to emulate the luxuriance of the French court by maintaining these European dances in the New World and performing them in the courtly style of a half-toe position, in which the body weight was centered on the ball of the foot (Daniel, 2002: 32). The European dances that arrived in Cuba originated in Paris, the international capital of fashionable dances. Parisian styles spread throughout Europe and then to the Atlantic, first reaching the major port of Havana (in addition to Rio and

Buenos Aires) and eventually spreading to other cities, towns, and villages. Although European dances were initially learned by the upper class, they eventually trickled down to the lower social strata (Chasteen, 2004: 116).

Among the court dances brought to the island, the most persistent was the English country dance, or *contredanse*, which was a salon or parlor dance. The basic group formation of the *contredanse* consists of lines of couples who change places, creating complex floor patterns. As the couples walk to the rhythm of the music, their only contact with one another is the occasional touch of the fingers and the hands (Daniel, 2002: 32). In the 1800s there existed in Cuba a strong dissatisfaction with the corruption and incompetence of the ruling government from Spain, which was then a feudal and despotic nation. The *contredanse* appealed to Cubans during this era, as Peter Manuel suggests, because it stemmed from the cultures of the more open societies of western Europe: France, for instance, was emerging as a liberal bourgeois nation with a cosmopolitan culture (Manuel, 1995: 31).

First danced in the eighteenth century, the *contredanse* attained widespread popularity before adopting characteristics that transformed it into a distinct Cuban genre known as the *contradanza criolla*. The oldest known musical piece of the *contradanza criolla* is the *San Pascual Bailón*, an anonymous work published in 1803. A key characteristic of the *contradanza criolla* is the *ritmo de tango*, a musical configuration derived from African music (Balbuena, 2003: 25). This *ritmo de tango*, later referred to as the *ritmo de habanera*, consisted of a rhythmic figure of five pulses, known as *cinquillo*, in a three-beat frame and is connected to the development of the Cuban clave. In particular, the *cinquillo* rhythm is the first section of the *son* clave (Daniel, 2002: 51). The term "tango" was used in nineteenth-century Cuba to indicate any kind of African dancing (Chasteen, 2004: 26). Haitian blacks integrated this specific rhythm, which distinguished the Cuban variation from its European heir. The movements of the dance therefore developed to express these African-derived rhythms. Nonetheless, European choreographic influences remained prominent; dancers, for instance, retained the upright posture of the European heritage (Daniel, 2002: 33). When the lower strata of Cuban society, whose members were often poor and black, adopted elite international dances such as the *contredanse*, they altered them by adding African-derived rhythms and moves to these European forms (Chasteen, 2004: 135). These modified versions of European-derived dances were eventually imitated by the higher social classes (135).

The *contradanza criolla* is the first of a set of related Cuban dances that stem from the French *contredanse* and the Haitian *tumba francesca* (Daniel, 2002: 51). Yvonne Daniel refers to the *contradanza criolla* as the *contradanza cubana*, which is also referred to as the *contradanza*. The *tumba francesca* is a music and dance tradition dating back to the 1700s that still exists in Cuba today. It refers to the dance culture introduced by Haitians of African descent who were brought to Cuba. They performed imitations of European court dances, such as the *contredanse*, *quadrilles*, *minuets*, and *cotillions*, to the accompaniment of drums as opposed to the string and wood instrumentation of the European tradition (33).

The basic step of *son*-based contemporary salsa dance can be traced back to the basic step of the *contradanza criolla* (Balbuena, 2003: 25). It consists of a forward and backward movement, in which the placement of the feet are alternated in time with four musical beats. On the first three beats, the foot is placed completely on the floor, and on the fourth beat, the heel simply rests. This basic step has been carried through the ages by the heirs of the *contredanza*, which include the *danza*, the *danzón*, the *son*, the Cuban *casino*, and various contemporary salsa styles. Although the core of the basic step remained the same, with each new dance, this step was and continues to be performed differently, incorporating various bodily and rhythmic accents as well as myriad footwork and figure patterns (25–26).

By the beginning of the nineteenth century, the *contradanza* had developed into a Cuban dance called the *contradanza habanera,* or *danza,* which incorporated the disparate cultural elements comprising the national identity (Daniel, 1995: 39). As the *danza* had a musical form similar to that of the *contredanza,* for a period of time the two forms were considered synonymous (Balbuena, 2003: 28). The *danza* includes the body part isolation of African dance, a European musical form, and a French Haitian dance structure (Daniel, 1995: 39). This dance was the most significant musical and dance form in the development of nineteenth-century Cuban Creole national culture: it was danced in all corners of the island by all classes (Chasteen, 2004: 157). The *danza* also marked the first time in the history of Cuban dance that the couple danced in the closed social dance position, or *positión de baile social cerrado* (Balbuena, 2003: 28). The closed-couple hold arrived in Cuba in the nineteenth century through international elite dances, such as the waltz and the polka (Chasteen, 2004: 122, 125).[2] The popularity of the *danza* endured from the 1840s to the 1870s, exhibiting a longevity that can be attributed to the desire on the part of elite Cubans born on the island, referred to as *criollos,* to distinguish themselves from their Spanish overlords. By adopting a Cuban popular dance form that had been mixed with African culture, they defied the Spanish, and hence European, dominance of their overseers (162).

Various principal figures of the *danza* remain today in salsa's predecessor, the *son,* as well as in the Cuban version of salsa, the *casino.* These include the *paseo, ocho,* and *caja y cedazo.* The *paseo,* for instance, has prevailed in Cuban dances such as the *danzón, danzonete, son,* and *casino* as well as in contemporary salsa dance outside the Cuban context. The *paseo* consists of a displacement of the basic step in order to move forward on the dance floor. The *paseo* can be compared to two figures—*vamos arriba* (let's go up) and *vamos abajo* (let's go down)—of the *rueda de casino,* the circular group version of the *casino,* in which the basic step is performed with a displacement so that the dancing couples can move from partner to partner in a circle formation (Balbuena, 2003: 29). In the case of the *vamos arriba,* for instance, while the couples are positioned in the *casino* circle, the men perform the basic step with a displacement in a counterclockwise direction, with the women moving clockwise (53).

In the 1880s the *danza* was replaced by the *danzón,* which remained the national dance of Cuba until the 1930s. Although this dance maintained European elements, Afro-Cuban rhythms were evident in the continuation of the African Cuban syncopations, or *cinquillo ostinato* (Manuel, 1995: 34). Despite the *danzón's* incorporation of African-derived rhythmic patterns, it was considered more cultivated and restrained than the rumba, whose highly rhythmic movements were associated with proletarian Afro-Cuban culture (37). The body movements and spatial dynamics of the danzón were slower and more rhythmic than those of the dances that had come before, and they allowed greater creative freedom (Balbuena, 2003: 30). The musical creation of the *danzón* is attributed to Miguel Failde (1852–1921). The first *danzón,* called *Las Alturas de Simpson,* was performed in 1879 (30).

The *danzón* constantly repeated the *ritmo de tango,* later referred to as the *ritmo habanera,* which incited the dancers to move their hips (Daniel, 2002: 52). This rhythm, a syncopated pattern, or *cinquillo,* enabled the dancers to emphasize the hip motion and to lower their center of gravity in the dance, resulting in the creation of a sinuous form. European set dances, for instance, required a higher center of gravity than this African-inspired Cuban dance. While the *danza* was marked by a choreography comprised of a multitude of figures, *danzón* couples often danced simply cheek-to-cheek (Chasteen, 2004: 20). The sensuality of the *danzón* rendered it a risqué genre (80). Its provocative quality also lay in its strong African influences. Consequently, the presence of the *danzón* at a white event in the late nineteenth century could, according to John Charles Chasteen, still provoke scandal (76). This dance was not part of either black or white society but thrived at racially mixed events. Consequently, the *danzón* was developed and enjoyed by people of mixed racial backgrounds (31). Because of the independence movements in Cuba, many *criollos* did not associate with Spaniards. And a growing sentiment again emerged that patriotism could be expressed through adoption of Afro-Cuban forms. This embrace of African-influenced Cuban genres meant that the *danzón* eventually became acceptable in middle-class society (73). Even middle-class women danced the *danzón* in the mid-1880s (80). White middle-class men typically had greater entry into African-influenced culture than did middle-class women since men were at greater liberty to frequent popular dance events, providing them with exposure and knowledge of black culture as well as sexual access to black women (204).

The *chachachá* is regarded by some dance scholars as a descendant of the *danzón* and consequently as part of the family of dances originating with the *contredanse*. The *chachachá* dance is quite different even though its musical structure and instrumentation resemble the *danzón* and its derivatives, the *danzonete* and *dazonchá*. In the *chachachá*, the dancers move with three quick steps and two slow ones. This dance developed in the early part of the century, yet it became popular with Enrique Jorrin's composition at the beginning of the 1950s (Daniel, 2002: 52–53). Jorrin's *La Enganadora*, written in 1949 and popularized by a widely diffused record in 1951, stands as the pivotal musical piece of the *chachachá* (Balbuena, 2003: 37). The *chachachá* has been danced in the Caribbean and in Central and South America and performed and diffused by people of Caribbean descent living in North America, Europe, and Africa (Daniel, 2002: 53).

Traces of the *chachachá* remain in contemporary *casino*, the Cuban version of salsa (Balbuena, 2003: 37). In the 1950s, Cuban dance culture traveled via migration and media—for example, films—to New York as well as to parts of Latin America and the Caribbean. Consequently, the *chachachá* also probably influenced the salsa that would develop in New York in the 1960s from a blend of Cuban genres transported to the city by people of diverse Caribbean backgrounds. The choreographic contribution of the *chachachá* to the *casino* lies not in the performance of the basic step but in the figures of the dance. The *chachachá* can be danced by couples in the closed social dance position but also by male and female dancing pairs, who simply face one another without touching. This loosening of the couple hold was to have an influence on the choreographic development of the Cuban *casino* (38). Furthermore, various figures of the *chachachá* can be found in the Cuban *casino*, such as the opening and closing of the couple, which is also a figure of the *son*, and certain rapid turns of the couple and turn combinations (38).

One key influence of the *chachachá* on the Cuban *casino* that did not mark versions of salsa outside Cuba was the performance of the *rueda* (circle). At the end of the 1950s, the *rueda* developed as a new variation of the *chachachá*, known as the *chachachá en rueda*. It was called the *rueda* because the dance formation consisted of couples performing the figures in unison while forming a circle that advanced either clockwise or counterclockwise. The *rueda* was directed by a man who signaled to the dancers the changes of partners and the combinations of turns and figures. According to Bárbara Balbuena, the formation of the *rueda* could have come from the *danzón,* in which partners formed a circle moving in a clockwise or counterclockwise direction but without changing partners as in the *chachachá* (Balbuena, 2003: 38–39).

The *son* developed in the middle of the nineteenth century, influenced by the *danzón* and the rumba. As the *son* evolved into its mature version, it blended sophisticated harmonies and the European instruments (horn and piano) with gradual intergration of faster tempos and heavy percussive rhythms. Because of this fusion, Peter Manuel states that "the mature *son* was as much an heir to the proletarian rumba as to the suave and genteel *danzón*" (Manuel, 1995: 37). This dance and music complex marks the equal blending of white and black cultural forces that characterized Cuban society (36). Combining European-derived and African Cuban musical elements, the *son* became the most influential dance and music within Cuba as well as within the nations of the Spanish Caribbean (36). Since the middle of the nineteenth century, the *son* had been evolving in the Oriente Province, which was peopled by Haitian refugees of African and European background who had fled the rebellious wars of Haiti. Black and mulatto musicians of both Haitian and Cuban backgrounds came together to create this genre (Fairley, 2000: 389). The *son* originated in various cities in the Oriente Province, such as Guantánamo, Baracoa, Manzanillo, and Santiago de Cuba (Balbuena, 2003: 35). It arrived in Havana around 1909 through diverse migrations as well as via the soldiers of an established permanent army (35). Although the *son* was developed and initially enjoyed by the lower classes, it eventually crossed class lines and was performed in elegant venues. The *son* enjoyed its golden age in the 1920s and 1930s, when it was played by trios, sextets, and septets; in the 1950s, the period of its greatest popularity, the *son* was performed with jazz orchestras (35). Early developments of this genre had more pronounced European features, including the dominant presence of string instruments, such as guitars and the guitar-like *tres*, a more restrained tempo, and a song-like first section, called the *largo*, which was characterized by an extended harmonic progression and by a melody often sung "in a bel canto style" (Manuel, 1995: 36). African Cuban influences on the *son* emerge in the use of bongo drums and an African-derived instrument called the *marimbula* as well as in the inclusion of an extensive *montuno*, "the final and, usually, longest part of a rumba, *son*, or other Afro-Cuban derived dance-music

piece, employing call-and-response vocals over a rhythmic and harmonic ostinato" (252). The similarities between the *son* and the rumba lie in the *son's*
integration of the *largo-montuno* structure, its use of claves, or sticks, and its
integration of ostinato. Most *son* musicians and dancers were black or mulatto; the lyrics of the *son* expressed the barrio street life of African Cuban
society (36).

Varieties of the *son*, such as the *changüí*, *sucu sucu*, and *son habanero*, developed in different areas of Cuba. From a choreographic perspective, there
are two principal ways to dance the *son:* the *son montuno* and the *son urbano*.
The *son montuno* is characterized by an accented movement of the torso toward the sides, a deep bending of the legs that creates a constant raising and
lowering of the body, and frequent up and down arm gestures, which have
been referred to by dance connoisseurs as *sacar aqua del pozo* (drawing water
from the well) (Balbuena, 2003: 35; Santos Gracia and Armas Rigal, 2002:
230). Before the emergence of the *chachachá* in the 1950s, the *son montuno*
was performed in a *rueda* (circle) with simple changes in dancing partners
(Balbuena, 2003: 39). According to Bárbara Balbuena, the movements of the
son urbano are slower, smoother, and more elegant than those of the *son montuno*. In contrast to the *son montuno*, dancers performing the *son urbano* assume a more erect dance position, bend the knees in a less pronounced manner, and do not display the continuous movements of the arms. Bárbara
Balbuena further explains how the movement style of this latter version of
the *son* is a precursor to the *casino* (35). Contemporary salsa probably also derives from the *son urbano*, as this urban version of the *son* migrated from Havana to New York as well as to certain cities in Latin America.

Both today's salsa and the Cuban *casino* retain various choreographic and
musical aspects of the *son*. For instance, throughout a performance of the *son*,
the dancer must maintain the rhythm of the music with the basic step. The
basic step of the *son* can be danced either with the beat of the clave, which
is also with the melody of the music, or *contratiempo* (against the rhythm or
counter-rhythm) of the clave. Performing the *son* against the rhythm of the
clave is considered to be the most authentic and enriched version of the
dance (Balbuena, 2003: 36). The ability of a dancer to move with, as well as
against, the rhythm of the music is essential in the *son* and its successors: salsa
and the *casino*. As already mentioned, the *son* is characterized by a rhythmic
scheme that stems from the clave, termed the *son* clave, which has been
maintained in contemporary salsa. The *son's* inseparable link between
rhythm, melody, and keeping time with the basic step has endured in contemporary performances of the Cuban *casino* (36) as well as in the various
forms of contemporary salsa outside Cuba.

The *son*'s basic step can be found in a similar version in the Cuban *casino* and in contemporary salsa styles. These similarities lie in the musical time in which the basic step is performed as well as in the spatial and corporeal patterns that embellish it. The *son*, like the *casino* and salsa, is performed in four beats, the first three of which correspond to a step and the fourth of which is a pause. As noted above, this basic step dates back to the *contradanza*. The closed social dance position of *son* couples has been retained in contemporary salsa styles and the Cuban *casino*. In the *son* and its heirs, the dancers perform a variety of figures that are repeated throughout the dance. Some of these include turns of the woman on her own axis as well as around the male dancer, fast and slow turns of the couple, arm combinations to perform the turns, and the opening and closing of the couple's embrace (Balbuena, 2003: 36).

Cuban dance structure can be distinguished from other non-Hispanic patterns in the Caribbean: there is more focus in Cuba on elaborate footwork that extends beyond a repeated walking step. In many of the dances of Cuba, of which the *son* and its heirs provide examples, the footwork is syncopated rather than marked by an even rhythm. Dance manuals have simplified the syncopation of the *son* through step instructions that describe the footwork as "short, short, long." In contrast, the basic step of other Caribbean dances, such as the merengue, *zouk, compass,* and calypso, is a two-beat walking step that is alternated; according to Yvonne Daniel, it can be identified as a "one, two" or "walk, walk" basic step (Daniel, 2002: 24).

In the first half of the twentieth century, the *son* enjoyed immense popularity in both Havana and New York. Just as America adopted Cuban forms, U.S. cultural influence became more pronounced within Cuba during this era. With the defeat of Spain in the Spanish-American War (1898), Cuba eventually became independent in 1902. Cuba in turn began to establish links with the United States. With its strong political, economic, and cultural connections with the United States, Cuba entered an era of North American domination. There were also various periods in this epoch when United States Marines occupied the island: 1906–1909, 1912, 1917–1920, and 1933–1934 (Manuel, 1995: 35).

This U.S. presence seeped into Cuban dance. In the early twentieth century, jazz dances such as the one step, two step, fox trot, and charleston were performed in dance halls on the island (Linares, 1974: 133). This North American cultural presence was strengthened at the beginning of the 1930s by the mass media's dissemination of cultural forms and by international concert tours that further exposed Cuban artists to American culture. By the 1950s, North American music and dances were extremely popular in Cuba. Rock and roll, for instance, enjoyed a strong youth following during this decade (Balbuena, 2003: 40). At this time, according to Roberto Sánchez Vignot, the younger generation of Cubans favored American popular music and dances, such as the twist, rock and roll, and rhythm and blues, over the Cuban *son*, *mambo*, *danzón*, and *chachachá* (Sánchez Vignot, 2004).

Vestiges of rock are visible in Cuban dances, particularly the *casino*. The incorporation of this North American genre into Cuban culture took place in the 1950s (Balbuena, 2003: 40). In early developments of the *casino* during this decade, dancers performed specific acrobatic turns and moves that came from rock and roll. For instance, they added a little leap to the opening and closing figure (40) as well as a circular movement of the arms performed while the man holds the woman's right hand with his left hand. Furthermore, early forms of the *chachachá* also exhibited traces of rock's influence, particularly in the performance of two figures called the *cojito* and the *suiza* (41). Rock and roll entered the Cuban movement vernacular that was being recreated and transformed within the North American context in the late 1940s and 1950s. Rock steps, for instance, could be found in Cuban dances such as the mambo being performed in the Palladium Ballroom in New York City in the 1950s (Stearns and Stearns, 1968: 360). Marshall and Jean Stearns cite the example of New York mambo dancer Pedro Aguilar, who incorporated rock and roll in addition to other American vernacular steps into his Afro-Cuban creations (360).

Cuban popular genres consequently had considerable influence on popular dance culture in North America. Following America's takeover of Puerto Rico in 1917 and the resulting migration of Puerto Ricans to New York (Duany, 2000: 5–6), Cuban music and dance, particularly the *son*, arrived in the city of New York, where Cuban and Puerto Rican musicians and composers kept Cuban music alive while transforming it in the American context. In Puerto Rico, Cuban music was and continues to be popular. According to Peter Manuel, "From the early 1800s until today, Puerto Ricans have avidly borrowed and mastered various Cuban music styles, including the Cuban *danzón*, *son*, *guaracha*, rumba and *bolero*" (Manuel, 1995: 52; italics added).

Ruth Glasser criticizes such salsa historians as Peter Manuel (1995) and John Storm Roberts (1979) because they do not recognize the significant contribution by Puerto Rican musicians and composers to the development of the *son*. Puerto Ricans are considered to have merely adopted and recycled Cuban music without having a hand in its creative evolution (Glasser, 1998: 10–11). Puerto Ricans, however, were not the only people in the Caribbean who borrowed Cuban music: musicians and dancers in the Dominican Republic, Guadeloupe, Haiti, Martinique, and Columbia produced the "*son Caribeno*," a version popularized throughout the Caribbean (Angeloro, 1992:

305). The *son* was embraced in the United States, Africa, and Latin America (Manuel, 1995: 43).

Nonetheless, the musical transformation of the *son* by both Cubans and Puerto Ricans altered the musical genre through the introduction of more complex jazz-influenced harmonies and European instruments, such as horns and piano. The tempo increased, and the rhythm section became more percussive (Manuel, 1995: 36–37). The most dramatic transfiguration of the *son* occurred in the 1940s in New York in the music of Conjunto Casino, whose bandleader, Arsenio Rodriguez, broadened the *son* ensemble by incorporating a conga, a piano, and a second trumpet. Further, musicians were to play regulated parts, a most radical change. The horn players, for example, played composed arrangements, while the rhythm section (piano, bass, and percussion) produced standardized accompaniment patterns. The mature modern *son* lost a certain amount of the musical improvisation that characterizes the traditional *son*. At the same time, these transformations created a concise and complex rhythm, with a driving force that compelled dancers to move with excitement and fervour. Th :se innovations laid the foundations for the birth of salsa, which was to emerge in the 1960s (37).

Salsa also evolved from the mambo, a blend of Afro-Cuban rhythms combined with the big band format of swing jazz. Cuban bandleader Dámaso Perez Prádo is credited with inventing the mambo in Havana in the 1940s, having introduced it to La Tropicana nightclub in Havana in 1943 (Manuel, 1995: 38). But Odilio Urfé claims that Prádo has been mistakenly credited with being the creator of the mambo. He cites documentation showing that it was actually created by Orestes López, a Cuban pianist, double bassist, and composer (Urfé, 1974: 71). The mambo was combined with the *son* and the *guaracha*, which is similar to the *son* but has a more upbeat tempo (Manuel, 1995: 72). As African Americans and Hispanics lived in close proximity in New York, their musical styles influenced one another. The mambo that thrived in New York brought together Cuban-influenced Puerto Rican styles, Afro-Cuban rhythms, and African American Jazz (Boggs, 1992a: 99). It also gave rise to a highly celebrated dance and music scene forged by famous bands led by Cubans Frank "Machito" Grillo and his brother-in-law Mario Bauza, as well as Puerto Ricans Ernesto "Tito" Puente and Pablo "Tito" Rodriguez (100). As New York musicians were often not directly influenced by Cuba, the migration of Cuban music to New York meant that the "typical" Cuban sound became altered to suit American tastes. The collaboration between African Cuban musician Mario Bauza and African American jazz musician Dizzy Gillespie illustrates how Cuban and American music began to fuse (102). Contemporary salsa, particularly the New York style, has been influenced by the New York mambo of the late 1940s and 1950s.

Mambo dance developed from the *son*. Although born in Cuba, it enjoyed a widespread craze in New York and throughout the world in the 1950s. As the mambo was transported to different parts of the globe, it transformed. Nonetheless, a version of the dance remains specific to Cuba. In the Cuban mambo, the foot pattern is not the *son*, characterized by the "short, short, long" basic step, but involves a "touch, step" repetitive sequence. In this pattern, the toe of the right foot, for instance, just touches the floor lightly, and then an entire step is executed with the right foot. The dancer repeats this step to the left. As the foot touches the floor, the hips and pelvis move forward and backward. There is a continuous alternation of the right and left foot sequence (Daniel, 2002: 44). The mambo's basic step has been identified with a dance originating in the Congo. Ferdinand Ortiz notes that the word "mambo" itself has a Congolese origin (Stearns and Stearns, 1968: 12). The mambo's count can be in either two (1-2) or four (1-2-3-4). The arms are bent at the dancers' sides and positioned slightly away from the body. The effect of this hold is natural, not stiff or overly stylized. Palms down and extended forward, mambo dancers sway their bent arms forward and back (Fernández, 1974: 73). The arm that swings is in opposition to the foot that steps. Yvonne Daniel describes the Cuban version as a "bouncy" dance that gives the impression that the entire body is moving up and down. Mambo is danced with occasional shimmeys of the shoulders, kicks, swift turns, and little jumps. Mambo traveled outside Cuba via a number of routes. Cuban musicians performing in cities throughout the world made it an international phenomenon. Puerto Ricans took the dance to New York City, and Cuban-born Pérez Prado brought it to Mexico. With these migrations came a change in the core step of the mambo: it went back to the basic step of the *son* foot pattern, described by Yvonne Daniel as "short short long." The international version no longer conveyed the lively and spirited feel of the Cuban mambo but emulated the smooth and alluring aura of its predecessor: the *son* (Daniel, 2002: 44).

Both within and outside Cuba, the mambo developed turns executed by dancing couples. This further differentiated the mambo from its antecendent *son* tradition, in which partners held one another closely as they moved around the dance floor. In the mambo, the male dancer, his arm upheld, guided the woman while she performed complex and smooth turns. The dancers either performed such turns or moved together with sensuous grace in a closed-couple hold. In the international version of mambo, dancers would also break the closed-couple embrace and dance separately. Once disunited from the couple hold, the solo dancers could then improvise their individual movements, which involved rhythmically executed gestures of the arms, head, and chest, while continuing the *son*-based basic step (Daniel, 2002: 45).

Large ballrooms, such as the Palladium, featured Latin music stars (Boggs, 1992a: 99). Machito, Tito Puente, and Tito Rodriguez performed the mambo with their bands in these venues for Latino and Anglo audiences as well as for New Yorkers from varied backgrounds (101). Blacks, Anglos, Latinos, Jews, Italians, and Chinese frequented the Palladium (Manuel, 1995: 69). Paolo Torres discloses how diverse the audience was at this Latin music venue of the 1950s: "The audience was never exclusively Latin. A pattern soon established itself. On Wednesday nights when 'Killer Joe' Piro gave dance lessons, the crowd was Jewish and Italian. Friday was for Puerto Ricans, Saturday for Hispanics of all origins . . . and Sunday . . . was for American blacks. *Everybody* danced to Latin music" (quoted in Boggs, 1992c: 129, emphasis in the original). Ernie Ensley, one of New York's most famous *mamberos* of the 1950s, suggests that the audience was not only diverse but also occasionally mixed. In an interview with Vernon Boggs, Ensley states that this was actually the case on Friday nights at the Palladium: "Friday night was the regular dancing crowd. Black, white, Spanish; everybody would get up there Friday night" (147).

Just as African American Jazz was fused with Cuban music in New York, so were steps from Jazz dance incorporated into Cuban dances, such as the mambo, *chachachá*, and other styles popular during the late 1940s and throughout the 1950s. This merging took place as jazz dancers from the Savoy Ballroom came to the Palladium Ballroom on Broadway and 53rd Street in New York City. Marshall and Jean Stearns provide examples of dancers during this epoch who blended various genres with the Cuban forms. The young dancer Teddy Hill, for instance, added lindy and charleston steps to the mambo. Cuban Pete (Pedro) Aguilar, who came to New York from Puerto Rico when he was three years old, blended tap, acrobatics, and, as noted above, rock and roll dances in his rendition of the mambo (Stearns and Stearns, 1968: 360). A dance team from the Palladium known as the Cha Cha Taps, formed by male dancing pair Charles Arroyo and Michael Ramos, combined an array of dance forms in their version of Cuban dance. For instance, they added a number of jazz moves, such as the buck-and-wing, brush, and slap, to their Cuban dancing (360). The buck-and-wing dates back to the vernacular dance of minstrel shows and consists of an integration of clogs and jigs (50). In the brush, a step from tap dance, "one foot is moved forward, out, and around and back, followed by a quick Catch Step, in which the weight is transferred from one foot to the other with a stamp on the *off* beat" (177). The slap is a brush step without a transfer of weight. This dance team also incorporated ballet arm and hand gestures along with Afro-Cuban corporeal movement and the footwork of tap (360).

In the 1940s the artistry of star dancer and teacher Frank "Killer Joe" Piro brought together thirty years of popular jazz dance and other American forms and incorporated them into the mambo. Piro was famous as a jitterbug dancer at the Savoy. After the Second World War, he taught Afro-Cuban dances at the Palladium, incorporating the African American jazz dancing of his earlier days at the Savoy. In the 1960s, when the twist was a dance craze, he modified this popular dance by adding steps from his days doing the jitterbug at the Savoy and teaching mambo at the Palladium (Stearns and Stearns, 1968: 361). The Afro-Cuban dances of the 1950s were being refashioned by and fused with the dance culture in which they were being performed and taught. This process forshadowed how salsa itself would become a dance that brought together not only diverse Cuban forms but also dances from the specific local contexts in which it developed. American Jazz had an influence on Cuban cultural forms not only within the United States—with the arrival of the *son* in New York in the 1920s and of the mambo and the *chachachá* in the 1940s and 1950s—but within Cuba itself. As previously noted, the one step, two step, charleston, and fox trot came to Cuba in the 1920s through either recorded music or performances by American orchestras (Linares, 1974: 133; Valenzuela, 2005). American genres had a deep impact on Cuban culture. In addition to the *son*, the popularity of the fox trot, for instance, during this era led to a decline in popular taste for the *danzón* (Linares, 1974: 135).

The Cuban revolution of 1959, which resulted in a Communist dictatorship under the leadership of Fidel Castro, disconnected Cuba from the rest of the world. The American embargo against Cuba meant that North Americans and Puerto Ricans were cut off from musical and cultural developments in Cuba. The influence of Cuban music on popular music in the United States vanished as a result of the *Trading with the Enemy Act*, which completely prohibited the entry of Cuban music and musicians into the United States (Pacini Hernández, 1998: 111). Breaking economic ties with Cuba would eventually provide a creative space for Latinos within the United States to develop U.S.-based dance and music cultural forms and industries. Prior to 1959 most of the dance crazes popular in Europe and the United States, such as the *son*, ballroom rumba, mambo, and *chachachá*, had their roots in Cuba (Moore, 2002: 58).

Salsa appeared on the popular music scene in the mid 1960s in New York. The early sixties had not been a favorable time for Latin music in the city. The mambo craze had vanished. Small ensembles and rock and roll were replacing big bands (Manuel, 1995: 72). In New York there was growing discontent among Latinos, especially Puerto Ricans, who wished to change the social conditions in which they lived (Marre and Charlton, 1985: 71–73). Inspired by the Black Panthers of the black power movement of the 1960s, Latinos in New York formed the Young Lords, a group of socially and politically motivated activists. They fought for the just treatment of Latinos and sought to change how Puerto Ricans viewed themselves. The Young Lords advocated Latino pride in their cultural heritage and rejected the assimilation of Puerto Ricans into Anglo-centric American society, a phenomenon that had been partially triggered by the shame that many Puerto Ricans felt regarding their language and culture. Certain issues were on the agenda: the civil rights movement, new interest in cultural roots, and the Puerto Rican independence movement (Manuel, 1995: 73). In a sense, salsa's development captured this self-awareness and political consciousness that was stirring Puerto Ricans in New York.

Rather than their traditional music forms, such as the *bomba* and the *plena*, Puerto Ricans chose modernized Cuban dance music to express Latin identity and pride, particularly the *son*, which they had played and composed since the 1920s. The *son* expressed the urban life of Puerto Ricans in New York barrios more poignantly than did the folkloric music of their homeland. The Cuban origins of the *son* and the rumba were downplayed, and these pre-Revolutionary Cuban sounds became a symbol of the barrio's rebellious atmosphere and of Puerto Rican identity. This music, which represented Latinos—particularly Puerto Ricans—in New York, eventually began to signify Puerto Rican identity in general. Migration influenced the development of Puerto Rican culture off the island: since the 1920s, 44 percent of Puerto Ricans had moved to the United States (Duany, 2000: 6). The majority of Puerto Rican music was written and recorded in New York. As music historian Jorge Javariz writes, "Puerto Rico is the only Latin American country whose popular music was mainly created on foreign soil" (quoted in Manuel, 1995: 67).

The sounds of the *son*, mambo, and rumba as well as other Cuban rhythms and forms, such as the *guaracha*,[3] *chachachá*, and *bolero*[4] (Waxer, 2002c: 5), were fused under the single designation "salsa," a new name for a musical style that had existed since the 1950s, made famous by such artists as Puerto Rican Tito Puente and Cuban Celia Cruz. The use of "salsa" as a marketable term became widespread with Johnny Pacheco's founding of Fania Records in 1964 (Boggs, 1992a: 103–4; Marre and Charlton, 1985: 81), which promoted the *son*-mambo-rumba complex as salsa to downplay the Cuban origins of the music. Yet Fania Records did not invent the term.

Rather, this Hispanic Caribbean music started to be termed "salsa" after the release in 1966 of a record produced in Venezuela entitled *Llegó la Salsa*

(Salsa Arrived) by Federico y su Combo (Arias Satizábal, 2002: 251). This was the first album to employ the term "salsa" to denote this Hispanic Caribbean music (Rondón, 1980: 33; Waxer, 2002b: 219). Medardo Arias Satizábal writes, "Curiously, after that LP and with the homogenization of Caribbean rhythms into a commercial formula that allowed for a rapid identification from this part of the world, everything was converted into 'Salsa'" (Arias Satizábal, 2002: 251). In 1962 Radio Difusora, a radio station in Caracas, Venezuela, featured a radio show called *La Hora del Sabor, la Salsa y el Bembe*, in which the latest releases by new artists such as Tito Puente and Eddie Palmieri were played. This radio program is considered to be the first instance in which the label "salsa" is used to refer to a particular genre of Hispanic Caribbean music (Waxer, 2002b: 225). It is often said that the Venezuelan disc jockey Phidias Danilo Escalona was one of the earliest users of the term "salsa" to refer to this Hispanic Caribbean music (Waxer, 2002c: 4; Rondón, 1980: 33). Many artists saw the term "salsa" merely as a commercial title: Tito Puente, for instance, who eventually accepted the term, was known to have said, "The only salsa I know comes in a bottle. I play Cuban music" (quoted in Manuel, 1995: 74).

Salsa follows the structural patterns of the modern *son*, described above: a typical salsa begins with a songlike initial section, followed by a prolonged *montuno*, the longest part of the song, characterized by call-and-response vocals. Then an instrumental break section referred to as the mambo or *mona* steps in, followed by improvised jazz-influenced solos. A harmonic-rhythmic ostinato repeats over these sections (Manuel, 1995: 83). A salsa band comprises ten to fourteen members, including the leader (who in contemporary bands is also the singer), two to four horn players, and musicians who play piano, bass, conga, bongo, and timbales (a set of two drums and a cowbell). There are also sometimes one or two *coro*, or choral refrain singers, one of whom might also play the clave, guiro, or maracas. A number of horn instruments can be found in a typical salsa band: a set of two trumpets known as the conjunto, a four-trumpet assemblage, or the most common arrangement of two trumpets with one or more saxophones and trombones (83).

Many Cuban musicians, according to Lise Waxer, often view salsa as simply "Cuban music in new clothes" (Waxer, 2002c: 5). A number of musicologists counter this Cuban-centered perspective, claiming that it downplays the musical innovations that occurred outside Cuba. They stress instead how stylistic changes rendered salsa quite different from its origins in various Cuban music and dance forms of the 1940s and 1950s (Berríos-Miranda, 2002; Waxer, 2002c: 5). Lise Waxer notes how the salsa from the 1960s and 1970s, for instance, features a more extensive horn section and uses more percussion than did the majority of the Cuban groups in the 1940s and 1950s (Waxer, 2002c: 5). Marisol Berríos-Miranda elaborates how the Puerto Rican musician Eddie Palmieri has been a key figure in creating a new Latin sound by adding trombones to the traditional piano, violin, flute, and percussion (Berríos-Miranda, 2002: 28).

In the 1960s and 1970s, this Latin music spread to the Spanish-speaking nations of the Caribbean basin, most notably to Colombia, Venezuela, and Panama. In particular, both Venezuela and Colombia had a part to play in the development of contemporary salsa, transforming this music and dance according to their specific national identities while simultaneously enhancing its status as transnational music and dance. Beginning in the 1960s in Caracas, Venezuela, and Cali, Colombia, salsa started to become part of the local popular culture. Both Caracas and Cali had previously been exposed to Cuban-derived rhythms in the 1920s, when Cuban *son* was popular in these two cities (Waxer, 2002b: 231).

Salsa became a part of working-class youth culture in Caracas in the 1960s and 1970s (Waxer, 2002b: 224). Venezuela had undergone drastic and rapid urbanization, and the resulting social problems, such as urban alienation and malevolent barrio conditions, were echoed in salsa. Salsa became the preferred music of the lower classes in Venezuela (Manuel, 1995: 79). This music was denigrated by middle-class and upper-class teenagers, who referred to it as *música de malandros* or *música de monos* (music of lowlifes or music of apes) because of its class and racial associations, identities that have been collapsed in Venezuelan society. Not only were *caraqueños* (citizens of Caracas) who danced and listened to salsa adopting an Afro-Caribbean cultural practice, but they were also Venezuelans of full or partial African heritage (Waxer, 2002b: 225). Similarly, Puerto Ricans in New York who listened and danced to salsa were called by a racist term, *cocolos*, to differentiate them from *rockeros*, Puerto Ricans who adopted mainstream American culture, particularly rock music (Sánchez González, 1999: 246); the term *cocolos*, which means "coconut-heads," was used by affluent "Yankophilic" *rockeros* to denigrate salsa fans (Manuel, 1994b: 23).

Through the meetings of working-class and middle-class intellectuals at the Universidad Central de Venezuela in the mid 1970s, salsa began to be adopted by the middle classes as a symbol of the authentic music of the people and a means to establish a pan-Latino identity throughout Latin America (Waxer, 2002b: 226). The salsa group Dimensión Latina, formed in 1972-73 and founded by Oscar D' León, is credited with bringing salsa music out of the barrios of Caracas and transforming this music into a style that evoked a pan-Latino identity in Venezuela. Drawing from Cesar Miguel Rondón's work, Lise Waxer writes, "as Rondón points out, the influence of New York salsa as a transnational style was key in the emergence of a pan-Latino identity in Venezuela" (Waxer, 2002b: 227; Rondón, 1980: 229). Dimensión Latina's invocation of "Latino" in its name drew upon a term imported from New York, signifying how intermixed peoples of diverse Latin and Caribbean heritages created a pan-Latinness that crossed national and regional boundaries. In Venezuela and other South American countries, identity was based on national affiliations as opposed to the notion of Latinidad. The Dimensión Latina musical style was inspired by the New York sound of Willie Colón and Héctor Lavoe (Waxer, 2002b: 226). From the mid 1970s to the early 1980s, salsa in Venezuela found its influences in groups from New York and Puerto Rico. Lise Waxer consequently argues that at the musical level, Venezuelan groups resembled those of New York and Puerto Rico. She writes, "Generally, Venezuelan salsa groups of this period were distinguished by a preference for many trombones in the brass section, and a tight rhythmic swing similar to that of New York and Puerto Rican salsa bands, where the beat feels like it is propelled from behind" (228). As the salsa scene burgeoned in Venezuela, it garnered international acclaim as a result of such superstars as Oscar D' León (Steward, 1994: 489–91).

Although New York–style salsa spread to Colombia, particularly Cali, in the 1960s, the appearance of Caribbean music in Colombia, according to Lise Waxer, dates back to the 1930s, when black Caribbean merchant sailors, called *chombos*, brought recordings of Cuban and Puerto Rican music to the seaport of Buenaventura. These sailors also brought with them ways of dancing to this music that eventually became part of the Buenaventura dance culture. These Caribbean recordings were played and danced to in bars and brothels in the city. Between the 1930s and 1950s, this music spread to Cali, which became passionately receptive to music and dance genres of Afro-Cuban and Puerto Rican origin (Waxer, 2002b: 231–32).

In the 1960s and 1970s, unlike Caracas, Cali did not have an evolved live music salsa scene. Rather, Cali was distinguished by the devotion of its salsa audience to dancing to music recordings by groups from Cuba, New York, and Puerto Rico. From its origins in neighborhood parties, the dancing moved to clubs that played a variety of recorded rhythms: 1950s Cuban *son*, *guaracha*, *bolero*, and mambo in addition to the more contemporary New York rhythms of the *pachanga*[5] and *boogaloo*.[6] A thriving record-based youth dance scene had developed in Cali by the late 1960s primarily because youths were barred from nightclubs. Instead, they set up their own dance spaces, called *agüelülos*. By the late 1960s and 1970s, salsa dancing expanded into a performance genre with dance competitions and salsa floor shows

(Waxer, 2002b: 235). During this era, salsa ceased to be solely a part of working-class culture when it entered the middle classes primarily through the interaction between middle-class leftist intellectuals and the working-classes within the university context (235). The conditions leading to the middle-class adoption of salsa were similar in Venezuela and Colombia. Colombia eventually surpassed Venezuela as a salsa center and in the 1980s developed a live music scene fostering such international stars as Joe Arroyo and Grupo Niche (Waxer, 2002b: 236). With the rise of the Cali cocaine cartel, a wealthy class began to take shape in the city in the 1980s and 1990s (235). The resulting boost in the city's economy facilitated the rise of a live music scene previously prohibited by limited economic resources (236).

Salsa's international urban appeal transformed a dance and music characterized by traditional Cuban cultural origins into a widespread metropolitan practice. Indeed, Reuben Blades saw his salsa music as the folklore of cities in Latin America (Marre and Charleton, 1985: 80). Born as an expression of Puerto Rican self-awareness and New York Latino pride, salsa music and dance came to signify a pan-Latin consciousness throughout the Americas. The lyrics of Fania-produced salsa songs evoked the experiences and concerns of people living in Latin American cities. The salseros of the 1960s and 1970s sang of love, but also cried out against American imperialism, urban alienation, violence, and the destitution of living in Latin ghettos, or barrios (Manuel, 1995: 75). Through the migration experience and mass media, Latinos throughout urban Latin America became increasingly conscious of one another and identified with the shared hardships, discontents, and pleasures conveyed through salsa. Salsa became both international and transnational, bringing together people of diverse backgrounds as it cut across national barriers in Latin America and the Caribbean. This combined international and transnational flavor was also apparent in New York, where Latino musicians and composers from a variety of backgrounds were involved in the evolution of salsa. For instance, Reuben Blades was of Panamanian descent, and Johnny Pacheco and José Alberto were Dominicans (Marre and Charlton, 1995: 80). Jewish American musicians, such as Larry Harlow and Marty Shellar, were also active in the salsa scene (Manuel, 1995: 78).

Salsa's transnationalism emerged in one of its distinguishing characteristics: its absorption of diverse national styles and rhythms as the music developed audiences in various nations and cities in the Americas. Rafael Cortijo and Ismael Rivera are credited with first including the Afro–Puerto Rican forms the *plena* and the *bomba* within Cuban-style combos, a technique that was then employed by other salsa bands, arrangers, and singers, such as El Gran Combo de Puerto Rico, Willie Colón, and Cheo Feliciano (Berríos-

Miranda, 2002: 28). Another example is Grupo Niche, a salsa group from Colombia, which incorporates *cumbia*, Colombia's national musical style, as well as *porro*, a variation of *cumbia* (36).

By the end of the 1970s, the salsa explosion had begun to wane. Fania Records folded in 1978. Salsa no longer dominated the Latin music market and was forced to compete with other types of music, most notably merengue from the Dominican Republic. The burgeoning demand for merengue was partially a result of the increased number of Dominicans in New York, which had reached 900,000 by 1990, representing 12 percent of the Dominican population (Austerlitz, 1997: 123). Many Latin music lovers in the United States and Latin America preferred merengue to salsa, as merengue has a punchier beat and is easier to dance to. Moreover, merengue bands are smaller and consequently cheaper than salsa bands (Manuel, 1995: 90). Salsa also had to compete with other American music styles, including hip-hop, rap, and rock. As second- and third-generation Americans of Latin descent assimilated into Anglo- or African American society and lost their Spanish, their tastes in music changed. Many young Latinos regarded salsa as a style of their parents' generation, associating it with quaint music from the islands (90). Another factor in salsa's downswing was the impact of large record companies, the so-called "majors," which have been involved in the Latin market in the United States since the 1980s. They helped to create a homogenized Latin music market dominated by Latino pop and sentimental ballads rather than by specific national and regional music, such as the Mexican *rancheras* and the Colombian *cumbia*. Even on radio, salsa was relegated to the margins of the musical spectrum.

Not until the 1990s did commercial salsa find a more central presence on the airwaves of New York and other U.S. cities, such as Miami and Los Angeles (Manuel, 1995: 90), where twenty-four-hour Spanish-language radio stations were established to air Latin music. The inception of these radio stations in the 1990s could be linked to advertisers' belief that Latinos are important consumers in the United States. As both the population and buying power of Latinos in the United States have been increasing since the 1990s (Farley, 1999: 43), Latinos are being increasingly targeted by advertisers. Citing the *Yankelovich Hispanic Monitor*, Arlene Dávila notes that from 1982 to 1993 the purchasing power of U.S. Latinos rose from $104 to $221 billion (Dávila, 2001: 68). In the article "Latin Music Pops," Christopher John Farley cites a 1999 report revealing that in the past advertisers in the United States were often instructed not to advertise on Spanish-language radio stations because of the perception that Latinos had little buying power. Without advertisements, commercial Spanish-language radio programs could not flourish. In the United States the rise in Latino buying power as well as advertisers' confidence in the Latino consumer's potential to spend have spearheaded the burgeoning of commercial Spanish-language radio devoted to Latin music (Farley, 1999: 43).

The salsa that has been popular since the late 1970s differs significantly from the music that reigned during the explosive years of the 1960s and 1970s. Concern with the working-class conditions of barrio life and the issue of Latin solidarity, related in Fania-produced salsa, has been replaced by sentimental love lyrics. Salsa has lost its political edge. According to Deborah Pacini Hernandez, salsa's initial expressions of race consciousness have been transformed into the "insipid lyrical concerns of its stylistic successor, *salsa romántica*" (Pacini Hernández, 1998: 113–14). Modern salsa is marked by a mechanical and flawless polished sound produced by recording different parts of the music separately. Cuban classics or early Fania records were often recorded live, giving the music of the 1960s and 1970s a raw, vital, spontaneous sound that has vanished from modern commercial salsa (Manuel, 1995: 87). The 1980s marked the emergence of *salsa romántica,* whose slick sentimentality contrasts with the forceful working-class African Caribbean *salsa caliente* (91). The production and promotion of *salsa romántica* became a means to challenge the rising commercial popularity of merengue and to reinstate salsa's commercial viability and popularity (Waxer, 2002b: 231).

Despite the criticisms leveled at *salsa romántica*, the marketing and promotion of this version of salsa helped revive the declining salsa scene of the 1980s. The stagnation can be partly attributed to Fania Records, whose monopolization of the salsa market in the 1960s and 1970s meant that no business infrastructure existed to rekindle the scene when Fania folded (Washburne, 2002: 102). *Salsa romántica,* the dominant style of the late 1980s and the 1990s, is marked by particular qualities of composition, arrangement, recording, lyrics, and performance (102). During the 1980s, two styles of *salsa romántica* developed that were almost comparable: New York and Puerto Rican. Both styles were designed for the purpose of revitalizing the salsa scene and increasing salsa's potential as a marketable product (102). To appeal to the musical tastes of Latino youths both in New York and Puerto Rico, salsa promoters incorporated pop elements into this new salsa style. The New York–based producer Louie Ramirez first introduced this version of salsa in 1982 and 1983 with a two-volume release for K-Tel Records entitled *Noche Calientes* (102). In contrast to the forceful and exuberant sounds as well as the less restrained and somewhat rough recordings of salsa during the Fania years, known as *salsa dura,* the style of *salsa romántica* was calmer and tamer, being characterized by extremely polished studio productions (102). As noted above, lyrics in this new style were romantic, with less focus on telling stories of barrio life and advancing Latino unity. Audiences for this version of salsa extended from New York to the middle-class Latinos in the United States as well as to various nations in Latin America and the Caribbean.

In 1987 Ralph Mercado founded Ralph Mercado Music (RMM), furthering the development of *salsa romántica* in New York City (Washburne, 2002: 103) and eventually replacing the position once held by Fania Records as the most prominent record company and concert promotor of salsa music (103). The image of salsa that was promoted through this record company emerged in the visual aesthetics of their lead singers: good-looking, young, white or light-skinned male and female singers with sex appeal (103). Salsa became a pop-influenced, whitened Hispanic Caribbean music, its African-Caribbean side rendered virtually invisible.

In the 1990s RMM began to record and produce a large number of its productions in Puerto Rico as opposed to New York, a shift that brought about financial losses for those involved in salsa music in this city. Therefore, to be competitive, many New York arrangers and musicians had to learn the Puerto Rican style of production (Washburne, 2002: 117). One of the key changes in Puerto Rican productions was a move toward a more delicate and refined brass sound. Because musicians lacked adequate electronic amplification, salsa brass had typically been strong and rich partly so that the horn section could be heard over the extensive rhythm section (117). *Salsa romántica* is also characterized by soothing vocals and toned-down percussion playing (119). These changes, which took place gradually through the 1980s and 1990s, resulted from a key transformation: the previously noted interdependence of the Puerto Rican and New York salsa scenes (118). Other factors that replaced salsa's raw, gritty New York sound with the subdued, softer, and slicker *salsa romántica* include the need to sell records and the monopoly that RMM exercised over salsa recording and concert promotion (118).

Since the late 1980s, salsa has swept throughout the world, developing audiences in such South American nations as Ecuador and Peru (Waxer, 2002a: 221) as well as in such western European nations as Sweden, Spain, Denmark, and Britain. Salsa is also popular in Australia (Clifford, 2001) and Israel (Edie, 1999), and in the early 1990s, a Japanese group, Orchestra de la Luz, took the Latin American salsa market by storm (Steward, 1994: 489). Salsa has also been integrated into the music of various nations in West Africa: in the 1950s and 1960s, musicians from such nations as Angola, Ivory Coast, Mali, and Senegal adopted Cuban/Caribbean sounds into their indigenous music. This West African reinterpretation of Afro-Cuban rhythms has been viewed as a return to the African roots of salsa (Angeloro, 1992:

305). Lise Waxer, however, envisions African salsa less as a restoration of this dance and music complex to its origins and more as an example of how cultural appropriation can occur between developing nations without the influence of North American or European cultural industries (Waxer, 2002c: 12). Today, for instance, the Senegalese band Africando garners international acclaim, specifically with its modern renditions of traditional Cuban songs.

Salsa is both a contemporary global and transnational phenomenon. Not only does it interconnect diverse peoples and nations of Latin American and Latin Caribbean origin, but it has developed audiences throughout the world. The promotion of salsa by the major record companies—Sony, CBS, EMI, Polygram, BMG, and Warner/WEA—has enhanced its global distribution (Waxer, 2002c: 8; Negus, 1999: 142-43).

Although salsa has spread to many areas of the world, it has never crossed significantly into the Anglo and mainstream music markets. Peter Manuel claims that in the 1970s, many music promoters hoped that salsa would find a niche in the Anglo market, as reggae had done. This crossover never occurred, possibly because of the language barrier and the competition that salsa faced from disco and rock. Salsa remained primarily a music enjoyed by Latin ethnic groups (Manuel, 1995: 79). In the 1990s Latin music reached more deeply into mainstream markets via such artists as Ricky Martin and Jennifer Lopez. Consequently, a few salsa singers, such as Mark Anthony, have managed to obtain widespread recognition (Farley, 1999: 40-2). In the 1990s singers who had initially started out in more popular music genres, such as hip-hop, Latin house, and rhythm and blues, started to perform as salsa musicians, drawing younger Latin fans to this music. Both Mark Anthony and La India were former hip-hop singers, and Brenda K. Starr was a rhythm and blues singer. This increase in the number of salsa fans within younger audiences in the 1990s is significant, particularly as many young Latinos had moved from salsa to rock, hip-hop, and rap beginning in the 1970s. Since the 1980s, rap has represented the voice of the barrio, a status once occupied by salsa (Manuel, 1995: 91).

The dominant commercial salsa style, *salsa romántica*, has appealed to the Latin music market in the United States and throughout the globe since the 1980s but has not managed a crossover to world beat audiences in the United States (Pacini Hernández, 1998: 113). World beat refers to a branch of world music that represents modern versions of dance-oriented styles, combining influences from both First and Third World traditions. World music typically refers to traditional renditions of songs from the musical heritages of Third World peoples whose cultures have not been influenced by the First World. The majority of world beat styles are African-derived even though the term "world beat" is neutral and does not refer to a singular characteristic. In the texts of their songs and in their particular dress and hairstyles, world beat musicians often express the notion that black people are united by a global diaspora. This music's supposedly traditional purity and authenticity, uncorrupted by Western technology and capital, lies at the core of this genre's appeal to Western audiences. At the same time, world beat allows for the integration of Western-based styles. Both traditions appeal to white Western audiences in their claims to embody "authentic" cultural expression. World beat propagates the African roots that exist in the musical traditions of both the First and Third World, whereas world music emphasizes how the traditional sounds of non-Western cultures express either national, racial, regional, or ethnic identities (112).

The exclusion of Spanish Caribbean music such as salsa and merengue from the world beat market can be greatly attributed to how the African roots of Latin Caribbean music have been made invisible in the promotion and marketing of the music. The tendency to ignore or obscure the African cultural influence in Latin music can be traced to the longstanding tradition in the Spanish Caribbean of promoting an Iberocentric identity while disregarding or downplaying the role that African culture and people played in that region (Pacini Hernández, 1998: 113). The salsa of the 1960s and 1970s was a rare exception: ignited by the civil rights movements, salsa musicians used lyrics and an emphasis on Afro-Caribbean percussion to celebrate this music's African roots. When world beat came onto the music scene in the 1980s, the dominant sound of salsa at the time was *salsa romántica*, whose link to African-derived musical traditions had vanished, thus limiting its appeal to the world beat market (113). As Deborah Pacini Hernandez states, "Given world-beat consumers' desire for an exoticized racial authenticity, salsa and merengue were perceived as too commercial (i.e., inauthentic) and were simply ignored" (114).

Since the 1980s, salsa has been marketed by the major labels to Latin audiences as a primarily "white" musical practice presenting a racially homogenized Latin identity that extends throughout the Spanish-speaking Americas (Pacini Hernández, 1998: 121). Lisa Sánchez González, who is highly critical of how Puerto Rican, Cuban, and African American working-class roots are absent from contemporary salsa, argues that salsa has become a channel to promote racist and bourgeois attitudes in the United States and other areas of Latin America. She writes, "How else can we explain the way that '*música cocola*, plebeian music, lower-class music' (as salsa has been viewed within Puerto Rico's insular and upper and middle classes since its inception) is being transformed by Latina/os outside the Puerto Rican diasporic community into a site for uppity signifying practices" (Storm Roberts, 1999, cited in Sánchez González, 1999: 246). Since 1988 the United States has loosened some of the restrictions of the *Trading with the Enemy Act* and allowed certain Cuban music and performers to enter the United States. Consequently, Cuban salsa, or *salsa Cubana*, has been present in the Latin music scene since the 1990s. Cuba is the only country in the Spanish Caribbean that celebrates and nurtures African-derived roots and culture, so the influence of African Caribbean percussion emerges in Cuban salsa. The Afrocentric nature of this Cuban music has appealed to the world beat and world markets (Pacini Hernández, 1998: 116).

Societal changes in Cuban society enabled Cuban salsa to become prominent in the international music and dance scene. Around 1985 tourism developed in the country, and musical groups were granted the freedom to tour and become successful in other parts of the Americas as well as in Europe and Asia. This move toward a more open society meant that Cuban music started to have an extensive international audience. Cuban dance and music forms, such as salsa music, *casino* dance, and various music complexes of Afro-Cuban origin, began to be enjoyed worldwide. The success of Cuban music off the island also led to an increase in the number of venues devoted to dance music within the country (Balbuena, 2003: 90), nurturing a more pronounced local scene whose artists could possibly attain international recognition.

Cuban salsa dance, or *casino*, is promoted and taught in schools throughout the globe; information about the dance is also disseminated worldwide on the Internet. The use of the musical term "salsa" to denote the dance genre *casino* within Cuba is a relatively new phenomenon. Distinct from most Cuban forms that are music and dance complexes, *casino* is danced to various genres of music rather than to a single style (Balbuena, 2003: 43). Salsa's global popularity in addition to the widespread distribution of Cuban *son*-based salsa compositions on the international stage led to *casino* being referred to as salsa. Therefore, *casino* started to be called salsa only after 1985 (91). Robin Moore claims that until possibly the late 1980s this term would not have been comprehended by most Cubans owing in part to its limited use in the media (Moore, 2002: 58). For many years, the censuring of artistic practices in Cuba had meant that the nations' music and dance were highly exclusionary; only in the mid-1980s was non-Cuban music played on the radio (67). From the late 1960s to the early 1980s, there was a policy of informal censuring that banned the use of the desgination "salsa" in radio shows and musicology research (63). Furthermore, as the ban by capitalist countries on playing salsa music was lifted only recently, there was not much opportunity for the name "salsa" to circulate and become recognized and understood by Cubans (58). The salsa that developed in North America did have a certain impact on Cuban popular culture prior to the 1980s. Bárbara Balbuena, for instance, describes how the music created in the United States primarily by Puerto Rican and Cuban musicians was enjoyed and danced to by *casino* dancers in Cuba. With their politically conscious lyrics and distinguished musical style, the works particularly of artists Reuben Blades and Willie Colón were danced to with fervour by *casineros* in the 1970s (Balbuena, 2003: 70). According to Robin Moore, the dance and music referred to as "salsa" by New Yorkers and by the majority of Latin Americans today would be generally referred to within Cuba as *son*, *timba*, *música bailable*, or *casino*. Whereas the first three refer to both a dance and music complex, *casino* refers only to a dance (Moore, 2002: 58).

Casino, or Cuban salsa dance, has been flourishing and evolving in Cuba since the 1950s. Whereas Maria Teresa Linares records 1956 as the year that *casino* developed among the youth (Linares, 1974: 200), Bárbara Balbuena illustrates how she cannot pinpoint, from the results of her interviews, exactly when in the 1950s *casino* distinguished itself from its predecessors, such as the *son* and the *chachachá*, to emerge as a unique genre (Balbuena, 2003: 43). *Casino* dancers vary their moves in accordance with the music to which they are dancing. For instance, dancers move in particular ways at the climactic moment, which is marked by the hard-driving percussion of the *sonero-salsero* compositions, those referred to by Cuban musicians as *bomba* or *timba*. At such musical moments, the dancers, especially those of the young generation, separate from the partner formation and vibrate and shake their bodies in solo dancing. Their moves are complex and require the ability to isolate and move various parts of the body with distinct, controlled, yet frenzied gestures (95–96). At other musical moments, particularly those that are *son*-based, dancers may form solo couples or a *rueda* (circle), maintaining the basic step in rhythm to the music while performing myriad figures, arm movements, and turns.

Timba combines Cuba's contemporary *son* with salsa and hip-hop influences (Fairley, 2000: 398). According to Sue Steward, *timba* is "salsa, by any other name, but with an innovative jumped-up rhythm and phat, funky bass" (Steward, 2000: 494). A key player in the development of *timba* is Juan Formell, who started the group Los Van Van in 1969 (Fairley, 2000: 396). In the 1980s this band created a variation of *son*, termed *songo* (396), whose rhythm fueled the growth of *timba* in the 1990s (Steward, 2000: 49). Contemporary salsa music of the *timba* style is influencing the development of salsa at the level of dance: the high-paced rhythms of popular Cuban bands, such as Charanga Habanarra and Los Van Van, are partly transforming salsa into a nonpartner dance. Focusing on the first and third beats of the rhythm, the *timba* style puts less emphasis on the second beat, a rhythmic stress that characterizes the mambo-influenced salsa styles of New York and Puerto Rico. The faster rhythms of the music lead dancers to perform more solo styling than couple steps (Chasteen, 2004: 10).

Casino is a genre that absorbs a diversity of forms, drawing from the rich repertoire of dances that thrive in Cuba. Various choreographic patterns from dances of Afro-Cuban origin have also been integrated into *casino*. Some of these include the following: dances of the *santería* (a Yoruba-derived religion of Cuba), such as the *elegguá*, *ogún*, and *ochosi*; elements from the rumba dances *columbia* and *guaguancó*; and movements and steps from the *makuta* and *yuca* (Balbuena, 2003: 96). Furthermore, movements from dances that preceded *casino*, such as the mambo, *chachachá*, and *conga*, have also been integrated into *casino* (96). The *conga*, or *comparsa*,[7] is a collective processional dance that originated in secular celebrations during the time of slavery (Martínez Furé, 1974: 87) and was later used in colonial marches to display *cabildos* (Daniel, 2002: 34).

The musical divide between Cuba and the United States has been waning. As Cuba became increasingly less insular in the 1990s, Cuban bands were allowed to tour in the United States for "educational" purposes, and eventually these trips transformed into commercial ventures. No longer isolated, Cuban "salsa" music is being exposed to American audiences and external musical influences. In the songs of certain Cuban musicians, such as those of Isaac Delgado, can be heard the smooth arrangements of Puerto Rican and New York salsa (Steward, 2000: 494). The Cuban *timba* group Den Den, for instance, has also been modifying its music to resemble the more polished sound of New York. Furthermore, the *songo* rhythm of *timba* is being absorbed into New York salsa and Latin hip-hop primarily through the efforts of RMM producer Sergio George (494).

The musical interconnection between Cuba and New York is beginning to influence the salsa styles developing in these two music centers. A question needs to be asked: how will this musical connection influence how salsa is danced in Cuba and New York? It is clear that as more Cuban-style musicians enter the Latin music scene in New York, their influence will probably affect the style of dancing in the city (Edie, 1999). Reciprocally, perhaps the mambo-based dance style of New York will become one of the ways of dancing salsa in Cuba.

Cubans readily incorporate foreign forms in current cultural expressions. The absorption of foreign musical styles into contemporary Cuban music can also be a way to resist a government system that has promoted national and political aims by maintaining insular cultural forms (Moore, 2002: 67). Just as Cuban music today draws from an array of international sounds—jazz, rock, rap, funk, and pop—the dance styles themselves may also integrate outside influences (60).

Cuban dance culture is strong; it has not been weakened by outside culture. Robin Moore argues that Cuba's strong musical heritage enables artists to absorb foreign forms creatively without threat to the national culture (Moore, 2002: 60). A situation similar to that identified by Moore in music may occur in dance. At various instances in the history of *casino*, *casineros*, for instance, incorporated foreign dance moves, which enriched their local performance. In the 1950s, Cuban dance was influenced by outside genres. Foreign music, such as bossa nova, twist, beat, and rock, were diffused by the media more than were Cuban styles. Nonetheless, dancers at the time integrated both Cuban and imported movements into *casino* (Balbuena, 2003: 65). Prior to 1985, Cuban society was extremely isolated, and dancers consequently had little exposure to non-domestic ways of moving to salsa rhythms. A performance by the renowned *salsero* Oscar D'Leon of Venezuela in 1983 led to a new choreographic routine being added to *casino*. The Cuban audience, taken with his style of dancing while performing on stage, rapidly copied his movements and gestures. Many of the dancing public remembered one of Oscar D'Leon's particular choreographic routines, which he performed with other singers on stage. It consisted of marking the basic *casino* step while executing certain turns on the sides and embellishing these moves with rhythmic accents, various kicks, and a number of corporeal patterns. This routine captured the attention of the *casineros* to such an extent that it is still danced in *casino* today (87). *Casino* was enhanced by the various fusions of Cuban and foreign elements because the absorption of external influences resulted in dancers adding or inventing more complicated turns and figures.

Contact between Cuban and North American cultures also brought about North American adaptations of Cuban forms within the ballroom tradition. The version of the *son*, for instance, that was appropriated and transformed became known as *rumba teatral*, or ballroom rumba, and continues to be performed in competitions today. Ballroom dance also integrated the *chachachá*, renamed the chacha, as well as the mambo. The ballroom tradition essentially created new dances in its inclusion of Cuban forms, yet this appropriation of Caribbean genres is not always viewed in a favorable light. The *rumba teatral* is for Bárbara Balbuena a deformation of the original dance (Balbuena, 2003: 40). The contemporary Latin dances salsa and merengue are both danced in ballroom circles, and these renditions conform to the movement aesthetics of this dance tradition (see chapter 3).

Today Cuban salsa is regarded as one of the five main transnational music styles. The others include New York, Puerto Rican, Venezuelan, and Colombian. At times, Miami is regarded as a separate transnational style even though it is similar to the New York and Puerto Rican versions. As the salsa music produced in New York, Miami, and Puerto Rico draws from the same pool of arrangers and studio musicians, the sound of the music created in each of these locations resembles that found in the others (Waxer, 2002c: 10; Washburne, 2002: 117). Based on responses from musicians, composers, and arrangers of Colombian salsa, Lise Waxer concludes that the Colombian version has a quality that distinguishes it from Puerto Rican, New York, and Venezuelan styles: it is marked by a sonic simplicity. The unique sound of Cali salsa, for instance, is described by Waxer as exuding "a light texture, a crisp percussive attack and an on-the-beat rhythmic feel" (Waxer, 2002b: 237). Puerto Rican, New York, and Cuban styles have a slightly behind-the-beat rhythmic feel and a heavy groove that contrast with the "sprightliness" of Colombian salsa (237).

Salsa dance is generally classified as one of six styles: ballroom, New York, Puerto Rican, Colombian, Cuban, and Los Angeles. This mapping of salsa into these fixed forms reflects the historical development of contemporary salsa from its music and dance roots within specific nations, cities, and dance traditions. These predominant styles are also global products. The Venezuelan dance style is not commodified on a global scale and hence is not generally included as one of the six principal salsa styles. The styles that have become the most prominent as a result of their widespread circulation in dance schools, in practice videos, and on websites are ballroom, New York, Cuban, and Los Angeles.

Various elements distinguish these six styles despite their interconnection. The distinctive features of each style are not always fixed but have the potential to transform depending on how individual dancers interpret them. Popular dance is in constant flux and evolution. Despite the organic fluidity inherent in dance, certain key elements underlie each style. These include how the rhythm of the music is interpreted by the dancers and how the core of the dance, derived from the Cuban *son*, has been embellished and altered through the absorption of other dance forms. The inclusion of the mambo in the *son* and rumba complex distinguishes the Puerto Rican and New York styles from Cuban salsa. Although *casino* does incorporate moves from the mambo, *casino* is not nearly as influenced by the mambo as are the Puerto Rican and New York styles. How salsa is danced in the United States stems largely from the Puerto Rican style, which has evolved significantly from the mambo ("Salsa and Mambo Dance History," 9 November 2000). Salsa's count is 1-2-3-4 5-6-7-8. Styles differ in what beat dancers begin on and in the intricacy of the footwork. The Puerto Rican style can be danced on either the first or second beat of the music: dancers can start either on the "1" or the "2." This style incorporates a great deal of technical footwork; to execute these footwork patterns, dancers often break the couple hold and dance alone. Technical footwork is called "solo" in Los Angeles and "shines" in New York (Edie, 1999). The Puerto Rican style allows for more elaborate footwork than does the New York style. Since the mambo was reintroduced to the New York style in the late 1970s and early 1980s, mambo dancers in New York argue that their style embodies the same degree of intricacy and complexity as Puerto Rican salsa (Edie, 1999).

The Latin hustle has influenced the New York style of salsa. Edie, also known as the Salsa Freak, editor in chief of *Salsaweb Magazine*, surmises that during the late 1970s and early 1980s, salsa dancing was almost wiped out by the hustle (Edie, 1999). Popularized in the 1977 disco movie *Saturday Night Fever*, the hustle combined some of the patterns of the lindy (a swing dance) with salsa and a disco beat ("Sonny Watson's Dance History: The Hustle," 2001). During its heyday in the late 1970s and early 1980s, the hustle was an elaborate nightclub couple dance involving spins, complex steps, hand movements, inventive lifts, and creative drops ("Welcome to Streethustle," 2001). Despite the supposed "death" of disco in 1979 (Straw, 2001: 169), the hustle survived as a dance style in social dance circles and influenced how salsa was danced in clubs. Many dancers combined hustle moves with the mambo style during the transition back to salsa music in the late 1980s and early 1990s. Interest in mambo-influenced salsa has flourished since the late 1980s. During salsa's declining years in New York City, Eddie Torres, along with Tito Puente, was among the only instructors in New York to keep the mambo dance alive (Edie, 1999). Dancer, instructor, and choreographer Eddie Torres is known as the Mambo King of Latin Dance because of his aspirations to ensure that the mambo is supreme once again in New York. He is dedicated to reintroducing dancers to what he claims is "authentic nightclub mambo dancing," called salsa in the 1990s ("Salsa and Mambo Dance History," 9 November 2000), in which spins and fancy footwork, or shines, are prominent. As a result of the large number of Puerto Rican immigrants in New York city, the Puerto Rican style has come to resemble the New York style, also called the Latin hustle or what Torres terms "Mambo On-Two," or the New York mambo. According to Torres, the impact of the Puerto Rican style in New York has led to increased footwork, or shines, in the salsa that is danced in New York, where salsa dancers incorporate almost as many shines as do dancers in Puerto Rico (Edie, 1999).

Another American style, Los Angeles salsa, is characterized by showy moves and cabaret gestures, derived mainly from West Coast swing and Latin ballroom. Los Angeles salsa combines elements from swing, ballroom, and a mild Puerto Rican style to create its own unique rendition of the dance (Edie, 1999). Since the 1950s a version of the original mambo has been incorporated into the ballroom dance tradition. Ballroom mambo, the official term for ballroom-style salsa (Edie, 1999), differs from New York mambo in terms of which beats are held or danced on. In ballroom-style mambo, the dancers hold the 1 and 5 beats and step on the 2, 3, 4, and on the 6, 7, and 8. They also "break" on the 2 and 6, meaning that dancers either take a step forward or backward. In New York–style mambo the dancers hold the 4 and 8 beats and step on the 1, 2, 3 and on the 5, 6, 7; they also "break" on the 2 and 6. These two styles differ in the nature of the holds. In New York–style mambo, by holding on the 4 and 8 beats, the dancer is not really static but is moving the feet from the front ꜱ the back or from the back to the front in preparation to step on the 1 and 5. In ballroom the dancers hold themselves in place for the counts on which they do not step. Consequently, New York mambo is a more fluid dance than ballroom mambo (Friedler, 2000).

After the revolution in 1959, *casino* developed into a complex dance whose moves and patterns were basically unknown to the outside world until the gradual opening of Cuba in the early 1980s. Since the 1950s ever-evolving *casino* has developed an extensive repertoire of turns, moves, complicated arm movements, acrobatics, and figures. Because the music to which *casino* is danced today has very fast tempos and extensive polyrhythms in the percussion, dancers perform complex footwork patterns that adorn the basic step without altering this traditional form (Balbuena, 2003: 91).

There are various ways to create a relation in *casino* between the accent of the dance step and the musical accent. The first method is to accentuate the first eighth note with the initial step. A second technique is to wait on the first beat of the music and advance on the second eighth note. In this case, the accent falls on the third step in the fourth eighth of the music. As people in Havana come from diverse Cuban backgrounds, it is possible to see both dancing styles at at any given gathering (Chao Carbonero, 1996: 9; Balbuena, 2003: 92). In the last few years, *casino* dancers, particularly among the youth, have started to accentuate the third eighth note of the musical bar with the initial dance step. This recent development has raised some eyebrows among certain members of the popular dance community who wish to maintain traditional interpretations of the form (Chao Carbonero, 1996: 9; Balbuena, 2003: 92).

Today *casino* is danced in a variety of ways: in embraced couples using the closed social dance position; in two rows stratified by gender, the male and female partners facing one another in a placement called *en formación de calle* (the formation of a street); and in the *rueda* (circle) (Balbuena, 2003: 92). The other transnational styles are generally danced only by single couples moving separately on the dance floor. The multiple formations of Cuban *casino* distinguish it from versions outside Cuba. *Casino de la rueda* consists of couples who dance together while building a large circle and who synchronize their individual figure rotations with those of the group. The couples take turns dancing with each member of the circle until they have danced with each dancer of the opposite sex. The resulting effect is that the dance circle keeps spinning, with men moving in one direction and women in the other. A male caller, who is also an expert dancer, announces the changes in turns, dance patterns, and figures (Daniel, 2002: 45; Chasteen, 2004: 10). *Casino* dancers perform practised and previously acquired steps despite there always being room for improvisation (Daniel, 2002: 45). Dancers may also form two *ruedas* simultaneously, with a smaller circle of dancers contained within a larger one. Since the late 1990s, as noted above, at highly percussive moments in the music, dancers also separate from the couple formation and dance the *casino* alone (Balbuena, 2003: 92–93).

When couples dance *casino*, both the male and the female move with speed and virtuosity in continuously turning figures, with the female circulating the most frequently. A key trait distinguishes *casino* from styles taught in Montreal and other cities influenced by the New York and ballroom traditions: *casino* couples rotate completely around one another while still maintaining contact with one or both of their partners' hands. In the turning style taught in many of the New York– or ballroom-influenced salsa dance classes, the male dancer spins the female rather than both partners in the couple turning completely around in relation to one another (Chasteen, 2004: 10). The Cuban turning style also emphasizes a back placement of the foot as opposed to the forward movement that characterizes the mambo-influenced style of New York and Puerto Rico.

Salsa is danced in diverse ways in different parts of Colombia. In Cali, salsa is a more "showy" dance, whereas in the rural areas, it is performed in a closed-couple embrace in which dancers sometimes move with their heads touching. However, one central feature unites the Colombian style: salsa in Colombia does not include the forward and backward movement of the foot found in the mambo-influenced styles of Puerto Rico and New York. The foot patterns consist of alternations to the back or to the side in a step series known as the *cumbia* style. Most Colombian salsa dancers move to the rhythms without numerous turns and spins. Although professional dancers performing in bands or at competitions display a more extravagant style, Colombian social dancing is calm and close, with dancers touching one another from head to toe (Edie, 1999).

A consequence of the vibrant Cali dance in the 1960s and 1970s was the the development of an original dance style unique to Cali: *el paso caleno*, or the Cali dance step. This unique style was characterized by a "rapid, 'double-time' shuffle on the tips of the toes, combined with high kicks and rapid footwork" (Waxer, 2002b: 233). *Caleno* dancing became distinct from the salsa that is danced in various areas of Latin America as well as in the rest of Colombia, where salsa's core element is the basic step derived from the Cuban *son*. Salsa dancing in Cali was a mixture of various elements: the Cuban *guaracha* and mambo and the North American jitterbug, twist, and charleston (234).

The unique simplicity and on-the-beat rhythmic texture of Colombian salsa music is expressed by its dancers. Lise Waxer reveals how Colombian musicians, composers, and arrangers identify "simplicity" as the quality that distinguishes the Colombian salsa from Puerto Rican, New York, and Venezuelan versions, which share an emphasis on forceful percussive elements and intricate musical arrangements. Influenced by Colombian music genres such as *cumbia* and *currulao*, Colombian salsa emphasizes melody, exciting lyrics, and simple horn sections. Salsa from Cali has a light touch and an incisive but sprightly percussive feel that creates an on-the-beat rhythmic sensation. The rhythmic phrasing of playing on the beat is mirrored in the Colombian way of dancing the basic step: dancers step on the beat. Puerto Rican, New York, and Cuban dancers, by comparison, tend to step a little bit behind the beat (Waxer, 2002b: 237).

Contemporary salsa is the creation of diverse people in various historical times and locations. Despite the syncretism that is inherent in the genre, salsa historians and critics have often chosen to credit a particular group and place with the invention of salsa rather than taking into account the complex history that has formed and shaped this music and dance. Vernon Boggs, for instance, presents salsa as a primarily African Cuban tradition in which Cuban rhythms were influenced by African American jazz in New York in the 1950s. Lisa Sánchez González, offering another version of salsa's history, argues that Boggs's account of salsa is misleading. As she notes, many salsa historians claim that Puerto Ricans plagiarized and commodified the Afro-Cuban *son*. Puerto Ricans were excluded from the salsa story because they were falsely regarded as white and thus thought to have played no significant role in the creation of salsa as an expression of the African diaspora's artistic heritage (Sánchez González, 1999: 238). Sánchez González credits Puerto Ricans with the birth of salsa: "Salsa was born in the Puerto Rican colonial di-aspora during the first half of the twentieth century, and raised among segre-gated communities of Puerto Ricans, Cubans, African Americans and a va-riety of Caribbean peoples in and around Manhattan, whose rich aesthetic traditions coalesced in unique performative logics and logistics" (238). Some accounts of salsa call it an American phenomenon given that it evolved mu-sically and commercially in New York. Peter Catapano's online history of salsa, "Salsa: Made in New York," emphasizes that city as the birthplace of salsa (Catapano, 2001). Although salsa is a Cuban-derived style that devel-oped through the artistry of musicians and dancers of Cuban, Puerto Rican, and African American descent in New York, Jorge Duany argues that salsa must not be considered an American phenomenon, for its historical roots lie in the Caribbean (Duany, 1992: 72).

Many ethnic groups, races, and cultures have had a hand in salsa's long history of development. This history unfolds in the proliferation of salsa dance and music styles that circulate in the Americas and throughout the globe. Despite the desire on the part of music and culture critics to claim salsa for a particular group, it is difficult to locate a rightful owner or specific geographical birthplace for this genre. Cubans in Cuba and New York, Puerto Ricans in Puerto Rico and New York, African Americans, Jewish Americans, various people of Caribbean descent in New York and the Caribbean, Venezuelans, Panamanians, and Colombians have all con-tributed to the artistic production of salsa and have been its eager audience. New York is not the center of salsa in the United States today: Miami and Los Angeles have challenged its supremacy. There are many salsa capitals throughout Latin America, such as Cali and Caracas. Salsa has also spread throughout the globe to Europe, Canada, Australia, Israel, Africa, and Japan. Which of these peoples and places produces the authentic salsa? In the ex-ploration of Latin music, looking for the genuine salsa is a misdirected yet common pursuit.

The history of salsa can be grasped only when the various peoples and places that have contributed to its evolution are taken into account. Burying elements of its history results in the exclusion of a particular race, ethnicity, class, or culture, omissions that could have oppressive consequences in actual circumstances. Lisa Sánchez González shows how the contemporary por-trayal of salsa as an elite, white, bourgeois cultural practice in Los Angeles of-ten leads to "darker-skinned" clientele being covertly barred from salsa clubs through a number of policies, such as dress codes (Sánchez González, 1999: 245). Working-class people of color are also discriminated against through certain practices in some of Montreal's salsa clubs. For instance, the owner of one of the oldest salsa clubs in the city revealed in an interview that through high drink prices and cover charges, she plans to discourage working-class Montrealers who have immigrated from Latin nations from entering her club. Being of European descent, she wants to foster an affluent clientele, one with a more European and white North American background.

The tendency of historians to emphasize the African Cuban roots of salsa could possibly have arisen to redress the fact that African elements in the music of the Spanish Caribbean have often been "forgotten." Sánchez González claims that Vernon Boggs's decision to select only Afro-Cuban musicians, such as Mario Bauza and Machito, and to exclude Puerto Rican musicians as founding fathers of salsa stems from the vantage points of the bibliographical references from which he has drawn to weave his history of salsa. For instance, he relies on the anthropological work done in the 1970s by Cuban ethno-musicologist Fernando Ortiz, whose terrain is highly insular, including only the Cuban context. As previously mentioned, one of Ortiz's primary aims was to unearth Cuban music's connection to African culture, a link that had been previously denigrated and kept hidden. Fernando Ortiz's political agenda has been transferred into Vernon Boggs's perspective (Sánchez González, 1999: 247).

Privileging salsa's African-derived heritage should not lead to the erasure of the significant role that Puerto Ricans and others have played in the creative development of salsa. Today the promotion of *salsa romántica* obscures its African and working-class core and portrays this cultural practice as a predominantly white Spanish genre. The roots of salsa illuminate how both European elite and proletariat African cultures fused to create this dance and music.

Notes

1. Yvonne Daniel more precisely refers to this group as the Kongo-Angolan (Bantu) or the Kongo (Daniel, 2002: 35). Other authors, such as Marshall and Jean Stearns (1968), refer to this group as the Congo. I therefore use the terms "Kongo" or "Congo" depending on each author's use.

2. See chapter 4, "The Couple in Dance," for a more detailed look at the closed social dance position and a history of this gendered form in European dance history.

3. *Guaracha* is an up-tempo Cuban music and dance genre characterized by lively and brisk arrangements, cheerful and humourous lyrics, and invigorating dancing (Waxer, 2002d: 316).

4. The *bolero* is a slow, romantic Cuban song that developed in the late nineteenth century and attained international popularity from the 1920s through the 1940s (Waxer, 2002d: 313).

5. *Pachanga* is a lively tempo version of 1960s salsa popular in the early years of the decade (Waxer, 2002d: 317).

6. Boogaloo, or *bugalú*, is a salsa form popular during the mid- to late 1960s that combined elments from rhythm and blues with Cuban-derived sounds (Waxer, 2002d: 314).

7. For a discussion of the choreographic elements of the *conga*, see Fernández, 1974: 91–100.

CHAPTER TWO

~

Transnational Identities and
Multicultural Connections

Salsa seems an unlikely dance and music to be flourishing in the cold northern city of Montreal. It is one of those "exotic" styles that conjure images of hot, lush city nights and seductive dancing couples. This sultry vision diverges from the urban reality facing most citizens, who must bundle up in layers of clothing to face icy weather conditions. As Montrealers endure long harsh winters, this city is an unexpected setting for a thriving Caribbean music and dance scene. Yet Montreal is inhabited by people who have come from a variety of "tropical" climates in South America, Central America, the Caribbean, and West Africa. The music heard in clubs, in venues, at festivals, and on community radio stations throughout the city expresses the varied "ethnicities" that characterize the population. There is considerable demand for the world beat sounds of West Africa, as well as for Caribbean and Latin music. Although world beat music—such as *soukous* from Zaire, highlife from Ghana, and the Caribbean rhythms of calypso, *soca*, and *compass*—are often ghettoized in the city, Latin music, particularly salsa and merengue, has filtered into the mainstream. These styles can often be heard as background music in commercial venues; while strolling through the downtown retail district on St. Catherine Street, for instance, one commonly hears salsa in chain coffee shops such as Second Cup and in popular clothing boutiques and stores. Salsa is also disseminated through various Latin-oriented businesses and media, such as clubs, dance studios, music venues, select radio shows on community and university networks, and a local community television show, *Teleritmo*.

Salsa music has become part of the cultural and commercial fabric of Montreal for all peoples, although it bears a specific significance for those of Latin descent. Listening and dancing to salsa music has become an expression of identity for some Montrealers of Latin descent. Even though many of them have not been raised with this dance and music complex, salsa connects them to a transnational sense of Latinness, a shared distinction that has resulted from their migration to a new country. Collective identities are not necessarily those with which we are born but can be formed and fashioned within a new context (Bulmer and Solomos, 1998: 827). At the same time, Montrealers of diverse backgrounds are incorporating salsa into their cultural repertoire.

Although salsa is a cultural expression of several population groups, it is also a commodity bought and sold in studios and dance clubs in Montreal. One method of accessing salsa dancing is by taking lessons in one of the city's schools. Salsa dancing thrives in a multicultural context: its commodification enables diverse groups to meet and to form alliances. However, the multicultural connections in Montreal's dance scene are distinct from the use of dance to convey multicultural values in Canada. Immigrants in Canada are officially encouraged to maintain their cultural heritage by performing traditional dances from their countries of origin. The dominant perspective on multiculturalism, officially promoted since 1971, stresses how such "ethnic" practices link to the cultural heritage of immigrants' countries of origin rather than how these cultures develop within the Canadian context. I discuss this topic in detail later in this chapter.

To show how salsa dancing forges multicultural relations in Montreal, I first relate how this dance is both a cultural expression and a commodity. This analysis combines an ethnography of the salsa scene in Montreal, the history of this Latin music and of Latin immigration in Montreal, and research on culture and identity that draws on the concepts of multiculturalism, transnationalism, and diaspora.

"Multiculturalism" is commonly used as an overarching term for a wide array of differences. J. W. Berry and J. A. Laponce argue that in the Canadian context "multiculturalism" stands for both multiethnic and racial differences and conclude, "in the nineteenth century, race was used to mean culture as well as race. The twentieth may well end with culture meaning race, as well as culture" (Berry and Laponce, 1994: 7). The term "multiculturalism," used to describe differences in general, often eclipses the specificities that produce diversity. Wahneema Lubiano, for instance, discusses the effects of subsuming "race" under the rubric of multiculturalism in American-based critical enquiries (Lubiano, 1996: 69). The popular use of the term "multiculturalism" describes and celebrates diversity without exploring the connections that can arise when people of various cultural, ethnic, and racial backgrounds come in contact.

Although "race" and "ethnicity" are often presented as natural categories, they are actually social constructions in that their boundaries are not fixed and finite. Who is included within a particular "race" or "ethnicity" often depends upon historical, political, and cultural circumstances. These social definitions are imposed upon members of particular groups by others or are developed by the groups themselves. These ways of classifying individuals and groups are ideological entities, fabricated and transformed through processes of struggle (Bulmer and Solomos, 1998: 822–23). Racial distinctions such as "blackness" and "whiteness" do not refer to essential qualities but to how historical and political conflicts have defined their meanings (823). Although the differences delineated by the terms "race" and "ethnicity" are created in discourse, these ways of delineating difference nonetheless have material consequences. Racial categories, for instance, do not refer to fixed essences but need to be maintained, according to Diane Fuss, as political categories. Since the classification of people into particular races has real and often oppressive consequences, these discursive categories need to be sustained in order to fight against the reality of racism (Fuss, 1989: 91).

The classification of individuals as "white," for instance, varies in accordance with historical periods, cultural norms, and geographical locations. Racism depends on context. Before the Communist Revolution of 1959, for example, Cuba was marked by racial segregation: those of Spanish origin enjoyed greater status than those of African origin (Daniel, 1995: 42). From 1920 to 1940, Afro-Cuban musicians were prohibited from playing in popular venues because of their skin color. Cubans of Spanish descent were and are considered white (Boggs, 1992b: 113). In New York, however, Spanish-descended Latinos from South America, Central America, and the Caribbean are not considered white and are targets of racism. Marilyn Frye reveals how the category "white" applies only to certain ethnic groups in the United States, primarily individuals of northern European and Anglo-Saxon heritage. She argues that many people with white skin, such as some Mexican, black, Puerto Rican, or Mohawk individuals, would not be perceived as white by the average white North American. Although an individual can have pale skin, any non-European ancestry, such as African or South Asian, will preclude the white classification (Frye, 1983: 113–14). Puerto Ricans in New York, therefore, find themselves excluded from the dominant white society because they are defined as non-white.

When racial and ethnic categories are imposed on individuals, these markers of difference become exertions of power whereby the "dominated" envision and experience themselves as "other" (Bulmer and Solomos, 1998: 823). However, identities founded on racial and ethnic differences are not always imposed. A sense of racial or ethnic distinction often arises as a consequence of conflict and resistance to oppressive situations in which such minorities have been the crucial and central players (823). The word "Latino" is, in a sense, a marker of oppression, as it uses a generalized term to define people of diverse national, racial, and ethnic origins, with differences being subsumed under one totalizing definition. "Latinos" themselves use the word to assert their identity within the American context.[1] Eduardo Mendieta writes of the experiences of Latin Americans when they migrate to the United States: "One arrives a Guatemalan, Salvadorean, Colombian, Cuban, Venezuelan, Peruvian, Costa Rican or Dominican, and slowly, after painful experiences of oppression, marginalization, and isolation, starts to learn to become a Latino and Hispanic. But in the process of learning to become a Latino and Hispanic what were originally artificial and imposed labels now take on a different character. These terms become ways for us to claim and build a place in the political culture of the United States" (Mendieta, 2000: 47–48). It is in these contexts that such terms as "race," "ethnic," and "Latino," or "Latin," are used in this exploration of salsa dancing in Montreal.[2]

Dancing to the rhythms of salsa (as well as to other Latin music, such as merengue and *bachata*) gives all Montrealers an opportunity to participate in pockets of Latin culture: dance clubs and schools are sprinkled throughout the city. The originally Dominican merengue, popular since the 1980s, is played along with salsa in clubs, music venues, and dance studios and classes. Salsa is an intricate dance that can be performed at many levels of expertise. Its simplest form consists of a basic step. Dancers embellish the elementary movement with elaborate turns, figures, and footwork patterns. The body moves in undulating isolations, the most distinguished being the rhythmic hip movements of *salseros*. The hip rotates to the beat of the music in a distinct and separate move. In Montreal, salsa is a couple dance, but at times male and female dancers break apart and dance solos. Since the late 1980s, Montrealers who have not grown up dancing salsa have started learning its steps and turns; although a number of dance studios teach salsa, most lessons take place in Montreal's Latin clubs. The tropical atmosphere, the engaging rhythms of the music, and the joy of dancing draw fans into the salsa scene. For many Montrealers, going to Latin clubs is tantamount to entering another world, claims DJ Sánchez, a key player in the Latin music scene since 1988. (It should be noted that throughout this work, pseudonyms are used for the names of dance schools, instructors, musicians, music promoters, and disc jockeys.)

In my ethnographic work, I was initially interested primarily in what happens to salsa when people from non-Latin backgrounds learn it. I investigated whether cultural appropriation changed the movements of the dance and whether perceptions about salsa differed between dancers of non-Latin descent and those who grew up dancing to its rhythms. Through my research on the Montreal salsa scene, I realized that in this city, salsa does not express a people in the sense of reflecting the heritage of a specific group or ethnicity. As previously noted, the idea that a cultural practice reinforces and expresses a specific society or group is rooted in the symbolic anthropology of the 1960s. Research on musical cultures was once dominated by that perspective, which focused on how a cultural practice signified a particular identity. Jocelyne Guilbault asserts that ethno-musicology, as well as other fields of study, claimed that musical practices represented a specific group or ethnicity—that is, a group's identity was reflected in its musical practices (Guilbault, 1997: 33).

Implicit in the early stages of my ethnographic work was the assumption that salsa in Montreal reflected the cultural tradition of a specific group. Initially, I interviewed teachers and students of salsa dancing to determine how attitudes to the dance differ between non-Latin Montrealers who have learned the dance in the city and individuals of Latin descent who have grown up dancing to salsa in a Latin context. A binary split in beliefs about the dance emerged. People who learned salsa in Montreal have a tendency to sexualize it; those who have grown up dancing to salsa music do not. I documented student perceptions of the specific movements, such as the hand gestures, the footwork, and the hip rotation as well as the entire dance itself. Many Montrealers who learned salsa in clubs and studios find particular movements analogous to sexual activity. For instance, the closeness of the embrace and the hip isolation are viewed as highly sexual gestures. The hand movements have been compared to making love, and even the forward placement of the foot, which characterizes the basic salsa step, has been compared to sexual penetration. The following eloquent and vivid quotation, from an interview with Roxanna, a Montreal disk jockey who learned to dance salsa in the city, provides an example of the sexualizing of the dance:

> You can compare salsa to sexual intercourse, actually. The way the salsa starts. You have a preliminary in it. You hear only the clave. You hear some kinds of beats that call you in. This is like the preliminary in sex; when you start touching, you look at the person. And after that the first trumpets come in. The woman perks up her breasts. She plays with her hair and all this sexual preliminary we know. And after, the salsa progresses to a very high instrumentation so you have a kind of a climax. It builds up. For the dancer who follows

the beat onto the dance floor, the heat goes on. Until the song is over, you have reached some sort of an orgasm.

In contrast, salsa teachers born outside Canada tend not to sexualize the dance. Although they claim that it has the potential to be sensual, none of them equate the movements with sexual intercourse. As Rita, one of Montreal's salsa dance teachers, says, "I don't sexualize dancing at all. In my classes, some of the men might think that I am flirting with them. When they get to know the movements and feel more at ease, they find out that it's not true."

Regarding salsa as a sexual dance is pervasive. Those raised without salsa as part of their heritage often tend to view the dance as primarily sexual. Upon presenting the idea that salsa may not be simply about sexuality either at academic conferences, in university course settings, or during informal discussions, I often encountered considerable opposition from those both within and outside the academy. For those whose cultural connections lie in the Caribbean or parts of Latin America, the assertion that salsa is not just about sexuality seems to make sense. Salsa is read most commonly as a sexual dance because many of its movements and patterns, such as the continuous hip movement and the closeness of the embrace, do in fact look highly sexual. The work by Brenda Dixon Gottschild on Africanist aesthetic concepts in Caribbean dance could shed some light on how a dance that appears merely sexual, especially to those from outside the culture, does not just embody sexuality. One of the characteristics of Africanist aesthetics, defined by Gottschild as "High-Affect Juxtaposition," enables expressions to occur simultaneously whose combination in Europeanist criteria would seem perhaps unacceptable. An example is the simultaneous enunciation of the sexual and the spiritual, or the body and the soul, in dance (Dixon Gottschild, 2002: 6). Fernando Ortiz, for instance, reveals how voluptuousness and religious ritual were combined in the African-derived dances of Cuba (Ortiz, 1951: 256). When black dances were commercialized through tourism, they were transformed into sexual performances, rendering invisible the religious significance of their voluptuous displays (256).

As the origins of salsa do stem from dance traditions in the Caribbean, salsa has inherited the aesthetic that enables the dancer to simultaneously experience sensuality, sexuality, and spirituality. Sensuality often refers to the senses of the body, whereas sexuality denotes more specifically physical expressions that are sexual in nature. While moving the body even in ways that can be construed as sensual or sexual, the dancer can experience a sense of spirituality that could be defined as feelings related to the soul or spirit. Spiritual activities consequently renew, lift, express, comfort, heal, or inspire the soul or spirit. Dancing enables *casineros*, for instance, to enjoy themselves and to break all forms of social barriers, as well as to attain spiritual satisfaction, which is what dance, according to Bárbara Balbuena, represents for the majority of Cubans (Balbuena, 2003: 90). A sense of spirituality experienced through the performing of *casino* moves is not devoid of sexuality and sensuality. For instance, in one of the figures of the *casino*, called *recoge los frutos* (gather the fruits), the male dancer gestures as though to grasp his female partner's breasts while extending his arms toward her (Balbuena, 2003: 117). Sexual movements and a sense of spirituality can fuse together in the salsa of Cuba and most probably in other Latin contexts. The marketable appeal of salsa dance as a cultural commodity distributed throughout the world lies in its sexualized exoticism. Its potential spirituality, which takes shape only through the experience of dance, does not surface in its worldwide commodification. Highly visible sexual aspects of salsa therefore predominate and come to represent the dance as a whole for those who have been raised outside of a salsa culture. Expressing one's inner self or awakening a spiritual sensibility through dancing, even in sexual or sensual ways, is an interior awareness that cannot be easily discerned.

The perception that Latin dance is merely a sexual expression often fades as individuals become more involved with the dance. My interviews with individuals of non-Latin origin who learned salsa in Montreal indicate that the sexual significance that they ascribe to the dance diminishes once they become more familiar with salsa. They start to view dance as a practice with value in itself, rather than seeing it primarily as a precursor to sex or as a vehicle for sexual expression. This change in attitude stems from experiencing the dance more from the inside, the site of the dancer, and less from the outside, the position of the spectator (Cowan, 1990: 24). Consequently, such elements of salsa as its hip movement and close embrace, initially perceived as sexual in nature, are eventually viewed as components essential to performing the dance rather than to performing sexuality. Engaging in dance has the power to transform attitudes about salsa and Latin culture in general. Salsa dancing becomes a possible site for defiance of the dominating force of cultural stereotyping.

The potential of a dance practice to resist hegemonic social forces is based on my initial assumption that a group, such as a particular subculture or ethnicity, can be a fixed and finite entity with clear boundaries. Associating specific attitudes with a particular group demarcates it as a unified and cohesive whole. A recent extensive look at the relationship between salsa and identity, undertaken by Frances Aparicio, associates this cultural practice with specific groups. According to Aparicio, the meanings that salsa fans ascribe to this music and dance depend on whether these indi/iduals are characterized in the United States as being either Latinos or Anglos, which consequently establishes two clearly defined spheres. Her analysis of the meanings that Latinos and Anglos ascribe to salsa reflects my early ethnographic findings. She claims that Latinos find political and cultural implications in salsa but that it has no wider significance for the Anglo dancer than the pleasure of dancing to the rhythms. In setting up this opposition, Aparicio establishes "Latinos" and "Anglos" as two distinct categories of salsa fans: "Most of my Latina/o students in courses on popular music have reaffirmed the serious political value and cultural urgency underlying their identification with salsa music. This process of signifying, of producing meaning and reaffirming cultural identity and boundaries through the music, stands in sharp contrast to the controversial and much discussed 'intoxicating' effects that some Anglo students have described to me in their intercultural experience of dancing to salsa music" (Aparicio, 1998: 99). Frances Aparicio does not question her division of salsa dancers and listeners into two streams because she is dealing with a relatively finite sample of salsa aficionados, in which it is possible to mark two distinct groups. Her findings of differences in attitudes toward salsa are largely based on opinions of students at the University of Michigan as well as on interviews with four working-class Latinas in southeastern Michigan (99).

Setting up two separate groups at the outset of my research reflected a highly questionable division. I realized that the barrier between Montrealers of Latin descent who teach salsa and individuals of non-Latin descent who learn the dance is much more fluid than it may have initially appeared. A superficial understanding of this dance scene can lead to false assumptions about salsa teachers and novice dance students, such as the notion that the student is learning this "foreign" dance in an artificial North American setting, whereas the instructor has "brought" this dance from her or his country of origin. Although many Montrealers may choose a Latin teacher because they want to learn "real" salsa, most of the instructors of Latin origin actually learned the dance in Montreal. Of nine dance teachers of Latin descent in the city, only three—Rita, Elio, and Paolo—had knowledge of the dance before arriving in Canada. Three of the five female salsa dance instructors whom I interviewed were born in Quebec, and one was born in English Canada. All had learned to dance salsa in Montreal. Linking salsa dancing only to Montrealers of Latin descent was not always possible. Furthermore, most of the teachers, whether Canadian-born or of Latin descent, have honed their dance expertise in Montreal.

The adoption of salsa by Montrealers of both Latin and non-Latin descent is not unexpected given the genre's history. As previously noted, neither the music nor the dance as they are known today can be traced back to one specific nation or group of people, and salsa has today spread to so many cities throughout the world that it has become a global phenomenon. It is also not surprising that most salsa dance teachers of Latin descent have learned to dance salsa in Montreal; they did not emigrate from nations that had a significant role in the historical development of salsa. The first wave of Latin American immigration occurred between 1974 and 1978 with an influx of Chilean refugees. Since 1982 the city has experienced a dramatic increase in immigrants from Central and South America, most significantly, in terms of population, from El Salvador, Chile, Peru, Guatemala, Colombia, Argentina, Guyana, and Mexico (Manègre, 1994: 14). With the exception of Colombia, none of these nations played a crucial role in the history of salsa; for many Montrealers of Latin descent, salsa was not a part of the culture in their country of origin. The majority of the city's dance instructors of Latin descent have come from Guatemala and Peru, where *cumbia* and merengue are popular. In Peru, merengue is the most prevalent Caribbean music, even though Peruvians also listen and dance to salsa (DJ Sánchez).

In an interview, Carlos of Salsa Celeste, one of the youngest salsa teachers, disclosed that he had listened and danced to alternative rock while he was growing up in Peru. Only in Montreal did he start to listen and dance to salsa and eventually to teach the dance. Although Montrealers of Latin descent may have preferred North American popular styles before they immigrated, many became avid fans of salsa (as well as merengue) in Montreal. Listening and dancing to Latin music becomes a way for immigrants of Latin descent to assert their cultural identity and establish boundaries in a Canadian setting. Dance instructor Miguel of Tropical Salsa reveals how the incorporation of salsa and merengue in the lives of Latinos in Montreal provides them with a vehicle to express who they are: "The Latinos who immigrate become one thousand times more Latin than they were in their countries. It is a phenomenon that at the beginning I did not understand. You know. You can ask many Latinos what did they listen to in their countries. They only listened to music in English. Upon arriving here, they listen to 99.9 percent of the time music in Spanish—salsa and merengue. And why? It's because, above all, they are trying to find their roots. Who am I in this huge country? It's like ants on a planet" (my translation).[3]

Dancing to salsa music in Montreal does not bring back memories of a homeland for instructor Oscar of Salsa Plus, who prior to immigrating to Canada danced disco and traditional Guatemalan dances. Nonetheless, according to Oscar, salsa dancing in Montreal becomes both a cultural marker and commodity that envelops all of Latin America: "Salsa is our Latin American commercial label. It's salsa, the dance, the culture, the richness of the nations. When we change country, we integrate into the country but we don't assimilate. We bring our culture with our music and dance. We cannot forget that. We can speak another language, but we cannot forget dance. It's our roots" (my translation).[4]

Listening and dancing to salsa has come to represent Latino identity in Montreal among people for whom salsa is not part of their "traditional" culture. Immigration has brought about a new sense of cultural identity, with people of diverse backgrounds expressing a shared pan-Latinness through their affiliation with salsa. This experience of Montrealers of Latin descent is part of the processes in contemporary societies that enable immigrants to claim cultural identities. According to Michel Wieviorka, the mechanisms through which cultural identities are created must be understood in terms of change and invention rather than in terms of the host society and reproduction. Montrealers' adoption of salsa as part of their contemporary music and dance heritage reveals that not all cultural activities by immigrant groups have roots in their countries of origin. The host country is not merely a terrain on which they can keep their "ancestral" cultural practices alive, but also a fertile ground on which to develop new cultural affiliations (Wieviorka, 1998: 891).

That new identities and cultural connections are forged as a result of immigration is not a new phenomenon. Historian Rudolph Vecoli illustrates how Italians came together only under the national umbrella term "Italian" in the United States: prior to immigration, they identified with particular regions of Italy, such as Calabria or Sicily (Glasser, 1998: 12–13). The history of salsa reveals, for instance, how music that is not indigenous to Puerto Rico became a symbol of this nation in the context of New York City. Points of articulation and rearticulation characterize the dynamics by which cultures engage in fluid processes of continual self-redefiniton and reformulation (Guilbault, 1997: 34). As defined by Will Straw, articulation and rearticulation account for how the creation and reformulation of alliances between communities is one essential element of popular music (Straw, 1991: 370). People of diverse Latin origins in Montreal express a shared sense of Latin identity through listening and dancing to salsa as well as to other popular Latin music, such as merengue and *bachata*.

The desire on the part of immigrants to form collective affiliations with one another is not only motivated by a need for cultural connections; it is also a response to experiences of racism and marginalization (Bulmer and Solomos, 1998: 831). Although Montrealers of Latin descent occupy every socio-economic strata, the majority of Latino immigrants are in the lower echelon of the socio-economic bracket (Manègre, 1994: 349). Immigrants in Canada more often occupy undesirable jobs (Hiebert, 1999: 349) and obtain fewer economic benefits from education than do nonimmigrants (364). Discrimination and living on the periphery of the dominant society could lead immigrants to find themselves excluded from better jobs despite their educational qualifications. Many Latin immigrants in Montreal face these and similar conditions as a result of their status as immigrants and their classification in Canadian society as "visible minorities." These shared realities could lead them to form a collective even though they also have affiliations with their countries of origin. Using the example of how Algerians, Moroccans, and Tunisians have come together in France to form a "Maghrebi diasporic consciousness," James Clifford writes, "It is worth adding that a negative experience of racism and economic marginalization can also lead to new coalitions" (Clifford, 1994: 311–12).

Salsa appeals to a wide spectrum of the Latin community in Montreal. Since the historical evolution of salsa has led to its becoming an expression of pan-Latin identity, its embrace by Montrealers of Latin descent is not surprising. The nature of Montreal's Latin community has enabled salsa to spread widely throughout this community in the city. Montreal's Latin population is extremely diverse: not one single nation dominates this community of about 54,000.[5] The Latin population in Montreal is also strikingly multicultural: there are people from every Central American, Latin American, and Latin Caribbean nation. This diversity is not always taken into account within the Canadian context: the single unifying category of "Latin American" in the Canadian Census erases the differences between people of Latin origin. For instance, the 2001 Census categorized Latin Americans as the fourth-largest group among visible minorities in Montreal (Canadian Statistics, 2001.) According to Latin music promoter Alvaro, the diversity of Montreal's Latin community affects musical tastes in the city. There is no one group (or groups) with specific national affiliations in the city whose musical tastes dominate. Therefore, the types of music vary: Montrealers of both Latin and non-Latin origin listen and dance to a wide array of Latin music, such as salsa, merengue, *bachata, cumbia, bolero, vallenato,* and Latin rock and pop. As Alvaro discloses: "I have had a hard time with DJs [disk jockeys] because DJs here [in Montreal] don't put emphasis on the side that here we have to . . . we like everything. Here we like salsa. We like merengue. We like *bachata.* They dance to all different styles of music. I think it is peculiar. I think it makes Montreal a very unique place in the Latin music spectrum in North America."

The absence of Latin "ethnic" groups who dominate over others in terms of population and historical significance distinguishes Montreal from other Latin music centers in the United States, such as New York and Miami. Montreal stands in contrast to New York, where musical tastes can be rigidly polarized between those who listen only to salsa and others who listen only to merengue (Alvaro). Paul Austerlitz, who has done considerable work on merengue, elucidates how divisions between Latin ethnic groups in New York are expressed through allegiances to specific musical practices. He writes: "While merengue does represent pan-Latino identity to some non-Dominicans, my experiences indicate that this is less true in New York City than in Puerto Rico, Connecticut, and the midwestern United States. In New York, ethnic boundaries between Latino groups are tightly drawn, and merengue most often marks Dominican rather than pan-Latino identity" (Austerlitz, 1998: 56).[6]

This stratification in tastes is linked to the large number of Puerto Ricans and Dominicans who live in New York.[7] Unlike the Latin populations in Montreal who do not have deep historical roots in the city, the influence of Puerto Ricans in New York dates back to the beginning of the twentieth century. Furthermore, New York has a large Dominican population whose musical style of merengue has challenged the supremacy of salsa in New York since the early 1980s. Consequently, most Puerto Ricans could have a greater allegiance to salsa than to merengue. In Miami the Latin population is not a minority group as it is in Montreal.[8] Of the city's population of two million, more than half are of Latin descent. Further, 66 percent of all Latins in Miami are of Cuban origin (Nijman, 1997: 167). Consequently, Cuban-influenced genres would certainly prevail in Miami.

As no single Latin immigrant group in Montreal is credited with bringing salsa to the city and maintaining it (compared with Puerto Ricans in New York and Cubans in Miami), audiences in the Latin music scene come from many areas of the Caribbean and Latin America. Salsa and merengue, rather than other styles, such as *cumbia*, *vallenato*, and *bachata*, represent Latin identity in Montreal because these two styles predominate in the commercial Spanish-language music market in the United States. In Montreal, salsa and merengue are the Latin music styles most commonly heard at salsa clubs, on radio shows, and in music video television programming targeting the Latin community. Media directed at Montreal's Latin community are conducted either completely in Spanish or in conjunction with French and/or English. The process by which salsa has become an expression of Latinos is intertwined with its commodification. Since both the dance and music of salsa are not indigenous, Montrealers access this cultural practice by going to salsa clubs, buying compact music discs, watching how-to dance videos, taking dance lessons, going to concerts, listening to the radio, and watching Latin music television shows.

Given the prevailing influence that commodification exerts on the proliferation of salsa in the city and given salsa's establishment as a marker of Latin identity, I redirected my ethnographic focus to take into account the link between commodification and identity. Rather than looking at the meaning that individuals learning the dance ascribed to salsa, I focused on how salsa dancing is promoted and "sold" as a cultural commodity. I investigated how commodification influences salsa as an expression of Latin identity. My ethnographic research entailed taking dance lessons at twelve schools in the city and conducting in-depth interviews with the dance instructors. To further understand the Montreal music and dance scene, I also conducted various informal interviews and had discussions with several instructors and dance assistants in the city, and I completed an extensive ethnographic study of the channels of communication through which salsa is distributed.

Salsa is disseminated through various locations, events, and media outlets in the city: Latin clubs, clubs with a salsa night, community radio stations, Latin community parties, concerts, Latin music nights, gyms that feature salsa aerobics, and a community television station featuring the Latin show *Teleritmo*. I interviewed club owners, Latin music disc jockeys who work in salsa clubs and on community networks, music promoters, musicians, and people involved in the community television network. I wanted to see how people of both Latin and non-Latin descent were responsible for creating this music and dance scene. I conducted this ethnographic work over a four-year period, primarily from 1996 to 2000. Most of the work was carried out in the summers, from May to September, although I documented changes in the salsa scene throughout the year and maintained my salsa contacts.

Many of the community outlets for Latin cultural production in the city, such as the Spanish-language television show *Teleritmo* and the combined French-Spanish radio show *Rumba de Samedi*, play primarily commercial Latin music that is popularized and promoted in New York (DJ Juan; DJ Sánchez; DJ Leo). Given that the Spanish language is central to these two media outlets, both are geared toward the Latin community in the city and are produced by Montrealers of Latin descent. The extent to which music tastes are influenced, and perhaps controlled, by the Latin music disseminated in the United States could be viewed as an example of American cultural domination. This affiliation with the U.S. Latin music scene, and consequently, with other parts of the globe, suggests that Montrealers of Latin descent feel connected to a Latin identity that extends well beyond the island of Montreal.

There has not been any work done on a shared sense of Latin identity in the Canadian context. Juan Flores's understanding of how Latins in the United States can be configured in terms of Benedict Anderson's concept of an "imagined community" sheds light on the Montreal situation. Flores discusses the tension between perceiving Latinos as a singular entity and perceiving them as an aggregate of diverse peoples (Flores, 1997: 185). The impetus to group all Latinos in the United States into one "imagined community" stems from two disparate impulses: to create a Latin market and to mark the shared history that unifies Latin Americans. Concomitant with the distribution of Latin products throughout the world is the circulation of stereotypes that reduce Latin identity to a few marketable misrepresentations. Similarly, Flores claims that there exists a "Latino historical unconscious" unifying diverse Latin nations that is grounded in concrete past and present circumstances rather than in myths and stereotypes: the extensive history of colonial Spain, the enslavement and oppression of indigenous and African peoples, the unstable conglomeration of nations under the control of international power, and the continuous migration of peoples, cultural practices, and commodities (188). Although these common historical circumstances and contemporary realities connect Latin American nations, these diverse peoples view their commonalities through the prisms of their national perspectives (188).

As a symbol of Latin identity, salsa embodies Juan Flores's notion that Latinos share certain historical realities. Elements of salsa music, such as its rhythmic patterns and certain instruments, keep alive the memory of the enslavement and subjugation of African peoples and, to a lesser extent, that of the indigenous peoples of the Caribbean (Manuel, 1995: 2–9). The salsa music that emerged in the 1970s with such artists as Willie Colon and Reuben Blades ignited Latino resistance against the force of international powers, especially U.S. imperialism (76, 80). The extent to which the migration of "people, culture and things" binds Latins into a single force surfaces in the development of salsa, from its origins in the Caribbean and its evolution in New York to its transculturation in such South American nations as Venezuela and Colombia as well as a number of U.S. cities (Flores, 1997: 188).

Juan Flores maintains that Latinos in the United States are better described as a "diasporic community" or a "world tribe" than as an ethnic minority or immigrant group. Of all the terms available, he chooses to refer to Latins as a "delocalized transnation" because of specific historical circumstances in the United States. Spanish-speaking peoples' presence in the area called the United States actually preceded the arrival of the English. Flores argues that if the existence of the indigenous peoples in this region is taken into account, then it is the Anglo-Saxon culture, not the Latin culture, that is the "original illegal alien" (Flores, 1997: 190). Canada does not have a history of Latin inhabitance prior to the arrival of the French and then the English. People of Latin descent in Canada cannot be configured as a diasporic nation or "delocalized transnation" in the same way that historical circumstances in the United States allow for the "imagining" of Latin identity. Latin immigration to Canada became significant only in the 1970s.

Although the terms "ethnic minority" and "immigrant" are applicable in the Montreal context, Latins in Montreal identify with the phenomenon of Latins as a "diasporic" people whose cultural boundaries transcend the borders that separate nations. Frances Aparicio positions the act of listening and dancing to salsa music on the part of some Puerto Ricans in the United States as a sensorial recapturing of their homeland. Their past is brought into their present life through the physical sensations of music and dance (Aparicio, 1998: 91). For many Montrealers of Latin descent, salsa may not invoke memories of home since the desire to dance and listen to salsa has often developed from being in Montreal. Montrealers attach themselves to salsa to assert a sense of Latin identity within the vast multitude of identities that comprise the Canadian cultural panorama, even if salsa was not part of who they were in their country of origin. Jocelyn Guilbault shows how a number of authors, such as James Clifford and Deborah Pacini Hernandez, claim that the delimiting of cultures within national boundaries is becoming more and more gratuitous as commodities such as music are produced and consumed in multiple international contexts rather than only in a particular location or national space (Guilbault, 1997: 34). As homi k. bhabha states, "The very concepts of homogenous national cultures, the consensual or contiguous transmission of historical traditions, or 'organic' ethnic communities—*as the grounds of cultural comparativism*—are in profound process of redefinition" (bhabha, 1994: 5, emphasis in the original; Guilbault, 1997: 34). The transnational tastes of individuals in the Montreal Latin community transform them into a diaspora.

The Montreal Latin community can be viewed as diasporic, albeit not in the strict sense of the term. "Diaspora" was used in earlier times to describe the dispersion of Jews, Greeks, and Armenians but now captures the displacement of many peoples. Stanley Tambiah asserts that diasporic communities are forged by peoples who, through voluntary or forced migration, relocate to other countries and are involved in transnational experiences and relations with their host country or region (Tambiah, 2000: 164). To limit the definition of "diaspora," Will Safran has labeled key criteria to characterize an "ideal type." From Safran's perspective, diaspora should describe exiled minority communities, scattered from their initial site of origin or "center" to at least two "peripheral" locations, who preserve a recollection or myth of their first homeland and accept that they will probably never be accepted by their host nation. They regard their original homeland as a locus to which they will eventually return and as a place to conserve or rebuild. The common identities of these diaspora collectives are defined by an ongoing connection with their homeland (Tambiah, 2000: 169; Safran, 1991: 83–84). James Clifford is wary of this "ideal type" as a working definition for diaspora, for even the most quintessential, such as the Jewish diaspora, does not conform to all of Safan's characteristics. Clifford claims, for instance, that parts of the history of the Jews and other well-known diaspora collectives reveal that such communities did not necessarily have strong connections to a homeland and a desire to return to their place of origin (Clifford, 1994: 305). Stanley Tambiah cautions that the term "diaspora," in contemporary analysis, has become so widespread that it may become too elastic (Tambiah, 2000: 169). Clifford, by comparison, comprehends diaspora as "a discourse that is traveling or hybridizing in new global conditions" (Clifford, 1994: 306). The circumstances that have created a looser understanding of diaspora include decolonization, a rise in immigration, global communication and transport, and a host of factors that have resulted in individual and group connections to more than one location as people travel and live more readily within and across nations (306).

Listening and dancing to salsa does not create diasporic connections among the diverse Montreal Latin communities by evoking a cultural practice that triggers memories of an original homeland. Nonetheless, salsa links the diverse people of Latin origin in the city to a transnational Latin consciousness. Listening and dancing to salsa on the part of Latin Montrealers represents as much their willingness to connect with a spirit of Latin identity as it does their desire to establish cultural boundaries within the host city. Salsa in Montreal nurtures a diasporic consciousness that reflects James Clifford's concept of diaspora in contemporary global conditions: "Diaspora discourse articulates, or bends together, both roots *and* routes to construct what Gilroy describes as alternate public spheres (Gilroy, 1987), forms of community consciousness and solidarity that maintain identifications outside the national time/space in order to live inside, with difference" (Clifford, 1994: 308).

In modern diaspora, decentered lateral associations may be as crucial as connections based on a shared place of origin and desire to return to a real or mythical homeland (Clifford, 1994: 306). Transnational lateral bonds and networks between diaspora are maintained by modern communication and transport technology and by labor migration (Clifford, 1994: 304; Tambiah,

2000: 173). Disparate locations become a singular community through the ongoing dissemination of "people, money, goods and information" (Clifford, 1994: 303). Salsa in Montreal joins this city to the salsa world of New York as well as to music centers in Latin America and the Caribbean; Montreal connects to transnational networks linking the United States to parts of the Americas and vice versa.

American cities such as New York or Miami connect to the Caribbean through the circular migration of people to these two areas. Discussing the strong bonds that many Miami residents of Latin descent have with specific areas in the Caribbean and Latin America, Jan Nijman elucidates how their migration to the United States has not led to a fixed and one-way inhabitance. These residents often live in two cultures simultaneously, transforming their status into "global villagers" (Nijman, 1997: 173). Large areas of New York are considered to be part of the Caribbean and are influenced by New York Caribbean culture (Clifford, 1994: 311). For many people of Caribbean descent who live in New York and other parts of the United States, the borders separating them from their "homelands" are deteriorating (Kaplan, 1996–1997: 58). Although many Caribbean people migrate to the United States to find work, their countries of origin remain readily available through travel and communication technology.

In addition to the connection between the Caribbean and such important salsa centers as Miami and New York, the Latin music world connects many cities throughout the Americas, such as Cali, Caracas, San Juan, Los Angeles, and Toronto. Although Montreal salsa is predominantly influenced by taste patterns in New York, other salsa centers also exert an influence. Many dance instructors in the city travel to parts of Latin America and the Caribbean to hone the styles that they teach or take frequent trips to clubs and studios in New York, spreading the New York style throughout Montreal. Non-Latin instructors also travel to cities in the United States and Latin America: a Canadian-born instructor related in an interview that she travels to Cali, Colombia, to learn more about the dance. Through travel and the migration of Latin peoples to Montreal, multiple communities of dispersed populations gather in this Canadian city: salsa has become a means for them both to evoke a pan-Latin consciousness and to mark their difference within Quebec and Canada. Their shared cultural affiliation with salsa (and merengue) elucidates Georges Lipsitz's understanding of how popular music practices can transcend the confines of geography. Diverse Montrealers partake of the same cultural practice as people in cities throughout the Americas. As Lipsitz writes, "Today, shared cultural space no longer depends upon shared geographic place" (Lipsitz, 1994: 6).

That Latin music primarily from New York is deployed to elicit and nour-ish an overarching Latin consciousness and diaspora in Montreal creates a paradox. The portrayal of Latin culture disseminated through music videos, CD covers, and salsa lyrics may reproduce sexual stereotypes. Commonly fea-tured on *Teleritmo*, videos of mainstream stars such as Ricky Martin and Glo-ria Estevan often depict exaggerated sexuality.[9] Juan Flores contends that stereotypical representations of Latin culture are used to sell Latin products in the United States and on a global level. He writes, "Whatever the partic-ular purpose, though, the means and result are the same—stereotypes: dis-torted, usually offensive, and in any case artificial, portrayals of Latino peo-ple. And these are the only images of Latinos that most people in the United States and around the world are ever exposed to which makes it difficult to test their accuracy" (Flores, 1997: 186). This perspective of Latin culture, predominant in the Western imagination, filters into the promotion of Latin cultural products to Latin consumers.

It is true that Montrealers from outside the Latin communities who have not had much exposure to salsa perceive the movements of the dance in highly sexual ways; it is also true that a number of salsa dance teachers of Latin descent use an overtly sexual image of salsa to promote the dance. Some male Latin dancers cultivate a portrayal of salsa as sexy and enticing: both Miguel of Tropical Salsa and Carlos of Salsa Celeste, for example, pre-sent a portrait of sensuality in their advertising. A dancing couple in Salsa Celeste's ad depicts an electrifying sensation as the bodies of the male and fe-male dancers touch. Carlos revealed in an interview that this representation, a sketch of actual choreography, is intended to be alluring. Although Paolo of Caribe dance school does not use sexual imagery to sell dance lessons, the female dancers' costumes of the school's dance troupe are highly suggestive. Thongs and bra tops, with calves and forearms wrapped in layers of flowing fabric, adorn the well-toned bodies of the Caribe dancers. Salsa teachers por-tray the dance variously. Some male Latin teachers, such as Gustavo of Salsa Brava and Oscar of Salsa Plus, do not foster sexuality in their advertisements. Two Canadian-born teachers, Catherine of Simply Salsa and Daphne of Riv-iera, actively try to downplay salsa's association with sex and the pick-up scene. Catherine's advertisement for Simply Salsa stresses the exercise aspect of dance. Daphne avoids giving the impression in the Riviera ad that the school is a venue in which to find dates and sexual partners but admits that the result of strategically downplaying the sexual element associated with the dance is an ad that is too unassuming.[10] Alvaro, a Latin music promoter and organizer of Bamboleo,[11] monthly Latin nights that lasted from 1993 to 1998, notes that in his artistic and inventive ads for these events, he wanted to portray a different image of Latin culture than the widespread depiction of women in bikinis. Many music promoters in the city use scantily clad women to sell their events, which reflect the advertising strategy of plastering female bodies on CD covers and in videos to sell Latin cultural products throughout the United States and in international markets. Montrealers of both Latin and non-Latin descent reinforce or resist the sexual stereotype of Latin culture in their dance promotions.

The stereotypical framing of Latin culture by Latins themselves is a form of "autoexoticism," a term that I borrow from Marta Savagliano's insightful writings on tango. Savagliano articulates how she finds herself being exoticized, as well as exoticizing herself, because of her foreign identity; her research on tango could further illuminate the phenomenon of individuals of Latin descent attaching themselves to stereotypes of their own culture. Marta Savagliano writes: "Reflecting on the disciplining/promotion to which I was subjecting myself in academia, I saw tango's process of disciplining/promotion in the hands of dance masters and spectacle entrepreneurs. Looking at tango's endless search for origins and authenticity, I came to understand the colonized nature of this attempt. Amazed at tango's colonizing appropriation through exoticism, I found myself transformed into an exotic object: colonized. Even more stunned by tango's achievements at home as a result of playing the exotic game, I put into question my own autoexoticism" (Savagliano, 1995a: 5).

Exoticizing one's own culture could result from migration to a new country and transnational identity constructions. Since those outside Latin culture in Montreal often sensationalize it, an exoticizing reinforced by marketing strategies, individuals of Latin descent may sensualize themselves to sell salsa, appealing to prevailing conceptions of the dance. The theme of autoexoticism surfaced a number of times in interviews with dance teachers of Latin descent. Miguel, for instance, disclosed how he unwittingly assumes the persona of a romantic and sensual Latin dance instructor in his classes.

The proliferation of sexual images to sell salsa dancing partly relates to the commodification of the dance in Montreal. As a commodified practice, dancing can also influence the production and distribution of other cultural commodities. Sarah Thornton illustrates the link between dance and cultural commodities by describing how, in the mid-1950s, jukebox manufacturer Seeburg proposed that discotheque would survive as a form of entertainment only if it offered "uninterrupted music." The "Little LP" was issued, offering seven and half minutes of continuous dance music, thus "the practice of dancing to discs began to affect the design of the record itself" (Thornton, 1995: 58).

The commodification of salsa is most apparent in the dance lessons offered in all the Latin clubs in the city, in some mainstream clubs, which have Latin nights, and in the two major dance studios, Riviera and Caribe. Dancing to salsa also directly affects the marketing of cultural commodities such as concerts, music videos, and compact discs. Alvaro reveals how audience dance participation facilitated selling the monthly Bamboleo Latin events: "The crowd is also a big part of the event. You have got to see the people dancing and swinging around the dance floor. That gives the whole event an ambiance. And when you don't have that, you can put as many artificial elements as you want, but it is not the same." DJ Sánchez notes that when he plays Latin hits from New York in the clubs in Montreal, the life span of a particular track depends on whether the crowd dances to it. The ultimate expression of appreciation for salsa music is dance. Leonardo, a Montreal Latin musician, claims that "The difference between Latin American and other North American music is when we play well and, you know, they say in the pocket or in the groove, we know right away. You can definitely see it on the dance floor. People will dance more. The excitement on the dance floor will increase. It will be more crowded and the better dancers will be there. Whereas if you are playing poorly you tend to see more poor dancing. You really get an immediate feedback. It's an automatic response." Peter Manuel illustrates how salsa is, above all, dance music. Live bands adapt recorded versions of commercial salsa tracks by enlivening the rhythm section and the vocals in order to keep the dancers moving on the floor and the musicians energized by the music. Manuel writes, "But if many modern records tend to sound rather slick and commercial, it should be remembered that the dance club scene is more important than the records, both to the audiences and to band members" (Manuel, 1995: 88).

The commercialization and commodification of salsa is often associated with its demise as an "authentic" cultural practice that expresses the heritage of a people. Although Deborah Pacini Hernandez and Peter Manuel do not evaluate salsa styles in terms of an overt discourse of authenticity, their claim that the highly commercial *salsa romántica* is a pale version of the earlier "revolutionary" salsa implicitly grants the previous style a degree of legitimacy. The musical and lyrical qualities of early salsa saluted the rebellious spirit of the working-class Puerto Rican diaspora and its African-derived cultural heritage. Pacini Hernandez writes, "But by the 1980s, when the world-beat phenomenon emerged, salsa's racial consciousness had been replaced by the lush orchestral arrangements and insipid lyrical concerns of its stylistic successor, *salsa romantica*" (Pacini Hernández, 1998: 113–14). According to Peter Manuel, as salsa gradually established a place in the entertainment industry, it lost its character as a rebellious expression of the proletarian Puerto Rican experience and transformed into a flavorless, non-political Latin pop music (Manuel, 1995: 91).

In cultural analysis, a binary division is often drawn between a "meaningful" and "authentic" cultural practice that flourishes in actual circumstances and the appropriated and consequently impoverished version of it that is exploited by cultural industries and the mass media. Referring to the work of Walter Benjamin, George Lipsitz relates how folk cultures, stripped from their sites of "origin" by processes of mass production and transformed into marketable commodities, lose their original significance and become mere novelties for unaware consumers (Lipsitz, 1994: 161). The appropriation of folk cultures that are today being distributed around the globe by cultural industries deprives them of their local meanings (161). People in developed Western countries have long consumed cultural products created by colonized people, using such racist and sexist terms to describe these products as "primitive," "exotic," "sexual," and "enticing" (4–5). Latin dances, ripped out of their cultural and historical contexts as cultural commodities to be enjoyed by mainstream North American society, are often framed in terms of a discourse of sexuality. Gaylyn Studlar reveals, for instance, how the popularity of tango teas in the United States during the 1910s was fueled by the sexual image of the dark foreign lover and further emphasized through Rudolph Valentino's cinematic persona of a tango dancer (Studlar, 1993: 26). Jane Desmond notes that in the North American context, Latin American dances such as the tango and the *lambada* are described as "fiery," "hot," "sultry," and "passionate" (Desmond, 1993–1994: 47).

Since the 1980s the increased commodification and commercialization of salsa has furthered its popularity in many parts of the world. This globalization has stripped the dance and music of much of its political significance and reduced it to the exotic and sensually alluring. Lisa Sánchez González claims that the transformation of salsa from a genuine expression of proletarian Puerto Rican diasporic experience into a practice in Los Angeles nightclubs has converted listening and dancing to salsa into an exotic thrill with racist and sexist implications. She discloses, for instance, how policies in Los Angeles salsa clubs are designed to foster a white elite clientele, while salsas and merengues with such lyrics as "*el negro allí, el negro sigue allí* ('the darkie over there, the darkie keeps it up over there')" and "*el negro bembón* ('the darkie with the big bottom lip')" are frequently heard in clubs (Sánchez González, 1999: 245).

It is indeed true that since the 1980s, the growing commercialization of salsa has rendered it void of a sense of racial consciousness and has encouraged the proliferation of sexist/racist stereotyping of Latin culture. Nevertheless, the history of salsa shows how the commodification of this musical form helped to develop this dance and music into an expression of a heritage of a people. As noted, salsa, which is not indigenous to Puerto Rico, came to represent the proletarian consciousness of the Puerto Rican diaspora. Music produced in New York by Fania Records was disseminated to the Caribbean. This circulation of musical commodities contributed to the growth of a Puerto Rican proletariat identity in New York and on the island. The transformation of salsa from an "authentic" culture into a cultural commodity that could be distributed and consumed nurtured its growth as a rebellious cultural expression. We might ask, however, whether there ever was a time when salsa was a truly "authentic" cultural expression in the sense that it had not been "corrupted" by some form of commodification. Tracing the history of salsa since the 1960s exposes how commodification has played a part in its incarnation as an "authentic" cultural practice. Transforming the practices of a people into a cultural commodity that can be distributed outside of its "origins" could also have positive effects. George Lipsitz points out that the political and moral context in which certain folk cultures thrive are both retained and strengthened by circulation outside their sites of origin. Reggae artists, for example, have been able to vocalize and spread the aspirations of the African diaspora beyond the music's birthplace, Jamaica (Lipsitz, 1994: 161).

In Montreal the commodification of salsa, particularly the transformation of the dance into a commodity that is "bought and sold" in dance schools, enables people from diverse backgrounds to connect. The multicultural flavor of the Montreal salsa scene is created by the diversity of individuals involved in promoting, teaching, and dancing salsa. Both Montrealers of Latin backgrounds and those born in Canada teach and promote salsa dancing. The dance clubs and studios are truly multicultural. One of the most striking aspects of salsa clubs is their lack of homogeneity: "I've noticed the clients in these clubs are multi-generational and multicultural" comments Marites Carino in the Valentine's Day article "Flirty Dancing: Lookin' for Love in all the Latin Places," which describes her first visit to Latin clubs in the city (Carino, 1999: 41). Latin clubs and dance studios are comprised of immigrant groups of both Latin and non-Latin descent as well as Canadian-born Montrealers of both Latin and non-Latin origin. On any night at Cactus, one of the city's popular Latin clubs, for instance, there are Montrealers from such Latin nations as Guatemala, El Salvador, Chile, Bolivia, the Dominican Republic, Colombia, Cuba, and Panama. Canadian-born Montrealers with European backgrounds such as Italian, Portuguese, and Greek, in addition to

Montrealers from various Asian and Middle Eastern backgrounds, dance to Latin rhythms. Montrealers born in Haiti as well as Canadian-born Montrealers of Haitian descent frequent salsa clubs, as do West Africans from such nations as Senegal, Cameroon, and the Ivory Coast. Canadian-born Montrealers who identify themselves as Quebecois or Canadian also frequent salsa clubs. Some clubs, such as Club 649 and Salsateque, have more diverse populations, whereas others, such as Casa Nacho and the Conga Room, cater more to a Latin clientele.

The history of salsa shows how exemplary this music and dance has been in bringing people of varied backgrounds together. As noted earlier, during the 1950s New Yorkers of diverse backgrounds frequented the Palladium, one of the hallmarks of Latin music. African Americans, Anglos, Latinos, Jews, Italians, and Chinese danced to the rhythms of the mambo and the *son* (Manuel, 1995: 69). The contemporary Latin scene in the United States emulates how salsa's Latin Caribbean precursors had fostered a multicultural following. Discussing Latin clubs in the 1990s, Peter Manuel writes, "Moreover, blacks, whites, mulattoes, and even some Asians are all dancing and mingling together, with an ease and naturalness that reflects the racial synthesis that produced Cuban dance music in the first place" (89).

Dance as an expression of multicultural values has a history in Canada. Since the introduction of the official policy of multiculturalism in 1971, which seeks to recognize and maintain the culture of ethnic groups in Canada who are not of French, English, or First Nations origin, the federal government has allocated funds to promote the development of "traditional" dances by community organizations and performances of these dances in culture shows. The need to officially recognize "other" ethnic groups was voiced most fervently by descendants of Ukrainian immigrants, who wanted to be included in Canadian political, economic, and social life while maintaining their historical and cultural heritage (Roy, 1995: 200). The multiculturalism policy was the government's response to recommendations by the Royal Commission on Bilingualism and Biculturalism, appointed in 1963 (Li, 1994: 377). Canada created this policy to help immigrant and cultural groups maintain and nurture their cultural heritage (376–77). In enacting the policy, Pierre Trudeau stated in his speech to the House of Commons in 1971 that "The policy that I am announcing today accepts the contention of the other cultural communities that they, too, are essential elements in Canada and deserve government assistance in order to contribute to regional and national life in ways that derive from their heritage yet are distinctly Canadian" (House of Commons Debates, 8 October 1971: 8545, quoted in Li, 1994: 377).

Canada has become a pluralist nation largely as a result of circumstances rather than because of any innate quality in the dominant Canadian and Quebecois cultures (Smith, 1970: 273). Prior to the Second World War, English Canadians who received immigrants manifested strong Anglo-centric sentiments that precluded immigrants keeping their languages and cultures. Immigrants were encouraged to assimilate and conform to English Canadian values. French Canadians were no more receptive to the immigrants, fearing that these newcomers would demographically threaten French Canadian survival as a people, which depended on a growing and significant population (Thompson and Weinfeld, 1995: 187–88). Amendments in 1962 and 1966 to the Immigration Act of 1952 eliminated a system that had barred immigrants from entering Canada on the grounds that they lacked certain characteristics. A universal point system was put into place, which allowed a more equitable selection of immigrants. Canada increasingly admitted immigrants from Asia, North Africa, Latin America, and the Caribbean, along with the "traditional" ones who were primarily white and of European descent (189). Prior to the large influx of non-Europeans, immigrants could assimilate into Canadian society because of their racial and ethnic similarity to the dominant culture. Speaking about the American experience, Eduardo Mendieta states that immigrants of eastern or southern European origin were initially viewed as a racial "other," compared to Americans of Anglo-Saxon descent. Eventually Irish, German, and Italian people were deracialized and assimilated into dominant American society (Mendieta, 2000: 48). Similarly, in Canada, in the first half of the twentieth century, southern and eastern European immigrants were perceived as a racial "other," then gradually as "white" by the dominant discourse of racial categorizations (Weinfeld, 1988: 590). Canadians of European descent do not fall under the euphemistic category of "visible minority," a term denoting individuals and groups who are not perceived as white. The narrative of assimilation, which relates how newcomers eventually adopt the culture and practices of their host country to the extent of complete conformity, has been shattered by new immigrations of "non-European peoples of color" (Clifford, 1994: 311). Because of race, these new immigrants cannot assimilate completely, as they are considered by the dominant discourse to be "other." The idea of Canada as a nation comprised of diverse groups who maintain their own culture has arisen partly because of these new immigrants, who cannot be assimilated into the "dominant" Canadian society comprised of individuals of white-European descent.

The image conveyed by Canada's multicultural policy is one of a "cultural mosaic," in which the ethnic panorama is comprised of diverse cultures living side by side, each developing its own distinct heritage. The cultures of ethnic groups in Canada have been maintained by official funding of national regional festivals, including folkloric dancing, ethnic theater performances and craft exhibitions (Li, 1994: 378), heritage language classes, special radio and television shows, and community culture centers (Kalin and Berry, 1994: 296). Certain assumptions underlie the promotion of the multicultural mosaic in which Canada's "ethnic" groups are given expression: groups whose entire national cultures can be represented by a few practices are regarded as homogenous. These practices, brandished to foster multiculturalism, express allegiances to nations or groups with a collective past; thus the traditional practices of ethnic groups in Canada today are bounded by primordial national allegiances.

Despite the aims of official multiculturalism to embrace ethnic Canadians, this policy actually envelops ethnic groups in the myth that their cultures are equal to the dominant cultures rooted in Canada's two founding nations. In reality "other" cultures have little power to affect and influence the prevailing cultures. Official multiculturalism policy is under fire for being a containment policy that keeps ethnic groups in "their place" and renders them unable to significantly influence Canadian society (Paquet, 1994: 63, 64). The multiculturalism policy remains merely decorative because it neither grants immigrants any "real ethnic rights" nor requires them to fulfill "multicultural obligations." The promotion of multicultural values without actual resources to support diversity can only create a split between what is expected from the official policy and what it can actually put into place in concrete circumstances (68). Without ethnic rights or obligations, groups in Canada that comprise the multicultural panorama cannot exert significant impact on Canada through the mechanisms of federal policy. Gilles Paquet demonstrates that the ten million Canadians who do not come from the charter groups have no real power in mainstream media and are unable to represent themselves from their own cultural standpoint. He unveils a possible hidden agenda in the official policy of multiculturalism when he states, "Indeed, recognizing the cultural identity of a minority group and promoting its maintenance through official financial support may well be an indirect and Machiavellian technique to consecrate exclusion of the minority group, or more appropriately to continue to dominate it" (68).

Promoting and funding dance cultures of minority groups to realize Canada's multicultural policy has received mixed responses. Kazukimi Ebuchi's anthropological work on Ukrainian dance exemplifies a positive look at the role of dance. For Ukrainian immigrants and Canadians of Ukrainian descent, dance is an ethnic symbol that answers the Ukrainian desire for a "root" experience, even though many non-Ukrainian Canadians participate (Ebuchi, 1986: 137–42). Critics who claim that dance and other cultural practices of ethnic groups have been manipulated by the policy of multiculturalism perceive officially funded displays of culture not as promoting ethnic identity but as containing the cultures of "other" Canadians. Myrna Kostash suggests that the image of dancing ethnic Canadians celebrating what she terms the "rather innocuous" cultural mosaic camouflages the mandate of ensuring that minority Canadians do not threaten the reigning cultural fabric of Canada: "Canadian sociologists have argued, as soon as the growing numerical and economic strength and cultural vitality of ethnic collectives began to threaten the entrenched superiority of the ruling élites, the élites and their media allies acted to defend themselves. They began the process of "de-clawing" multiculturalism. According to this argument, it is *they*, and not the minority groups who insisted on the 'singing and dancing' of the cultural heritage spectacles" (Kostash, 1995: 128).

Peter S. Li discloses how the official practices of funding ethnic art and culture have both controlled and trivialized the artistic expressions of minority groups in Canada. In Canada's art world, a two-tiered system exists. Since 1957 the Canada Council has primarily funded art stemming from European and American traditions, such as orchestral music and ballet (Li, 1994: 378). At the same time, the federal multicultural policy has aided and cultivated the artistic and cultural practices of visible minorities. However, rather than advancing artistic creativity, multicultural-based funding has supported artistic organizations whose expressions celebrate Canadian diversity. Money has been granted for national and regional festivals that feature the dances, theater performances, and crafts of various communities in Canada (378). Artists funded through the Canada Council are given greater freedom of expression than those supported by multicultural assistance. Further, the official multiculturalism policy selects groups for financial support that conform to its implicit political agenda. This marriage between art and state policy has influenced the kinds of cultural and artistic practices displayed in ethnic festivals.

Official multiculturalism policies overlook the impact that the traditions of ethnic groups can have on contemporary Canadian art. The celebration of artistic expressions featured in multicultural shows, such as the Canada Day parade, accentuates how ethnic groups' heritages represent primordial remote countries to which immigrants once belonged. These folkloric performances stress the exotic characteristics of traditional cultures and seriously downplay the artistic merit and potential of minority arts. Li comments, "The basis of their official support and their public endorsement is cultural novelty and ethnic exoticism, but not necessarily aesthetic value"

(Li, 1994: 381). The ethnic art cultivated evokes the stereotypes propagated by multiculturalism; potentially complex and organic art is not encouraged to flourish and become enriched within a new context but is transformed into mechanical, rigid, and static expressions emphasizing links to a past heritage. The Canadian policy of multiculturalism presents immigrants' cultural heritages as a way for ethnic Canadians to maintain the cultures of their countries of origin. Li offers the alternative view that reinscribing distant and remote cultures on Canadian soil is influenced to a greater extent by the context in which immigrants live than by the cultural heritage that they have allegedly brought to this "new" world (Li, 1994: 385). He states, "the analysis of ethnic art and minority culture in Canada clearly shows that their form and content are largely constrained by material and social forces of the immigrant-receiving society, rather than a primordial source" (385).

The federal government promotes dance displays that exhibit the ancestral heritage of specific groups, such as Canadians of Chinese or Ukrainian descent. Critics claim that these exhibitions fossilize cultural practices; the performances reduce rich and complex dance traditions to such stereotypes as the Chinese Lion dance and Ukrainian Cossack dancing (Roy, 1995: 203). The philosophy presented through the culture show is one of the mosaic, in which each group expresses its heritage separately without influencing the "dominant" cultures or the cultures of "other" ethnic groups (Li, 1994: 376–78).

Mooring these dances to the folkloric past of Canada's immigrant populations conveys the myth that dances funded by the official multiculturalism policy are "pure" cultural expressions that have not been "corrupted" by commercialism. However, the assumption that these dances flourish under conditions that are free from commercial restraints is problematic. Kazukimi Ebuchi, for instance, reveals that although the Ukrainian national dance that thrives in Canada was once part of the "natural village environment," it is today a cultural industry that includes dance schools and theatrical performances (Ebuchi, 1986: 137–42).

Salsa dancing cannot be attributed to the folkloric past of any ethnic group within Canada's multicultural panorama. Although salsa expresses Latin heritage for many Canadians of Latin descent, the commodification of this music and dance on the global level and in Montreal also contributes to its signaling of Latin identity. Salsa's blatant connection to commercialism and consumer society excludes its inclusion in the terrain of folkloric dances heralded for preserving the ancestry of Canada's ethnic groups.

Reuben Blades has proclaimed salsa to be the folklore that united the cities of Latin America. His words communicate an innovative and far-reaching understanding of folkloric culture that extends the term beyond the

expression of a rural ancestral culture to position folklore within contemporary urban life. As previously noted, salsa in contemporary contexts becomes
folklore because it is a dance that thrives and evolves through collective
artistry. Salsa exemplifies how folkloric cultures can come to represent the
practices of urban societies in diverse locations and historical times. As salsa
continuously evolves, it cannot be frozen into a folklore that portrays an ancestral heritage. Nonetheless, it does express the urban contemporary "folkloric" culture of some members of Montreal's Latin population. Furthermore,
as people of non-Latin origin are also involved in Montreal's scene, salsa
brings Latins and non-Latins together. The connections created through this
Latin dance style provide insight into a multicultural society that extends beyond the image of diversity promoted by the federal government's funding of
"traditional" ethnic dances.

The multiculturalism policy considers neither how the cultural practices of
ethnic groups interconnect nor the influence that dominant and ethnic cultures can exert on each other. Ethnic groups in Canada are funded to promote
and develop unique heritages that supposedly thrive separately, distinct from
other cultures. Quebec's policy, called interculturalism, which distinguishes
the province's stance on ethnic relations from the Canadian policy, appears to
incorporate the possibility of contact between cultures while maintaining cultural hierarchy. Interculturalism allows that different ethnic communities may
influence the dominant culture while recognizing that there is a prevailing
culture (Paquet, 1994: 70). Gilles Paquet argues that a hierarchy is implicit
through reference to minority groups in Quebec as "cultural communities."
He contends that the term *communautés culturelles* gives members of ethnic
groups a status between that of a full citizen and an outsider (75).

The Quebec government has developed a branch within the Ministry of
Immigration based on a new concept of cultural communities. The recognition of cultural communities within Quebec was implemented, at the policy
level, to mobilize and organize immigrants. Quebec's immigration policy and
the province's attitudes regarding cultural communities are informed by the
nationalist aims of the province. The concept of cultural communities has
arisen largely as a consequence of constitutional rivalry and battles for legitimacy between Quebec and Ottawa (Fontaine, 1995: 1041). From the Quebecois perspective, the federal government's policy of multiculturalism coun-
teracts Quebec nationalism. The province's immigration policies can be
regarded as steps and measures that differentiate the province from the federal system yet maintain its general direction (1042). The Cultural Development Policy of 1978 describes the notion of a "culture of convergence,"
which is now referred to as "the Quebec nation" (1044), defined as a "tradi-

tionally French Quebec culture" or as a "Quebec culture, French in tradition (culture Québécois de tradition française)" (Government of Quebec, 1978, vol. 1: 58). Three types of minorities exist around the culture of convergence: the "Anglo-Saxon" or "colonial minority"; Native minorities, referred to as "societies of former times"; and "other minorities," defined as "all those who join an already constituted nation." Louise Fontaine argues that this policy promotes a segmented society that excludes those who are not members of the "Quebec francophone majority" (Fontaine, 1995: 1045). Just before the 1981 elections, the government of Quebec declared a plan of action for the cultural communities. At the level of rhetoric, this proposal departed from the federal government's notion of multiculturalism and the American ideal of the "melting pot," which favors immigrants' assimilation into the dominant culture. The cultural communities concept has three objectives: "To insure the maintenance and the development of the cultural communities and their specificity, to foster increased awareness among francophone Quebeckers of the contribution of the cultural communities . . . and to favor the integration of the cultural communities into Quebec society" (Government of Quebec, 1981: 12, quoted in Fontaine, 1995: 1045).

Quebec's 1981 plan for cultural communities departs from the federal government's concept of multiculturalism in that it favors, at the policy level, the integration of cultural communities into Quebec society (Government of Quebec, 1981, cited in Fontaine, 1995: 1045). In this aspect, the plan resembles the situation in Montreal, where cultural interaction occurs through the experience of everyday practices such as salsa dance. Nonetheless, just as the official multiculturalism policy can limit the expressions of immigrant groups to their former national allegiances, potentially creating stereotypes that prevail in the host context, the policy of cultural communities tends to homogenize diverse peoples under restrictive, overarching "ethnic" labels. For instance, in citing the contribution that specific ethno-cultural communities have made to Quebec's heritage and contemporary society, a government publication by the Advisory Committee on Quebec's Cultural Heritage Policy presents ethno-culturally diverse groups as providing singular and unifying contributions to Quebec society: "The Latin American communities, for their part, have contributed to stimulating our interest in issues of solidarity, whereas the African communities have made us aware of the demands of cultural development and the Asian communities have led us to maintain interreligious and intercultural dialogue" (Government of Quebec, 2000, my translation).[12]

The concept of cultural communities is problematic, as what exactly constitutes a cultural community has never been clearly defined (Fontaine,

1995: 1045). According to Louise Fontaine, the term has been employed to incorporate Quebec Anglophones and the members of what are termed "visible minorities" (1045). Fontaine adds that the term "cultural communities" includes such disparate groups as recent arrivals to Quebec, some permanent residents, some Canadian citizens, and some whose mother tongue is French, although they are not considered members of the francophone majority. Even descendants of Irish immigrants of 1840 have fallen under the category of cultural community in order to get grants within the mandates of the policy. Louise Fontaine points out that since 1990 "cultural communities" has been replaced as the official term in government documents by "Quebeckers of the cultural communities (*Québécois des communautés culturelles*)." The change in name did not change the problem of definition. Fontaine comments, "we still do not know what a 'Cultural-Communities-Quebecker' is. Nor do we know what a cultural community is" (1046).

The lack of definitions for these terms leads Fontaine to suspect the motivation behind the development of the concept of cultural community. These categories may in fact be political categories created to obtain votes. Consequently, both the "minorities" and the bureaucratic and political elites in Quebec, as well as in Ottawa, are simply realizing their own interests rather than striving for the goal of cultural diversity (Fontaine, 1995: 1046). The cultural communities policy provides Quebec's nationalist elite the opportunity to be central to the decision-making process. This policy also positions the ethnic elite, which comprises Quebeckers of French descent, at a higher social level (1046).

There is a difference between the facts of multiculturalism and the articulation of cultural connections through the policies of multiculturalism and cultural communities (Kalin and Berry, 1994: 294). Containing the cultural productions of diverse ethnic groups so that they do not influence one another is not always possible in concrete circumstances. The cultures of diverse groups can fuse to produce new, or hybrid, expressions. Transculturalism may happen, if only infrequently, between groups who occupy positions outside the centers of power. Minority group cultures can also be usurped and reformulated by the dominant ones. A central characteristic of multicultural society is a meaningful exchange between diverse cultures (Bulmer and Solomos, 1998: 830). Amy Gutman describes the politics of multiculturalism when she asserts: "By multiculturalism, I refer to the state of a society or the world containing many cultures that interact in some significant way with each other. A culture is a human community larger than a few families that is associated with ongoing ways of seeing, doing, and thinking about things" (Gutman, 1993: 171).

The Montreal salsa scene also exemplifies Amy Gutman's vision of multiculturalism as facilitating the interaction of diverse cultures in a meaningful way (Gutman, 1993: 171). How does the salsa dance scene cultivate vital connections between cultures? The multicultural context of Latin dance has the potential to foster alliances between diverse groups and individuals, alliances with the potential for positive and negative dimensions. The distribution of this dance enables people of varied backgrounds and cultural heritages to form connections, eradicating barriers that separate groups from one another. The dissemination of salsa dancing in the city can also construct social hierarchies based on such distinctions as race, ethnicity, and cultural heritage. The following chapter provides an in-depth look at how the production of salsa dancing embodies multicultural interactions that yield both positive and negative consequences. This analysis draws from a sociological approach to the issue of multiculturalism, which, according to Michel Wieviorka, concerns mainly the workings of the society in which multiculturalism flourishes (Wieviorka, 1998: 883). I also incorporate the ideas of political theorists Amy Gutman and Charles Taylor.

Canada's official multiculturalism policy also perceives the cultural practices of particular ethnic groups to be bounded by specific national allegiances. However, many current dance and music heritages, such as salsa, are produced and enjoyed by people from a variety of nations, rendering these cultural expressions transnational. The federal government only supports the cultural practices of ethnic groups that can be traced to a given nation or people. Canada's willingness to allow diverse cultures to flourish alongside a national Canadian culture shows how the concept of multiculturalism in Canada transcends the idea that a singular culture defines a nation-state (Thompson and Weinfeld, 1995: 195).[13] As Christian Joppke states, "the very notion of multiculturalism conveys that not one but multiple cultures coexist within a limited, state-bounded territory" (Joppke, 1996: 450). Yet, at the same time, this official support has the effect of ghettoizing ethnic cultures and hindering their potential for meaningful impact on other cultures. State control is antithetical to a truly multicultural environment: as Joppke notes, "Multiculturalism reflects a novel situation where culture is no longer contained, controlled, and homogenized by the national state" (450).

Diverse cultures interact in a multicultural setting, breaching social barriers that are based on national affiliations. New alliances between groups are fashioned that construct identities and group affiliations in ways resembling the establishment of national identities. However, there is a difference: multicultural communities do not perceive themselves as "sovereign," a condition that applies only to territorial groups who aspire to become nations

(Joppke, 1996: 451). The proliferation of salsa in Montreal has helped to forge a transnational Latin identity, one that reflects Benedict Anderson's idea of "imagined communities." Montrealers of diverse Latin backgrounds create a pan-Latin connection, which in turn links to Spanish-speaking peoples of various nations and cities in the Americas. This connection is "imagined" since members of this vast community can never know one another. Montrealers of Latin descent establish boundaries that are narrower than those of the nation-state, Canada, and the province, Quebec, and yet broader in that they foster a transnational allegiance to a pan-Latin identity that crosses the Americas. Identities and cultures that are formed in multicultural contexts are either "underinclusive," incorporating affiliations narrower than those that define the nation-state, or "overinclusive," including groups that are larger than the nation-state (450).

The tendency to form allegiances and groups in multicultural societies produces two paradoxical impulses. In a multicultural setting, people actively claim identities rather than having them imposed, as is the case when individuals develop an allegiance to a nation. Categories can transcend the traditional restraints of class, nationality, and region in the modern production of identities. Consequently, by listening and dancing to salsa music, many Montrealers of Latin descent voluntarily choose to connect with a transnational Latin population. At the same time, identities forged in multicultural situations are essentialist, prescribed, and all-encompassing (Joppke, 1996: 449). A specific characteristic, such as ethnic heritage, sexual orientation, or race, becomes the predominant quality for collecting seemingly diverse individuals under one overarching identity. This tendency for individuals to feel united with others because they have certain traits in common resembles the manner in which nations are built upon myths of commonly shared characteristics. Montrealers of Latin descent experience a sense of connection because of their shared Latin ethnicity. As Joppke states "The world of multiculturalism is populated not by individuals with a multitude of overlapping, and often conflicting, group affiliations and interests, but by groups or "communities" that are inert, homogeneous, and mutually exclusive, such as gays, Latinos, or Muslims" (449). Defining identity in terms of a single characteristic and excluding others because they lack the characteristic defies principles of inclusion and functional differentiation and opens the door for multiculturalism to foster fundamental tendencies and antimodern extremism (449). Multicultural connections are inspired by the need for equal rights and recognition of ethnic, racial, and religious or sexually defined groups, yet at the same time multiculturalism has the potential to generate exclusionary and rigid groups based on common identities (449).

Contradictions in the formation of identities and group affiliations can re-sult from multicultural circumstances. Salsa-based alliances between individ-uals from various Latin American nations in Montreal have the potential to broaden the scope of ethnic affiliations. As identity categories become more inclusive, an appeal to a sense of differentiation distinguishes a particular group. As previously mentioned, the desire on the part of many Montrealers to listen and dance to salsa music stems in part from a need to define who they are within Canada. Moreover, they define themselves, in an overarch-ing sense, as belonging to the Spanish-speaking Americas. As more Mon-trealers from outside the city's Latin community become involved in this sub-culture, the boundaries defining the group again broaden. There is some concern in the field of ethnic and racial studies with the paradox that lies at the heart of the production of cultural identities. Martin Bulmer and John Solomos state: "The preoccupation in much of the recent literature in this field with issues of identity and the assertion of the relevance and importance of understanding the role of new ethnicities has not resolved the fundamen-tal question of how to balance the quest for ever more specific identities with the need to allow for broader and less fixed cultural identities" (Bulmer and Solomos, 1998: 834).

Charles Taylor's political philosophy provides a possible response to the dangers inherent in the building of identities in multicultural societies. The quest for differentiation can lead to forming identity categories that promote exclusion and ethno-centrism. The desire for distinction can even pave the way to such drastic measures as genocide, euphemistically termed "ethnic cleansing," whereby the virtual extermination of an "outside" group is sought (Bulmer and Solomos, 1998: 825). Charles Taylor proposes the politics of dif-ference in which individual and group identities are recognized as distinct. He states, "with the politics of difference, what we are asked to recognize is the unique identity of this individual or group, their distinctiveness from everyone else. The idea is that it is precisely this distinctness that has been ignored, glossed over, assimilated to a dominant or majority identity" (Tay-lor, 1994: 38).

The recognition approach is more than simply a tolerance of cultural dif-ference. It ensures a balance between an acknowledgment of difference and universal rights and values (Wieviorka, 1998: 895), such that differentia-tion cannot be dissolved through assimilation or even annihilation. Fur-thermore, distinct groups need to flourish within society so that they are not relegated to the margins through ghettoization. According to Wiev-iorka, "multiculturalism" refers to the navigation between the two obstacles that hinder the proliferation of cultural difference within a given society:

restricting minorities to ghettoes and eradicating difference through the process of assimilation (895).

Charles Taylor's concept of the "politics of recognition" may seem unrealistic, for if a society acknowledges all group distinctions, it could simply dissolve into a proliferation of differences without a central core to hold it together. Nonetheless, Taylor argues that given how modern societies are increasingly multicultural, it has become difficult to appeal to a "neutral" culture that dictates how society as a whole should deal with issues and problems. In a nation such as Canada there are people who live within national borders yet also belong to cultures that question the philosophical boundaries of this nation. Rather than responding to differences through the dominant culture's norms, or in Taylor's words by stating, "*this is how we do things here,*" he proposes that a nation meet the challenge of cultural differences without jeopardizing basic political principles (Taylor, 1994: 63, emphasis in the original). Taylor claims that in a liberal democracy, individuals and groups should not have to relinquish their identities (LaForest, 1993: xv, cited in Birnbaum, 1996: 39). According to Stanley J. Tambiah, Charles Taylor pleads for acknowledgment of the importance of recognizing difference on the grounds that societies are becoming more and more multicultural (Tambiah, 2000: 169). Taylor notes "that all societies are becoming increasingly multicultural, while at the same time becoming more porous. Indeed, these two developments go together. Their porousness means that they are more open to multinational migration; more of their members live the life of diaspora whose center is elsewhere" (Taylor, 1994: 63).

The salsa dance scene in Montreal exemplifies Charles Taylor's vision of the multicultural nature of contemporary societies. Although many Montrealers of Latin descent live and function within Quebecois society, they may also feel the need to connect with the Latin diaspora that crosses the Americas. Listening and dancing to salsa becomes a means to identify with a pan-Latin consciousness that transcends Canadian national boundaries. The image of multiculturalism that is promoted through the federal government's official multiculturalism policy is surpassed in how identities are produced within the Montreal salsa dance scene. This policy funds and fosters the traditional heritages of ethnic groups in Canada whose cultures are clearly defined by their allegiance to a primordial nation or region outside of Canada. The production of identities in the actual circumstances of multicultural urban centers illustrates how immigrants' ethnic affiliations and cultural practices cannot always be traced to their countries of origin. Many Montrealers of Latin descent choose to express their allegiance to the Spanish-speaking Americas by listening and dancing to salsa even though they may not have engaged in this practice in their country of origin. Furthermore, their desire to adopt salsa as part of their cultural heritage is influenced by the process of immigration and by the circumstances that they face within the host country. Given the multicultural nature of Montreal and Canada, immigrants in Canada often feel the need to define who they are within Canada's diverse ethnic terrain. Listening and dancing to salsa becomes a channel to establish boundaries within Canada.

The proliferation of Latin music in Montreal gives rise to the production of identities that reveal the contradictions and paradoxes of identity creation within multicultural societies. The practice of listening and dancing to salsa enables immigrants from diverse countries in Latin American, Central America, and the Caribbean to unite under the all-encompassing identity category of "Latin." Although new alliances that form around this popular music and dance practice transcend the borders of specific nations, these alliances are also exclusionary, as they are based on the restrictive ethnic category of "Latin." At the same time, through the commodification of salsa dancing in the city, many Montrealers who are not of Latin descent are exposed to this cultural practice. Montrealers of Latin and non-Latin descent are involved in teaching and promoting salsa. People from all backgrounds enjoy listening and dancing to its rhythms. Affiliations that arise through the commodification of salsa have the potential to bring diverse people together and consequently to be highly inclusive.

Conversely, the cultures of ethnic groups that are promoted by the official multiculturalism policy become ghettoized through the federal funding process. This policy seems to circumscribe the cultures of immigrant groups within national boundaries and restricts their expressions to the confines of church basements, culture shows, and community centers. Salsa is not ghettoized within specific Latin American and Caribbean enclaves in the city but forms an integral part of Montreal's commercial music and dance panorama. The commercialism of urban salsa has enabled this dance and music to become a symbolic tie to a cultural heritage for those of varied Latin American backgrounds while facilitating the widespread promotion and enjoyment of this cultural practice by Montrealers of both Latin and non-Latin descent. Through processes of commodification, this dance and music complex becomes a part of the cultural fabric of a wide spectrum of Montreal society. Salsa dancing is therefore being integrated into the cultural practices of mainstream Quebecois and Canadian society. Within multicultural circumstances, the process of immigration alters both the immigrants and their host nations, such that ethnic and national identities can become fluid concepts that are being continually created, negotiated, and transformed (Lipsitz, 1994: 121).

The following chapter provides a concrete example of how teaching and promoting salsa dancing in Montreal enables diverse cultures to come in contact with one another. This proximity has the potential to both create and eradicate hierarchies based on racial, ethnic, and cultural distinctions. The multicultural connections embodied in Montreal's salsa dance scene further transcend the image of the mosaic promoted by Canada's official policy. In Montreal's Latin dance scene, diverse cultures interact with one another as well as with the "dominant" culture. This salsa scene exemplifies Amy Gutman's description of multiculturalism as entailing the meaningful interaction of diverse cultures (Gutman, 1993: 171).

Notes

1. The designations "Latino" and "Hispanic" were first generally used in the 1970s by federal agencies in the United States. Since that time, their use in America has been maintained through census categories, state policies, and the media (Dávila, 2001: 2). In Montreal the terms "Latino" and "Latin" are used in both French and English. "Hispanic" is rarely used in Montreal, whereas in the United States it is often used interchangeably with "Latino." There is a subtle difference between the terms "Hispanic" (or "Hispano") and "Latino." The former has been regarded as a politically sanitized term because of the contexts in which it was used. For instance, in the western United States, such as New Mexico, it was adopted by elite Mexicans to stress their Spanish ancestry and to accentuate their class and racial superiority over Mexicans. In New York, however, "Hispanic" (or "Hispano") has been used as an overarching term for the city's diverse Latin American groups. Furthemore, "Hispanic" (or "Hispano") essentially means "derived from Spain or the Spanish." When applied to Latin American people living in the United States, this term stresses the Spanish heritage of Latin Americans over their indigenous roots and colonial history. During the 1960s and 1970s when Chicanos and Puerto Ricans in the United States were engaged in struggles to assert their identity rooted in indigeneous and colonial realities, the term "Hispanic" (or "Hispano") did not describe who they were. Consequently, political activists in the United States today often regard "Hispanic" as a less political term than "Latino/a" (15).

2. Scholars based in the United States draw a distinction between the terms "Latino" and "Latin" in regard to musical practices. Frances R. Aparicio and Cándida F. Jáquez, for instance, prefer not to use the term "Latin music" because "Latin music" does not describe the cultural agency of American Latino/as in the production of Latino musical practices but connotes how the Anglo-American public and market have socially constructed Latino popular music in the United States (Aparicio and Jáquez, 2003: 9-10). The term "Latino popular music" is often used for Latino productions in the United States, whereas "Latin Amerian music" denotes musical productions from Latin America. There is obviously an interconnection between these

two musical spheres. Deborah Pacini Hernández points out that she uses the less precise term "Latin music" to refer to the musical productions of Latin Americans and Latino/as. Although she emphasizes that the term "Latin American and Latino popular musics" is more precise, she opts for the less acurate term "Latin music" because it is less cumbersome (Pacini Hernández, 2003: 14). In this book, I use the terms "Latin" and "Latino" interchangeably for people and cultures from diverse Latin American origins within the context of Montreal as well as for Latino popular musics that thrive in the United States, taking into consideration that the use of these terms may not be the most precise. My use of both "Latin" and "Latino" also reflects their lived bilingual usage in Montreal, where "Latino" and "Latin" are often used interchangeably in both French and English for people of Latin American descent who live in the city as well as for the musical productions of "Latin Americans" and U.S. Latinos. It should be noted, however, that when I refer to Latino/as in the United States, I specify this group of people by referring to them specifically as U.S. or American Latinos.

3. Les Latinos qui immigrent deviennent mille fois plus Latinos que dans leurs pays. C'est un phénomène qu'au début je ne comprenais pas. Tu comprends? Tu peux demander à plusieurs Latinos qu'est ce qu'ils écoutaient dans leur pays. Ils écoutaient juste la musique en anglais. En venant ici, ils écoutent 99.9 percent du temps juste la musique en espagnol comme la salsa et le *merengue*. Et pourquoi? C'est parce qu'après tout, ils essaient de retrouver leurs racines. Qui suis-je dans ce grand pays? C'est comme des fourmis dans une planète.

4. La salsa est notre marque de commerce latino-américaine . . . c'est la salsa, la danse, la culture, la richesse des pays. Quand on change de pays on s'intègre au pays mais on ne s'assimile pas. Nous apportons notre culture avec la musique et la danse. On ne peut pas oublier ça. On peut parler une autre langue mais on ne peut pas oublier la danse. C'est enraciné.

5. This estimate is based on figures from Census Canada 2001, which makes it difficult to get an accurate figure of the population in Montreal because of the way that Census Canada classifies differences. For instance, the 2001 Census shows Latin Americans as the fourth-largest visible minority group in Quebec. The largest group is classified as Black; the second largest group as Arab/West Asian; and the third largest group as South Asian. In the same chart, entitled *Visible Minority Population, by census metropolitan areas*, this 2001 Census classifies people residing in Quebec by such disparate differences as racial identity (i.e., Black), ethnic identity (i.e., Arab), and geographic origin (i.e., Latin America). Consequently, it is possible that there are Latin Americans who classify themselves as blacks and vice versa as well as Latin Americans who do not classify themselves as a visible minority but see themselves as white. Consequently, the number of people in Montreal whose country of origin is Latin America may exceed the exact figure of the 2001 Census, which is 53,155 (Canadian Statistics 2001).

6. This bifurcation in musical tastes stratified along ethnic lines may be waning somewhat in the United States. For instance, the appearance of *merengueras*, Puerto

Rican female singers who perform the primarily Dominican-derived merengue, points to perhaps future trends in cultural cross-fertilization between Latino/a groups in the United States (Dávila, 2001: 120).

7. New York is the second largest Latino market in the United States. Prior to the 1960s, 80 percent of the Latino population in New York were Puerto Ricans. In 2001 Puerto Ricans represented 43 percent of the Latino population in the city, the rest being comprised of Dominicans and people from Central America (Dávila, 2001: 19).

8. Miami is the third-largest Latino market in the United States, and Los Angeles is the largest (Dávila, 2001: 19).

9. Not all the popular videos aired on this television show project a highly sexualized vision of Latin culture. The videos of the Cuban salsa group, *Bambolé*, which aired frequently on *Teleritmo* in 1999 provide an example of a less pronounced association of Latin dance and music with an erotic flavor.

10. Daphne has changed the advertisement for her school since our interview. Although her new advertisement is more alluring than her previous one, she has not compromised her initial position of not giving the impression that her school is a place to meet potential partners.

11. A pseudonym has been used for the name of these monthly Latin nights.

12. Les communautés latino-américaines, pour leur part, ont beaucoup contribué à stimuler notre intérêt pour la solidarité, alors que les communautés africaines nous ont sensibilisés aux exigences du développement culturel, et que les communautés asiatiques nous ont conduits à entretenir le dialogue interreligieux et interculturel.

13. Defining a national Canadian culture is not an easy task. Thompson and Weinfeld, for instance, argue that most immigrant groups, who are often perceived as threatening the fabric of Canadian society, share the values that lie at the core of Canadian identity. These values include freedom, liberty, the rule of law, respect for authority, piety, family, the importance of hard work, education, and civility (Thompson and Weinfeld, 1995: 195).

CHAPTER THREE

~

Staking Claims

Addressing the differences between Latin dances within a ballroom context and those flourishing in actual circumstances, Ruud Vermay says, "You will, of course, never see a Cuban Rumba or Brazilian Samba until you travel to the birthplace" (Vermay, 1994: 32). The authenticity of a popular dance is ultimately linked to its place of origin. Latin popular dance styles in a lived culture express the heritages of a people or a nation, as is the case with the rumba in Cuba, merengue in the Dominican Republic, and *cumbia* in Colombia. Originating in Caribbean nations, salsa has spread throughout so many parts of the globe that it is difficult to speak of an "authentic" salsa dance. Nonetheless, the exotic appeal of salsa outside of its sites of "origin" is founded on the belief—or perhaps the illusion—that a genuine dance can be reproduced. Salsa's connection with an authentic cultural expression "sells" the dance and transforms it into a cultural commodity in Montreal.

Although most salsa teachers have honed their dancing skills in Montreal, the rhetoric of "authenticity" cultivates the dance as a marketable product. The discourse of origins and authenticity is either invoked or rejected to legitimize the different dance styles that are promoted, taught, and sold in the city's schools. Tensions arising between instructors and schools result from differences both in the culture and dance traditions to which they link salsa and in the ways that they express the dance corporeally. Since salsa has not developed out of a lived context in Montreal, no solid dance heritage exists from which instructors can draw to legitimize their knowledge. Those involved in the promotion and teaching of the dance must carve out a place

111

for their particular form of salsa, choosing from an array of styles that circulate in the city. The various ways that schools and teachers justify their style express how diverse Latin groups, as well as people of non-Latin descent, interact in a multicultural setting. Depending on the school, salsa dancing is connected to an international phenomenon through a ballroom dance tradition, New York club dancing, a general Latin heritage, or a specific Latin Caribbean cultural practice.

Associating the Montreal dance styles with different areas of the globe reveals how salsa flourishes well beyond its Caribbean roots. Some instructors connect salsa to a general Latin heritage, a link that reinforces how this dance and music represents a Latino consciousness that extends throughout the Spanish-speaking Americas. Others connect salsa to New York since it evolved in that city during the late 1960s and 1970s; indeed, New York is often regarded as salsa's "birthplace." The connection between salsa dancing and the Latin component of ballroom dance reflects how modified versions of dances from Cuba, as well as from other Latin nations, were incorporated into British- and American-derived Latin competitive dance. Lastly, the establishment of the Caribbean as the "true" birthplace of salsa inaugurates a clear place of origin for a dance and music style that has become international.

As teachers "sell" the same commodity, they have a stake in distinguishing their version from that of others and in "exoticizing" and linking it to a source outside the city. Dance schools compete for a share of the market. There are, however, a few instructors who are open to the diverse styles that circulate in the city. The mapping out of variations among the schools exposes myriad possible phenomena that occur through the circulation of the dance: the celebration of diversity, the assimilation of a minority practice into the prevailing culture, the appropriation of minority practices by the dominant culture, and either the creation of hybrid forms or the resistance to hybridization to ensure cultural purity. This analysis of Montreal dance schools illustrates how multicultural relations in actual circumstances have the potential to bring diverse people together as well as to reproduce hierarchies based on such distinctions as culture, ethnicity, and race. The connections embodied in the Montreal salsa scene are always anchored to the commodification of the dance in the city.

I contrast how the discourse of authenticity and origins is either invoked or rejected by instructors in two popular schools in Montreal, Riviera and Caribe. (As in the previous chapter, pseudonyms are used here for the names of dance schools and instructors.) To a lesser degree, various other dance schools are included in the discussion. The differences between Riviera and

Caribe expose a key conflict in salsa dancing: the rupture between ballroom-influenced Latin dance and street salsa. "Street salsa," a term used to describe the general form of the dance that has developed from lived circumstances, distinguishes this version from ballroom renditions.

This analysis of Montreal's Latin dance schools draws from an extensive body of ethnographic work on the city's salsa scene. Although salsa dance teachers in the city come and go, my ethnographic study (1996–2000) looks at instructors who had been in business for at least three years prior to 2000. Many still offer classes today (2005). In this category are four schools started by Canadian-born instructors, all of whom are women, and nine salsa schools directed by Montrealers of Latin descent, all but one of whom are men. The interconnnection between issues of gender and ethnicity is explored in chapter 5. To document how the rhetoric of authenticity is deployed to sell different styles of salsa, I conducted open-ended in-depth interviews with these instructors. One of my goals was to ascertain how they perceive the style of salsa that they teach. Claims of "authenticity" are largely based on the kinds of movements taught and on how knowledge of the dance has been acquired. So that I could understand the style taught at each school, I took salsa lessons, comparing the movements that the dance instructors promote and teach. Having extensive background knowledge of each school prior to the interviews enabled me to ask well-informed questions and provided a context in which to interpret responses.

Some background on the forms of salsa dancing that have developed in a lived context and those that have been influenced by ballroom dance is needed before discussing how Montreal dance schools legitimize the styles of salsa that they teach and sell.

The acquisition of salsa by individuals who grow up moving to the rhythms of the dance differs from its acquisition by those who learn it in a studio or club. As salsa has evolved in many cities and countries throughout the Americas, it is difficult to delineate precisely the "true" and "authentic" salsa sites that develop this dance in actual circumstances. Identifying salsa in what I call a "lived context," I am less concerned with where individuals have learned the dance than with how the dance becomes a part of their cultural heritage. In a lived context, salsa is not formally learned but is passed on from generation to generation. Most people who grow up with the dance acquire it in childhood, its movements often being taught indirectly through the corporeal language of the body; thus they may not have a sense that they have learned it. Furthermore, in lived circumstances, dancing is done to music: there is no separation between the rhythm of the music and the steps of the dance. According to Yvonne Daniel, this inseparability stems from an

African-derived relation between these two expressive arts that has spread throughout the Americas (Daniel, 1995: 34).

One of the principal ways that the salsa body moves is through corporeal isolations. Specific parts of the body, such as the head, hands, hips, and shoulders, move separately to the rhythm of the music in coordination with steps and turns. Although executing body isolations may require more skill than the steps and turns of the dance, these isolations are often unconsciously learned. A child may be formally taught specific footwork and turn patterns of salsa, but body isolations are picked up by experiencing the family dance culture, similar to how we acquire everyday gestures. Although these subtle separations of parts of the body may seem effortless to the outside viewer, their performance involves a great deal of skill and dexterity. Individuals of Latin Caribbean descent, who are dispersed throughout the Americas, often learn the dance as an extension of their heritage. Such is the case for Lisa Sánchez González, whose acquisition of salsa in Los Angeles brought her closer to her ties with the Puerto Rican diaspora. She writes, "As a Boricua raised in Los Angeles, I learned salsa in my home and among our extended family. The music itself has been for me another home in what I came to understand as a species of exile, as part of the legacy of the Puerto Rican working-class diaspora" (Sánchez González, 1999: 244–45).

Adults who first learn salsa in the formal setting of a classroom do not acquire the dance in actual circumstances. Nonetheless, they have grown up in a dance or movement culture whose vernacular they may or may not have consciously learned. As they produce their movement heritage in the ways that they move their bodies, they transpose their bodily culture to the salsa dance class. Their corporeal vernacular, acquired in actual circumstances, exerts an influence on how they apprehend this new dance.

The idea that individuals grow up in a movement culture that patterns their everyday gestures finds resonance in Pierre Bourdieu's concept of habitus. The habitus of an individual is determined by the socializing practices of the group or class into which a child is born (Bourdieu, 1977: 167).

Consequently, a child is disposed to perceive the world in the same manner as the older generation and to see it in light of a certain myth (Mahar, Harker, and Wilkes, 1990: 11). The habitus, which constitutes a kind of logic, is framed in childhood: the child internalizes a set of determined objects directly through material connections and indirectly through the habitus of adults. Both the direct and indirect elements that form a child's habitus are material. The set of beliefs and attitudes learned in childhood produce the body as a "living memory pad" that makes the mind act (Bourdieu, 1990: 68). The child develops the habitus not by imitation, which presumes a conscious effort to mimic, but by what Bourdieu terms "practical mimesis," which implies unconscious acquisition—that is, the child acquires the habitus unconsciously (Garnham and Williams, 1986: 119). Bourdieu states, "The schemes of the habitus, the primary forms of classification, owe their specific efficacy to the fact that they function below the level of consciousness and language, beyond the reach of introspective scrutiny or control by the will" (Bourdieu, 1984: 466). What the body "learns" in childhood becomes not something that the individual acquires but something that the individual is (Bourdieu, 1990: 73). The child adopts the habitus of his environment by picking up the gestures, postures, and movements of those around him. These appropriated bodily movements are simultaneously individual and reflective of a larger social reality. Bourdieu discloses, "Body hexis speaks directly to the motor function, in the form of a pattern of postures that is both individual and systematic, being bound up with a whole system of objects, and charged with a host of special meanings and values" (74).

Bourdieu's concept of habitus structures individual behavior according to two classification schemes: the social division of labor and sexual division. Individuals of the same class and sex exhibit similar practices and bodily expressions as a result of their habitus. According to Bourdieu, the asymmetrical power relations between the sexes are embodied in masculine gestures of domination and in feminine ones of submission (Bourdieu, 1990: 72). Bourdieu acknowledges that it is not possible for every individual within a given class or sex to have parallel experiences. Nevertheless, he claims that members of the same class, for example, are more likely to confront similar situations than those outside their class (Bourdieu, 1977: 85). The habitus not only reproduces existing objective social conditions that maintain sexual and class differentiation, but also alters these conditions. The concept of habitus allows for both continuity and change within the system of class and sexual differentiation by reproducing regularities in the original objective condition while managing to adjust to continuously changing external conditions (78). The systematic nature of the habitus allows for class and sexual practices and attitudes to be objectively "regulated" and "regular" without being enforced by the organizing action of a conductor (72).

Although Bourdieu's theory of habitus applies primarily to the class system in a French society, it is also applicable to this exploration of salsa, for it helps to explain why individuals born into specific dance cultures unconsciously "learn" movements and practices without an "active" agent imposing the patterns. Bourdieu's theory concludes that individuals' gestures conform to those of their class; I modify his theory for this focus on salsa as a transnational phenomenon to reveal that individuals of diverse backgrounds may share similar dance heritages when they grow up dancing to the rhythms of this music.

Salsa dancing is now a transnational practice enjoyed by diverse classes, races, and ethnicities and cannot easily be linked to a particular group. However, the body isolations that characterize the dance can be traced to the African-derived heritage that flourishes in the Caribbean. Salsa's development in New York City in the late 1960s and 1970s is attributed to working-class Puerto Ricans, Cubans, and African Americans. Today those who claim salsa as their cultural heritage may not be from the proletariat working class and/or from the African Caribbean or African diaspora; individuals who have grown up with salsa now also come from middle-class white Latin American societies.

Norman Bryson defines dance in terms that take it well beyond the parameters delineated by dance historians, who privilege such performance dance styles as European ballet. According to Bryson, dance is part of a wide array of "socially-structured human movement" and can include forms of coded movement commonly not considered to be dance. He cites examples such as the movements of people at a cocktail party, a wedding, and a lecture hall (Bryson, 1997: 58). I advance Bryson's understanding of "socially-structured human movement" by including within its sphere such common gestures as walking and posturing. The manner in which dance movements are imprinted onto the bodies of individuals in a culture may correspond to the embodiment of kinetic models in everyday corporeal patterns.

When Montrealers see salsa dance for the first time, it appears to be composed of movements that are completely apart from everyday motion. Novice viewers frame these unfamiliar actions as an "exotic" collection of moves and turns completely distinct from quotidian corporeal expressions. The example of how the "dancing" of rock audiences comprises corporeal extensions of a culture illustrates how the dance patterns of salsa could be part of a vocabulary of everyday movement. Sarah Thornton points out that rock audiences "dance" to the music, but their gestures, such as "toe-tapping, finger-snapping, rhythmic clapping, pogoing, slamming and moshing" (Thornton, 1995: 71), are not categorized as dancing. Rock audiences are aware that none of these movements are formally learned, but what they may not know is that these corporealities involve a total posturing of the body that is culturally based. For instance, rock "dance" styles involve such bodily postures as hunching and curved shoulders that are also part of a daily stance. These movements may appear "natural" because they are a common part of a cultural group's repertoire of expressions, when, in fact, they have been informally learned. Similarly, total body moves in salsa dancing are often perceived as a "natural" and "spontaneous" response to music, when in reality these movements are steeped in years of informal dance training. Since many people who grew up dancing to salsa music started as children, they have acquired their dance tradition through numerous years of experience and practice. The movements of a vital dance culture are also never static but change through this lived practice.

When salsa is "brought" to a new setting, often just the steps and turns of the dance are culled. How the total body moves, particularly the posturing and isolations, cannot be easily reproduced, as these corporealities are a product of the years of acquired knowledge and informal practice that an individual garners from being part of a culture. Consequently, those elements that render the dance "authentic" can often never be fully seized. John Martin sums up the difficulties involved in assessing the authenticity of a dance style when it is has been transplanted to a new setting: "It is far easier to speak in a foreign language without a trace of an accent than it is to dance a foreign idiom with complete purity of style" (Martin, 1965: 76, quoted in Vermay, 1994: 32).

Various Latin dances that were integrated into British and American ballroom repertoires were altered as a result of their transplantation from their "original" context. The Cuban street dance style rumba, for instance, was incorporated into American popular culture in the 1920s and remains part of the Latin section of competitive ballroom dance. However, the dance that was exported under the name of rumba resembled more the Cuban *son*, as the rhythm and movements of the rumba were so anchored in the lived dance culture of Cuba at the time that this dance could not be easily learned and reproduced by white American society (Buckman, 1978: 197). Yvonne Daniel notes, "While both dance variations use traditional rumba rhythms, the popularized ballroom style does not resemble the original Cuban dance, sometimes contrasted as *rumba del campo*, or rumba from the countryside" (Daniel, 1995: 18).

Ballroom dance dates back to professional dance associations established in England and the United States in the 1870s. These associations codified dance steps and body posturing into clear rules of acceptable and unacceptable movement in dance. The establishment of these dance associations was triggered by the rise in popularity of the round dances—the waltz and the polka—which defied conventions with their speed, rhythm, and close embrace. A lack of formality in steps and deportment distinguished these dances from previous styles. People could also learn them by observing other dancers rather than spending a great deal of time and money taking dance lessons (Buckman, 1978: 118). These British and American dance associations created a ballroom style deemed "formal, elegant, and polished," which laid the foundation for contemporary competition dancing. This dance tradition rejected the revolutionary aspect of the round dances of their day—their spontaneity—and was subsequently unable to incorporate the improvisation and innovation of black-derived dance and music traditions, beginning with ragtime, which would revolutionize American popular culture (122).

Ballroom dance experienced an increase in popularity in the 1930s, which continues to the present day. It marked a departure from what were seen as uncouth, exhibitionist, wild, and uncontrollable dances of the swing era—the lindy or the jitterbug. British ballroom standardized dance steps from previous decades as a measure against what they deemed an anarchist strain in the dances of the young (Buckman, 1978: 192). In 1924 the first Ballroom Committee of the Imperial Society of Teachers of Dancing, which consisted of five principal dancers, including notables Josephine Bradley and Victor Sylvester, established guidelines for the fox trot, popularized in the 1910s, and the waltz, which flourished from 1800 to 1850 (Buckman, 1978: 193; Thomas and Miller, 1997: 94). Today's ballroom dance competitions are based on rules established by the official rulebook of the British Council of Ballroom Dancing (BCBD), which was compiled from a conference of various teachers' associations in 1929 that represented the Official Board of Ballroom Dancing. These established rules and regulations, which laid down the English style for the movement patterns of the waltz, fox trot, quickstep, and tango, were rooted in the 1924 meeting of the first Ballroom Committee. This English style, referred to as the "international style," characterizes ballroom dances performed in competitions today (Thomas and Miller, 1997: 94).

Beginning in the 1900s, the repertoire of British and American ballroom dance began to incorporate, modify, and standardize popular Latin dances. The Argentinean-derived tango, the first dance to be included in the ballroom realm, was popular in British and American dance cultures in the early twentieth century (Buckman, 1978: 172–73). The Brazilian *samba*, introduced in the United States in 1939 and made famous by the films of Carmen Miranda, was followed by the merengue in the 1950s (199, 201). The *son*, under the name of rumba, which reached the United States in the late 1920s, was standardized by British dance teachers in the ballroom tradition in 1946 (197). Then in the 1950s two other Cuban dances, the mambo and the *chachachá*, were modified and included in ballroom dance (199–200).

Latin American dances have been transformed to accord with the movement ideals of the European-based heritage of ballroom dance. The steps and turns of the prototypes have been culled and modified, but the total body moves of the "un-derived" forms have not been adopted. The Cuban dance styles that have been extended into the ballroom dance tradition are not contemporary but date back to the social life of Cuba in the 1920s (the *son*) and the 1940s (the *chachachá* and mambo) (Buckman, 1978: 196–201). When these dances were incorporated into ballroom dance, the steps and turns of the "original" dances were taken and modified, and the moves and posturing of the body changed from their renditions in the lived context. The movements of these transplanted Latin dances have been translated into the vernacular that characterizes ballroom dance. Jane Desmond argues that when Latin dances were incorporated into this tradition, they crossed racial lines, moving primarily from black to white culture in the United States. The dances underwent a transformation: a stiffening of the hip, quietude, a straightening of the torso, and increased focus on footwork (Desmond, 1993–1994: 39–40). Marta Savagliano notes a similar change in tango as it moved from black to white society. Although Savagliano does not specifically refer to the form of tango prevalent in British and American ballroom dance, her findings are relevant, as tango is an essential part of the Latin section of social dance. The fluid body movements, based in African influences on tango, gave way to a corporeal stiffness and concentration on footwork. Savagliano writes: "The stiff torsos of the black dances became stiffer; the swaying hip (*quebradas*) and the sharp interruptions of the dancing marches (*cortes*) lost their joyful fluidity and became grave, and so did the faces, concentrated in displaying filigrees of footwork (*figuras*) for an attentive audience of *pardas* and *chinas*" (Savagliano, 1995a: 31–32).

The transformation of Latin styles in the ballroom tradition reflects the body ideals of this dance heritage. Joann Kealiinohomoku's writings on how ballet elucidates the standards of a particular ethnic group—"Caucasians who speak Indo-European languages and who share a common European tradition" (Kealiinohomoku, 1983: 544)—could be applied to the ballroom dance world. Even though ballroom is today a global phenomenon, this dance tradition stemmed from the same ethnic group to which Kealiinohomoku links ballet. Although I do not want to completely equate classical ballet and ballroom dance, I incorporate Kealiinohomoku's interpretation of ballet as an expression of a particular ethnic group to point out that the corporeal ideals of these two diverse dance traditions may have some points of intersection.

Drawing a link between ballet and ballroom dance may cause a great deal of contention. Ballet stands as a pinnacle of Western performance art, while ballroom dance is not granted much status by the "serious" dance world. Given the importance that professional competitions play in ballroom dance, it seems to be more a sport than a dance (Thomas and Miller, 1997: 98). The International Olympic Committee recognized ballroom dancing as a legitimate Olympic sport in 1997, positioning it securely within the athletic sphere (Kornreich, 1998: 125). Nonetheless, the dance worlds of both ballroom and ballet intersect through their shared characteristic of highly structured rules and regulations. Writing about the ballroom branch of the Imperial Society of Teachers of Dancing, Paul Buckman draws a parallel between these two dance worlds: "Dance competitions for British, and then the world, championships made the English style the model for all good ballroom dancers. The details of performance were as minutely practiced and scrutinized as in ballet" (Buckman, 1978: 193). Although ballet may appear completely separate from popular dance styles, social dance was influenced by ballet just as ballet incorporated elements of social dance (93). Classical ballet, for instance, integrated and modified such popular dances as the polonaise and polka in its repertoire of traveling steps (Guillot and Prudhommeau, 1976: 81–82). To distinguish themselves from laboring sectors of society, French aristocrats in the seventeenth century walked with their feet turned out, a gait that became an integral part of French court dancing. As ballet was formalized as an art in this period, the turned-out foot became part of the basic ballet position that still characterizes classical ballet today (Buckman, 1978: 71–72). This unnatural foot placement was also integrated into the social dance of the seventeenth century (72–73). Of the fusion between ballet and social dance, Buckman notes: "Though we are not concerned with the history of ballet, its intimate connection with social dance in the seventeenth century can scarcely be ignored" (72–73). When the English ballroom style was developed by the Imperial Society of Teachers of Dancing in 1924, they replaced the turned-out foot of ballet, which had been the base position for all dancing, with the "natural" walking step, in which body weight was transferred on each step. The incorporation of this step in ballroom can be traced to the influence of the Boston, a dance first introduced in Britain in 1903, which incorporated a natural walking movement (Thomas and Miller, 1997: 102). The turned-out feet prescribed by ballet, which had persisted since the seventeenth century, was dropped altogether in 1924 (Buckman, 1978: 194). The adoption of this "natural" foot position in ballroom dance could be used to counter the claim of a correlation between the body movements of ballet and ballroom. Nonetheless, ballet's influence on social dance since the seventeenth century illustrates an affiliation between these two seemingly disparate dance worlds.

Pull-ups, body lifts, and body extensions, according to Joann Kealiinohomoku, comprise the corporeal ideals of ballet, which exemplifies the dance aesthetic of Caucasians of European descent (Kealiinohomoku, 1983: 542). Ballet body ideals translate into particular ways of moving the back, hip, and joints that surface, in a parallel way, in ballroom dance. Pull-ups and body lifts require that movements be executed with a straight and still back; the back does move forward and backward but, when bent, generally remains straight. There are two forward leanings, or *penché en avant*, in ballet. In the first, the back is not curved; the dancer bends at the hip, maintaining a straight back. The second, called the *dos rond*, does allow for a slightly curved back, but this deviation from the straight back position is not as pronounced as African-derived movement isolations of the back. In outlining the positions of the body in classical ballet, Genevieve Guillot and Germaine Prud-hommeau comment, "It should be noted that there are two kinds of *penché en avant*. The first, which is never very accentuated, is produced by curving the spinal column above the pelvis, which remains vertical; only the thoracic cage is bent" (Guillot and Prudhommeau, 1976: 17). The posturing and quietude of the back in ballroom dance resembles the vertical, still torso extolled in ballet. These corporealities are antithetical to the upper body and torso isolations that characterize African-derived movements in Latin Caribbean dance.

Ballet is distinguished by consistent vertical, rigid hip placement. When a dancer raises her or his leg, the hip should not change position or move from the vertical stance. This hip movement contrasts sharply with African-derived Latin dances, which are marked by pelvic rotations. Although the Latin section of ballroom dance includes hip movement, a ballroom-influenced hip movement is less pronounced than in the "original" version and is also triggered more by the action of the legs than by isolating and rotating pelvic and abdominal muscles. It can be asked to what extent ballroom dance has been influenced by the classical ballet dance, which prohibits hip motion. Guillot and Prudhommeau describe a "forbidden" position of the body in classical dance, called *ensellé*, which permits a hollowing of the back and hip displacement, highlighting ballet's insistence on a still back and motionless hips: "The *ensellé*, which we shall group with the positions of the body (although strictly speaking, it is not one of them), is attained by making the back hollow and thrusting the hips forward. Highly regarded in certain countries (e.g., in Africa, and among the comic characters of the ancient Greek stage), this position is formally forbidden in the classical dance" (Guillot and Prudhommeau, 1976: 28).

In elucidating ballet's taboos against back and hip movements, Guillot and Prudhommeau allude to how a displacement of these body parts is revered in African dance. Although the authors make a broad statement by generalizing about the dance tradition of an entire continent, their observations support the claim that one African-derived influence on Latin

Caribbean dances is an emphasis on considerable fluidity in the pelvis, an area of the body that must remain completely rigid in classical ballet. The hip does rotate in Latin ballroom dances but to a lesser degree and in a different manner than in the Latin dances that emerged in a lived context. Jane Desmond writes on dance styles rooted in a European-based heritage: "In dance traditions originating in Europe, both popular and theatrical, such as ballet, the torso tends toward quietude and verticality, and the pelvis rarely functions as an expressive bodily unit of its own" (Desmond, 1993–1994: 44–45).

Bodily extensions in ballet demand that the energy of the dancer be directed toward creating the impression that the dancing body, most notably the neck, head, back, legs, and feet, are all fully extended. Turned-out legs and fully pointed feet, which become pronounced in the wearing of point shoes by female dancers, accentuate the classical ballet style. Arms and wrists in classical ballet are not completely extended but are held with a slight curve. In referring to the position of the arm in this dance tradition, Guillot and Prudhommeau reveal that "The rules of linear aesthetics (which are those of the classical dance) prohibit angles, whatever they may be, including the 180-degree angle (which is a straight line). Thus the joints must neither form angles nor be completely straight, but rather 'sustained,' with the arm folding a gently curved line. When we speak of an arm *tendu* in classical terms, that means with the elbow and the wrist slightly bent" (Guillot and Prudhommeau, 1976: 198–99).

Traces of ballet's corporeal aesthetics are found in the rigid upper body, erect head, curved arms, extended leg, and straightened knees that characterize contemporary ballroom dance. According to Helen Thomas and Nicola Miller, the smooth and steady posturing of the upper body in ballroom is consistent with the rules of deportment outlined in James P. Cassidy's *A Treatise on the Theory and Practice of Dancing*, published in Dublin in 1810, prior to the introduction of the waltz in Britain: "In order to dance well, the body should be firm and steady; it should be particularly motionless, and free from wavering, while the legs are in exertion, for while the body follows the action of the feet, it displays as many ungraceful motions as the legs execute steps, the harmony, the exactness, firmness and perpendicularity, equilibrium in a word, of all those beauties and graces that are so essential to make dancing give pleasure and delight" (cited in Thomas and Miller, 1997: 101–2).

In 1885 Allen Dodworth attempted to codify the steps of new dances of the time, particularly the waltz, which was considered unruly because of its speed, rhythm, and close embrace. Dodworth outlined positions for good dancing, which resemble the corporeal ideals of both ballet and contemporary ballroom dance. In the 1870s Dodworth and other dance masters formed protective associations in England and the United States to establish a ball-room style that still governs contemporary competitive dancing (Buckman, 1978: 121–22). In *Dancing and Its Relation to Education and Social Life* (1900), Dodworth outlines a position of the body, for instance, that is regarded as the "correct" dance stance. He writes, "The upper part of the body should be slightly inclined forward, the hips backward—the forward inclination just enough to cause a tendency in the heels to rise from the floor; the head erect, legs straight, arms hanging by the sides, elbows very slightly turned outward, so that the arms will present gently curved lines to the front" (Dodworth, 1900: 24). The raised heel, erect head, straightened knees, and curved line of the arm (which he refers to as the "Grecian bend") intersect with ballet postures. Dodworth further provides illustrations in the same text of the "wrong way" to dance, which is marked by bent knees, bent back, lowered head, and raised bent elbows as well as by the "vulgar" stance of the close embrace. Dance manuals of the nineteenth century depicted ideal dance patterns that emulated class-based aesthetics. Jane Desmond comments that, "In manuals directed toward the middle and upper classes, bodies that pressed close, spines that relaxed and clutching arms were all denigrated as signs of lower-class dance style" (Desmond, 1993–1994: 38). The standardized movements of the English ballroom style accorded with rules specifying those bodily ideals deemed refined and upper class in resistance to what was perceived as the chaos and disorder of the heterogeneous unruly bodies of the dancing masses. Paradoxically, those responsible for constructing this "upper class" ideal were part of the vernacular culture, not from the upper social strata (Thomas and Miller, 1997: 103).

In tracing the influences of African dance in contemporary African American dance styles, Jacqui Malone argues that one of the influential corporeal traits is dancing with pronounced flexed joints. Work done on the African influence on North American dance styles can be adapted to the Latin Caribbean context. Bent knee positions such as the *plié*, which consists of a flexing of one or both knees, are not valued for themselves in ballet: Guillot and Prudhommeau write that, "On the whole, *pliés* are used more as exercise or as elements of a step than for their own sake in ballet" (Guillot and Prudhommeau, 1976: 83). The fully extended leg, celebrated in the ballet body, exceeds a naturally straightened leg. Guillot and Prudhommeau discuss how a ballet instructor should teach a child to straighten the leg: "Straighten up. The teacher says: 'Stretch as far as you can.' Most of the time, a leg considered to be stretched does not have its extensor muscles completely contracted. The child must become aware of just what a totally extended leg is, and he can only do it after the *plié*. The notion of the 'straightened leg' is not intuitive, contrary to what one might think" (Guillot and Prud-hommeau, 1976: 392).

The straightened hips and legs that are revered in ballet are completely antithetical to what Jacqui Malone describes as body ideals in the African dance styles that have influenced African Americans. Malone writes that "Africans brought to North America were no doubt affirming their ancestral values when they sang a slave song that urged dancers to 'gimme de knee-bone bent.' To many western and central Africans, flexed joints represented life and energy, while straightened hips, elbows, and knees epitomized rigidity and death" (Malone, 1996: 11–12). According to Jane Desmond, in America the movements of some black-derived dances, such as the turkey trot and the charleston, were "tamed and whitened," which further illuminates how straightened joints and extended backs characterize European-influenced dance patterns. Desmond notes that "Such revisions tended to make the dances more upright, taking the bend out of the legs and bringing the buttocks and chest into vertical alignment" (Desmond, 1993–1994: 40). The bent knee, flexed elbow, and fluid hip movements of the African-derived dance culture of the Americas sharply contrast with the celebrated ballet patterns of straight legs, extended curved arms, and still hips, which appear in a less pronounced form in ballroom dance. Questioning the beauty standards of the Latin section of ballroom dance, Ruud Vermay contrasts the corporeal aesthetics of Latin dances that are influenced by ballroom dance and Latin dances that are characterized by African-derived movements. He asks, "Do we find a stretched leg and high-heeled shoes more 'beautiful' than a bent leg and a bare foot?" (Vermay, 1994: 56).

Comparing African dance patterns with the "academic dance of Europe" exemplified by ballet, Brenda Dixon Gottschild identifies a key distinction between the two traditions. Movement of the ballet body is triggered from one corporeal center, the "upper center of the aligned torso" above the pelvis. The possibility of two or more corporeal centers from where movement emanates emerges in the polycentrism of African-derived dance. Polyrhythms further characterize African-influenced styles, which facilitate dancing to different rhythms with various parts of the body. Dancing to a number of rhythms is also facilitated by body isolations in Latin Caribbean dance. For instance, the feet may follow one rhythm while separate movements of the torso or head follow another. Contrasting the European and African dance aesthetics, Gottschild writes, "In this regard, Africanist dance aesthetics represent a democracy of body parts, rather than a monarchy dictated by the straight, centered spine" (Dixon Gottschild, 1995: 103, 106).

Modifications to Latin street dance in the ballroom tradition have created a style that reflects European-based dance aesthetics. Despite the evolution of a style of salsa dancing that is influenced by ballroom, salsa has not been firmly entrenched in the Latin section of this dance heritage. Although ballroom-modified versions of the *son*, mambo, and *chachachá* date back to the first half of the twentieth century, salsa remains a living dance that has not been fixed and structured, as have its predecessors. However, salsa is gradually being incorporated into the Latin section of the ballroom style, resulting in body modifications to express the ballroom dance ideals. Ballroom-influenced salsa dancing does not incorporate the complex body isolations that are part of the street dance style. The principal body isolation that has been transported into the ballroom-influenced style is the hip rotation, which Paul Bottomer describes in his how-to book on salsa dancing, *Salsa: Dance Crazy*: "The Salsa feel is given to the basic movement by a combination of keeping the upper body perfectly still and concentrating the energy into the waist and legs. The leg action is all-important because it is this which gives the characteristic hip movement of the dance. However, the hip movement is a by-product of correct leg action and is not an independent movement" (Bottomer, 1996: 14).

In interpretations of ballroom-influenced salsa, the hip movement is generally not created by separating and rotating the pelvic muscles but by leg movement. The "perfectly still" back that Bottomer identifies contrasts with salsa posturing that has emerged in a Latin Caribbean context. Although the back is held straight in the salsa of Latin Caribbean contexts, it is neither rigid nor completely motionless. A quiet, vertical torso, leg-triggered hip action, and leg extensions and straighter joints mark salsa within the ballroom dance tradition.

Salsa learned in a lived context does not distinguish between the steps and turns of the dance and how the total body moves in dance. In ballroom dance, which is not lived but must be formally learned, this separation exists. The disparity between ballroom salsa and the dance that emerges in a context is illustrated by Bottomer's mapping out of basic ballroom salsa steps for male and female dancers.

Man:
    Move the left foot back, leaving the right foot in place, releasing the heel of the right foot and flexing the right knee. The left leg straightens as the body weight moves over the foot.

Woman:
   Move the right foot back, leaving the left foot in place, releasing the heel of
the left foot and flexing the left knee. The right leg straightens as the body
weight moves over the foot. (Bottomer, 1996: 16)

In a written description of a dance style, the only parts of the dance that can
be easily transmitted are the steps and feet placement. How the entire body
moves cannot be easily translated into written language but needs to be conveyed visually.

Montreal's salsa dance schools display tensions between "lived context"
salsa and ballroom-influenced styles. Discrepancies among schools surface in
how instructors access information about changes to the dance, in the actual
movements that are taught, and in the specific culture with which salsa is associated. Dance schools may institute the contradictory relations of simultaneously maintaining and dissolving cultural hierarchies as a result of the
commodification of salsa in the city.

The Riviera school, one of the most successful in Montreal, is headed by
Canadian-born Daphne, who has a ballroom dance background. The school
promotes a version of salsa resembling more a ballroom style than a dance influenced by Latin Caribbean movements. With the exception of the hip
movement, the school does not incorporate many body isolations.[1] Beginner
salsa classes learn the hip movement as an extension of leg action rather than
as a pelvic rotation. Turns and steps are emphasized much more than entire
body moves, and Rivera's emphasis on still, straight torsos and extended legs
is consistent with the performance style of ballroom dance. Daphne is reluc-
tant to classify her school's salsa style as predominantly marked by ballroom
tradition; nevertheless, in an interview she alludes to a link between Latin
street styles and ballroom dance: "When people say ballroom, what ballroom
really means . . . back when there were ballrooms, when people used to go
dancing, they used to do the waltz . . . Viennese waltz, fox trot, and later
tango. That's what we mean by ballroom. Now we say ballroom and Latin.
Latin originated from the streets and people that were dancing it at parties,
and then people who were stretching ballroom picked it up and structured
it."

Daphne's reluctance to classify the Riviera style of salsa dancing as part of
the Latin side of ballroom dance could partly stem from the fact that salsa
dancing is not firmly anchored in this dance tradition. Her hesitation might
also be attributed to the fact that linking salsa dancing to a ballroom dance
tradition completely removes it from a lived context. Nonetheless, Daphne's
characterization of the Riviera brand of salsa positions it closer to the ball-

room dance tradition than to a street dance style. She points out that salsa has not been structured to the same extent as other Latin dances in ballroom, such as the tango, rumba, and chacha,[2] and that it is therefore less codified and open to interpretation. She says:

> Most of these dances [tango, rumba, chacha] are pretty well structured. They've been around for so long that now they are established. There is a standard. For instance, you can say now in the tango, this is the norm. Of course, like dance any art is open to interpretation. You cannot control what people do. They will do what they feel is right. For instruction, there are guidelines. We have certain rules. In tango, you move forward with this part of the foot. You move yourself like so. You move in this direction. If you are dancing here or if you are dancing in Europe or if you are dancing in Africa. You are doing the same thing. There is certain agreement. Salsa is pretty fresh. Because it is mainly coming from mambo, it is still open to interpretation. People are trying to structure it now.

When a dance flourishes in a lived context, developments and changes in the dance cannot be codified and imposed on the movements. Introduced into ballroom dance, however, Latin street dance movements become frozen and fixed, creating one of the key differences between ballroom and street dance styles. Furthermore, since a living dance develops in actual circumstances, transplanting it to other contexts will change the dance in accordance with the culture of the new location. Local styles influence how salsa is danced in different areas: for instance, salsa in Colombia is influenced by *cumbia*. However, according to Daphne, since the Latin side of ballroom has clearly prescribed rules, a Latin dance will be performed in the same way in Europe or Africa.

The manner in which the Riviera dance school learns about changes in salsa clearly links its method to ballroom style. In a lived context, modifications in dance occur informally by observing other dancers and adopting different styles. Changes arising at the level of movement are passed on through both corporeal and verbal language. In 1996 the Riviera introduced the Cuban *casino rueda* style, which was sometimes referred to as *salsa rueda* in Montreal and parts of the United States. In the following extract from our interview, Daphne reveals how her dance school learns about current changes in salsa:

> There are many ways. Primarily because we are a dance school and we are established, people know us. A lot of the time, the information finds us. Okay, it will be faxed to us or a friend will tell us or we have friends in the industry in

New York or whatever. They say this is what is going on. Do you want to join us in a conference on this new style? So a lot of the time, it just comes. If we want to find it, we call our contacts or we go ourselves to New York or Miami. And a percentage is innovative on our part.

Accessing information about a dance via technological modes of communication, such as faxes or possibly the Internet, clearly breaks with the oral and corporeal transmission of changes in lived dances. Nevertheless, one of the methods that Riviera uses to find out about shifts in dance does resemble how dances evolve in actual circumstances. As Daphne mentioned, dancers and teachers from the school travel to destinations such as New York and Miami to observe salsa dances in these locations. However, because the members of Daphne's dance school visit these cities only briefly, they are not part of the continuous evolution of salsa in Miami and New York. Daphne reveals that once a dance is transplanted from its original setting, there is a distinction between the dance that is learned and the un-derived form of the dance. To explain her point she refers to the Cuban dance *salsa rueda*, in which many couples dance in a circle, changing partners and performing numerous steps and turns called out by a (usually) male leader. Speaking about the introduction of *salsa rueda* to Montreal, Daphne says:

Now they [Montrealers] are bored of this [the Riviera style of salsa], so we have to show them something more. That is why we started showing the Montreal salsa scene *salsa rueda*, which is another way of calling *casino rueda*. There are two ways of saying it. A Cuban person would probably understand *casino rueda*. A more Americanized saying is *salsa rueda*. But it is like anything. In its own place, the locals see it and know it. It is nothing special. They do it every day. The moment it goes outside like in Miami and foreigners start to notice it, then it starts to suddenly be a fad. We'll push it. It is new and hot. They'll take pictures. They'll write up on it. They'll do research and suddenly everyone wants to do this, and meanwhile the people in Cuba have been doing it for ages. So it is always a situation like this. We say it is a new dance, but it is not. It is just new to everyone else.

Daphne does not fix her style of salsa to a clear origin or a specific dance culture. She is not concerned with establishing a true or authentic salsa style but embraces the myriad ways that salsa is danced in the city. Commenting on the Montreal style, Daphne says:

I feel Montreal salsa is kind of like its people—multicultural. Very different. You can look at one dancer and say it looks like he is doing the Colombian style,

and you can look at another one and say he looks like he is doing New York
[style], and you can look at another one. . . . You can see all styles in one club.
It is really nice. If you go to New York, you see that everyone is doing New York
style. And if someone is doing something different they are like . . . what style
is that. And they will look down on it. You'll go to Miami, and you will see a
very strong Cuban influence, and they will dance their style. Then you will see
some Puerto Ricans. There are Puerto Ricans in Miami. If you go to Puerto
Rico, you will see their style. What I am saying is in Montreal, it is nice because
you will see all styles. I like that because I am a person of variety. We have a variety troupe. We teach variety. I just love variety. I like the fact that another
teacher could teach something that is different from us and vice versa.

Daphne's celebration of the diversity of the Montreal scene could also be influenced by the image of Latin dance promoted at the school. Riviera teaches
salsa along with merengue and *bachata* as well as many other Latin dances derived from the Latin section of ballroom dance, such as the chacha, rumba,
mambo, samba, and tango. Daphne further configures salsa as a dance that
can incorporate diverse Latin dance styles besides the Cuban-derived predecessors of salsa, such as the rumba, mambo, *chachachá*, and the *son*. She adds
that, "Salsa and the reason it is called salsa is because there is a blend of roots
there and a blend of movement. Physical movement. . . . You can take tango
steps and put them in salsa. You can take merengue steps and put them in
salsa. You can take rumba steps and put them in salsa." Dancers at Riviera
also incorporate their own choreography when developing their style.
Daphne is not concerned about cultural purity in her company's rendition of
salsa; rather, in a sense, she creates a hybrid form by extending the interpretation of salsa movement well beyond its Cuban-derived patterns.

Raised in Canada and of non-Latin descent, Daphne learned salsa in
Montreal and cannot claim a "right" to teach an "authentic" salsa dance
based on a Latin heritage or on life in a Latin culture. On the other hand,
unlike many of the city's male dance teachers of Latin descent with very little dance training, Daphne has considerable background in dance stemming
from the ballroom tradition. She establishes distinctions based on her
school's dance expertise rather than on its "ethnic" origin and claims to authenticity. This distinguishes her school's "educational-structured method,"
based on rules, from the "natural" method of certain freelance dancers, based
on feeling and intuition. Daphne says:

We have a structure because we have a curriculum and we have names of steps
and a certain order. That is because we developed a curriculum. We do that because it is our business. But there are freelance teachers who will go out and

teach their theory of what they think is right in salsa. The steps might be similar to ours or they might be completely different. But that is good, too. Because you are getting a more natural view of someone basing their decisions on how it feels rather than on certain rules. It is good to have both. The dance school structured-educational method and the natural attitude. It creates a nice balance.

Just as Daphne embraces the multicultural potential of Montreal's salsa scene, she is also receptive to the different kinds of traditions that characterize instructors in the city. The "structured–educational method" refers to the technique used by instructors like herself who have ballroom dance training, whereas the natural attitude, based on feeling, is favored by those who do not have formal dance training but learned the dance through lived practice. In accepting that both teaching methods can contribute to the Montreal scene, Daphne further demonstrates her open attitude toward the multitude of styles and traditions that characterize the salsa dance milieu.

The idea of a salsa style that develops through feelings as opposed to rules and structures is consistent with how Western-based scholars have typically viewed the dances of non-Western people. According to Joann Kealiinohomoku, stereotyped perceptions that cast the dances of non-European peoples as "natural" and "unfettered" have been projected onto these dances (Kealiinohomoku, 1983: 535). Configuring the "natural dancer" as inspired strictly by emotions further echoes Kealiinohomoku's stance that the Western eye views the dances of the "other," particularly those of African and indigenous cultures, as "instinctive" responses to music. Kealiinohomoku mentions specifically how the dances of so-called "primitive" people are viewed not as choreographed but as expressions that occur "naturally" and thus without artistry (Kealiinohomoku, 1983: 535). Even though Kealiinohomoku is referring specifically to how Western scholars have projected a primitive stereotype onto the dances of non-Western peoples, the idea that the dances of "the other"—in this case, Latin popular dances—can be "natural" expressions places them on a less equal footing than styles from European culture.

Although salsa developing in a lived context may not be formally coded, this dance is not without structure. A salsa dancer who grew up with the dance can coordinate multiple levels of movement. Foot placements and turns are married to isolations of the entire dancing body. The ease with which many salseros dance this complex coordination of movement patterns often leads the outside viewer to the conclusion that salsa is a "natural" expression, when, in fact, knowledge of the dance has been acquired through extensive "informal" training. Positioning salsa as "natural" eclipses the intricacy that is embedded in the dance.

Reference to the teaching style of certain dance instructors in the city as "natural" does not completely describe the current situation in Montreal. Only two dance instructors of Latin descent in the city, Paolo and Rita, had danced to salsa music before arriving in the city. Although Paolo and Rita acquired the dance in lived Latin contexts, they both also have considerable dance training. Rita has background in Latin jazz dance and Latin Caribbean dances; Paolo has training in Latin Caribbean dances, such as salsa and merengue, as well as in the *son, chachachá,* and mambo. Some dance teachers of Latin descent in Montreal learned to dance salsa in the city and consequently did not learn it in the "natural" way—that is, in a society where salsa is part of the everyday cultural fabric. A number of instructors, however, have attained some of their knowledge of salsa through observing dancers in clubs in Montreal and elsewhere. This method of acquisition is less structured and formal that that of ballroom instruction.

The teaching of salsa in a ballroom-influenced dance school with no connection to the actual lived context of the dance could be viewed as a form of cultural appropriation; the practice continues in Montreal. Stemming from European cultures, ballroom dance is often perceived as more elegant and refined than the Latin street dances from which salsa derives. Therefore, downplaying body isolations, particularly movements of the hip and back, is intended to make the dance more aesthetically appropriate; the straighter joints, still backs, and extended legs in Latin ballroom dance are supposedly what renders the style graceful. As already noted, when Latin street dances were initially adopted into Western social dance, they were modified to comply with European-based aesthetics, thus privileging a European-derived movement vernacular above an African-derived one. Modifying salsa to accord with the standards of ballroom dance in Montreal maintains this cultural hierarchy in a contemporary context.

At a number of music and dance events in Montreal, Riviera has offered dance lessons and performed for the audiences. The school taught and performed regularly at the Bamboleo monthly Latin parties, which were featured for five years at one of the city's largest nightclubs. Although Bamboleo parties drew a mixed crowd, the events must be characterized as "Latin" since the master of ceremonies commonly addressed the crowd only in Spanish. Even though many Montrealers of Latin descent may never have danced to salsa music in their countries of origin, there are also many who have. In the monthly Bamboleo fiestas, salsa was demonstrated and taught by the dancers of a company disconnected from the lived culture of the dance's origins.

Daphne usually performed with her partner Alejandro, who learned salsa in Montreal. A bizarre reversal of positions occurs when those who grew up dancing to salsa are instructed and entertained by a performance that may have little bearing on how they envision salsa. Nevertheless, this version of the dance is presented as an expression of Latin culture.

Riviera does not claim to teach an "authentic" salsa or a rendition of the dance from a lived context; instead, the school encourages the development of variety in Montreal's salsa dancing. Daphne's open attitude toward cultural diversity demonstrates her celebration of the multicultural nature of the salsa dance scene. This embrace of diversity could also be partly motivated by strategies to sell the dance. Riviera promotes both diverse Latin styles and an interpretation of salsa that incorporates outside genres beyond its Cuban derivatives, creating a unique hybrid form of salsa. At the same time, the teaching style that is used at the school stems from a dance tradition that appropriated Latin dance styles, then established the ballroom style of these dances as more refined and elegant than the "originals."

A few salsa schools in the city promote a New York dance style. Catherine, for instance, grew up in Montreal and danced ballroom before she started teaching salsa in the summer of 1996 with Miguel. These two have two dance schools, Catherine's Simply Salsa and Miguel's Tropical Salsa, both of which advertise teaching the New York method. Miguel, originally from Peru, started dancing to salsa in Montreal. Carlos of Salsa Celeste, who also promotes the New York style, also began dancing to the salsa rhythms in Montreal. All three instructors hone their skills by learning from salsa dance videos and observing the New York club dance scene.[3] As none of these teachers grew up dancing salsa, linking their style to one that originates in New York gives their salsa lessons an authentic flair. The style that is taught in Montreal resembles the New York style in terms of the footwork and figures. However, none of the instructors whom I interviewed teach their students to dance on "2"—that is, to start on the second beat of the music. Instructors teach the New York style, in which their students start on "1," or the first beat of the music. Dancing on "2" is generally not taught in Montreal.

The link to New York salsa started in 1996 and did not characterize how salsa dancing was initially promoted in Montreal. In the late 1980s and early 1990s, Montreal salsa teachers came from Guatemala. They include Rita of Salsa Works, Marcus of Exclusive Salsa, Oscar of Salsa Plus, and Gustavo of Salsa Brava. With the exception of Rita, all of these instructors started to dance in Montreal: a precise origin of salsa or a specific style was not integral to the way these earlier salsa dance teachers "sold" their dance. Salsa was instead linked to a general Latin heritage. Since Guatemala is not a leading salsa nation, these first dance teachers could not claim an "authentic" link with a salsa heritage. As previously noted, only Rita had a dance background and teaching experience before her arrival in Canada. Being a Latin jazz dancer and choreographer, she integrated the African-derived body isolations that characterize this Latin dance in her salsa classes. Rita first learned these African-derived body isolations as a teenager when she learned to dance merengue in Livingston, Guatemala, an area peopled by the Garifuna, the descendents of escaped enslaved Africans.[4] Besides teaching the steps and turns of the dance, Rita included pelvic and hip rotations and upper body isolations, and knowing salsa's predecessors, she incorporated, for instance, the teaching of *chachachá*. Her notion of what constitutes "authentic" salsa expression is more closely tied to the actual execution of the movement level of the dance than to whether a dance style links to a leading salsa nation. With her incorporation of body isolations, Rita's version of salsa resembles a Latin Caribbean style more than do those of the other Montreal dance teachers of Latin descent.[5]

Those instructors who have taught it refer to the first Montreal salsa style as either the Colombian or the classical style. The Colombian style that developed outside of Cali and reached Montreal is characterized by small steps, in which dancers tap out the accents of the rhythm. Foot placement is directed primarily to the left and the right, and dancers often move laterally by crossing one foot over the other. According to dance instructors, forward and backward stepping characterizes the salsa style of New York and the Caribbean. However, this characteristic distinguishing the Colombian from the New York and Caribbean styles is open to dispute. Recent immigrants to Montreal from Cuba direct their dance steps to the left and right. However, as noted by Charlot, a Montreal dancer and instructor, in the Cuban style the feet are sometimes turned out at an angle of forty-five degrees, as opposed to the straight placement of the feet in the side-to-side stepping that characterizes the *cumbia*-influenced style. As there can be a certain degree of overlap between the various styles, I am less concerned with defining which movement patterns delineate which styles than with how these distinctions become markers of authenticity.

Some instructors in the city claim that the Colombian style is influenced by *cumbia*, a dance that was popular in Central America during the 1980s (DJ Sánchez). This Colombian dance and music style blends African, European, and indigenous musical heritages. The majority of the instruments used in the original folkloric version of *cumbia* are African-derived, with the exception of a type of clarinet and a recorder-like flute, which reveal the influence of the indigenous peoples (Burton, 1994: 550). The European aspect of *cumbia* is found in the forms of the melodies and patterns of the verses, which are modeled on medieval Spanish poetry. In the 1940s *cumbia* moved from its rural origins to become part of the dance culture of the urban middle and up-per classes (550). Since the 1970s, *cumbia* has been influenced by salsa, re-placing earlier offbeat chords with rhythmic piano patterns (550).

Cumbia's effect on the styles taught by Montreal's first salsa dance in-structors could also stem from how *cumbia*, which has been influenced by in-digenous peoples in Colombia, might intersect with the dance styles of the indigenous peoples of Central America. Leonardo, a former saxophone player in a local merengue and salsa band, refers to the salsa dance style with swings to the left and right as affected by indigenous dance influences in Central American Latin dance. Other salsa dance teachers, particularly Rita, adamantly oppose drawing a link between the salsa danced first in Montreal and indigenous dance traditions. Rita argues that the style that she first taught is the classical salsa style, which originated in Cuba and was adopted by nations in Latin America.

"Classical," a term not used today on the Internet or in popular discourse, refers to a style whose basic step derives from the Cuban *son*. This style of dancing is characteristic of Latin American countries and consists of the ba-sic "short-short-long" step (Waxer, 2002b: 233–34). Describing the basic step in terms of short or long movements stems from dance manuals and resem-bles the "quick, quick, slow" terminology used in ballroom manuals (The Dance Store Online, 2005). The basic "short-short-long" step, as previously mentioned, consists of dancers stepping on the three beats of the music and pausing for the fourth. Whereas the first steps are short steps, the last one ap-pears to be a long step because of the pause.

Some of these earlier dance teachers have gradually moved away from the Colombian, or classical, salsa style and have adopted the New York style. Gustavo of Salsa Brava, who has been teaching in Montreal since 1988, re-veals how his dance style has evolved. He teaches a method that combines his own vision of the dance with the New York style that he developed dur-ing frequent jaunts to the city.

Oscar, of Salsa Plus, who first taught what he terms the "Colombian" style, now incorporates a multitude of styles derived from various Latin nations. Before he began teaching salsa in 1987, he learned the dance by watching people in clubs in Montreal. In an interview, he told me that he would fre-quent a different club every night of the week. Since his early years as a salsa dancer, Oscar has continued this initial method of acquiring the dance, thereby expanding his movement repertoire beyond the Colombian style. Since near the beginning of his teaching, Oscar has given lessons at La

Palmera, one of the longest-running clubs in the city. (A pseudonym is used for the name of this club.) He has increased his knowledge of the dance by observing the styles of La Palmera club goers, who originate from various nations in Latin America and the Caribbean. Oscar says: "but right after the Colombian style, I learned from a Venezuelan who would come to the club [La Palmera]. He had another style, and I watched someone from New York who had another style, and after, I watched someone from Puerto Rico, and that way, at a given point, I learned. I mastered almost all the styles. My style is very personal, but that suits everyone. Because with all the styles that I can do, I can dance with everyone. That is the La Palmera style" (my translation).[6]

Although Oscar claims to teach a salsa style that has evolved from the dancing in the Montreal Latin club La Palmera, he does not want to link his style to Montreal. He legitimizes the style that he promotes at La Palmera by connecting it to a general Latin heritage. Oscar adds these further comments to link the "La Palmera" style that he is developing in Montreal to the dance that stems from leading salsa nations as well as from New York:

> Now [1999], there exists the influence of the Cuban style because it is in fashion. In the 1980s, *salsa romántica* was the most popular style. This style became influenced by mambo. In my opinion, the New York style is the mambo style mixed with the Cuban style. It's a beautiful style but is more of a performance style. The style that has been developed here [La Palmera], given that we have a limited space, it a style that is marked by small-step movement patterns. It's a Montreal style. But this Montreal style has not developed because of Montrealers but because of the mix of Latin Americans. There are Haitians, Cubans, Colombians, Venezuelans at the club. There are Panamanians. There are people from all the communities and all the styles. It's really very mixed. (My translation)[7]

Paolo of Caribe, who has lived in Montreal since 1991, clearly justifies his "right" to teach salsa on the basis that he grew up in a Latin Caribbean context and is of Caribbean origin. He claims expertise on the grounds that he is part of a wider Latin Caribbean cultural heritage, to which salsa belongs. His definition contrasts with Daphne's conception that salsa can incorporate the steps of the Argentinean-derived tango and the Dominican merengue; Paolo defines salsa as a blend of specifically Cuban dances: the mambo, *chachachá*, rumba, and *son*. He further justifies his right to teach salsa on the grounds of extensive experience, as both a dancer and a choreographer, with various Caribbean dances, particularly salsa and merengue, and is highly critical of teachers with neither a dance background nor a Caribbean dance heritage. Paolo says: "I am insulted because I have a dance background. I come from a Caribbean country, and I grew up with Caribbean dance. When I see people who do that [teach the dance without having a dance background], I take it as an insult. They insult my culture. It [salsa] comes from the Caribbean. It's as if someone took your culture and tried to destroy it in another country" (my translation).[8] Paolo's Latin Caribbean heritage and knowledge of the dance in a lived context are for him the elements that distinguish the salsa taught and promoted at Caribe from that found at the other schools in the city.

To legitimize the Caribe style of salsa, Paolo constructs a number of hierarchies based on ethnic, racial, and cultural differences. He launches an attack against other dance instructors of Latin descent in the city. He argues that they teach salsa but are ignorant of the dance because they do not come from Caribbean nations. Paolo says, "There are many Latinos who come from Central America . . . there are Chileans, Peruvians, Salvadorians. There people do not dance salsa because salsa is a mix [of cultures] from the Caribbean" (my translation).[9]

According to Paolo, these Latin dance teachers are in fact teaching *cumbia* under the guise of salsa. Paolo further claims that the style of *cumbia* that these dance teachers promote is much simpler than salsa. In a free trial class, which the school offers to potential students, Nancy, one of four dance teachers at the school, reiterated Paolo's claim. She danced a few steps of a salsa style to illustrate the dance taught by other instructors in the city and to expose how this dance is not salsa but in fact *cumbia*. Her demonstration of this "false" salsa was intended as a warning to the students that we would be deceived if we took lessons with Latin dance instructors who taught this version. I immediately recognized the style that Nancy was denigrating as the first rendition of salsa that I had learned from teachers primarily from Guatemala.

Caribe's criticism of other Latin teachers in the city sets up an ethnic hierarchy. As previously mentioned, the salsa taught by Central Americans is partly influenced by indigenous dance traditions. However, as also already noted, some Montrealers who teach and promote salsa would not agree with the above claim. Brigido Galvan, a musicologist and salsa musician, discloses how the impact of indigenous cultures on the music and dance traditions in Latin America is often denigrated. There is presently a heralding of African-derived elements in Latin music.[10] Unlike the musical traditions of Guatemala, which have indigenous influences (Guatemala, 1987), the effect of indigenous peoples on the culture of the Caribbean is not as strong because of the virtual extermination of the native populations by the sixteenth century. During Christopher Columbus's government of the region from 1496 until 1570, the Caribbean indigenous populations became completely extinct, with the exception of those found in a few areas of the Dominican Republic and the African-intermixed "Black Caribs" of St. Vincent, who were later exiled to Honduras (Manuel, 1995: 4). Paolo's criticism of indigenous-influenced salsa in Central America transports a Latin American cultural hierarchy into a new setting.

Further, Paolo is attempting to salvage a dance tradition that he argues is being usurped by North American domination. The claim by some Montreal dance teachers that they teach a New York style is a point of contention for Paolo: he is against using "New York" as a site of origin for a dance that he contends comes from Puerto Ricans, Cubans, and Dominican Republicans who are living in New York. He also considers the incorporation of Latin dances into the ballroom dance tradition as both an appropriation of Latin culture by white North Americans and a destruction of dance at the level of movement. In Paolo's opinion, ballroom dance has reduced salsa—and other dances that are continuously evolving—to a fixed set of rules in order to render feasible the teaching and consequently the "selling" of the dance. He asserts, "You can do anything in salsa, as there are not any rules. It's white people who regulated salsa. It was the white people here in North America who regulated it to make money" (my translation).[11]

Freezing Latin dance into fixed rules renders the dance mechanical and turns the dancers into robots. Comparing Caribe's style with social dance, Paolo says: "A mechanical dancer is a person who does one thing and that's all. An instructor who is natural will develop your dancing ability differently than a person who is mechanical like [a ballroom dancer]. That's American dance. It has been around for eighty years. . . . If you look at the dancers there [at ballroom dance schools], you'll think they are robots. If you look at the dancers here [Caribe], you see that they are natural. We grew up with that [Latin dance]" (my translation).[12]

Referring to a dancer as "natural" often reproduces the prevailing myth that Latin people are born with rhythm in their veins. Paolo employs the term "natural" to describe the style of dancing that has emerged from people who grew up in a Latin dance culture. The "robotic" style of ballroom dance is antithetical to Paolo's understanding of a "natural" form of salsa. By classifying the Caribe style as "natural," he privileges the Latin dance tradition that has emerged from actual circumstances. Paolo strongly believes that he has the expertise to teach salsa as a living vibrant dance, a skill, he contends, not shared by Montreal dance schools influenced by North American social dance, such as Riviera and Arthur Murray.

Paolo frames the difference between salsa as a Caribbean art form and the ballroom dance tradition of Latin dance in racial and cultural terms, as does

Elio, originally from Cuba, who was a dance instructor at Caribe for a number of years. Both denigrate the Latin dances that are structured by the ballroom dance tradition as products of white American society and draw a clear hierarchy that exalts the Caribbean form of Latin dances such as the mambo, rumba, and chachachá. With the exception of rumba, which is still popular in Cuba (Daniel, 1995: 7), these dances are not contemporary styles, but Latin section of ballroom dance maintains all three as contemporary. Elio discloses how the chachachá that has been modified in the social dance tradition is actually a simpler form of the "original" dance and does not fully adhere to the rhythm of the music. During my interview with Paolo, Elio joined the interview briefly, and spoke about the chachachá:

> The chachachá has its tropical rhythm, a Cuban rhythm which dates back to 1956. It was a popular dance that everyone on the streets danced. After the son comes the chachachá, and it's a way to show your spirit and who you are through music. And now we [Caribe] must show the public the real chachachá. I don't know if it is easier for you [North Americans] to say chacha instead of chachachá. The name was changed and the steps as well. The chachachá is a more rigorous and stylish dance because the chachachá (of the Carribean) is cha-cha-cha one-two. And everyone here dances it as one-two, cha-cha-cha. And when you listen to the music, you can see that you [North Americans] have made a mistake in the rhythm of the music because it is the contrary of what you do in the dance. (My translation)[13]

Despite Caribe's mandate to teach and promote Latin Caribbean popular dance styles, the school's instruction technique is similar to dance methods that are influenced by social dance. More attention is paid to steps, turns, figures, and elaborate footwork than to how the total body moves in dance. Further, Nancy, the director of Caribe and principal teacher in the company, was born in Quebec, and has a dance background in ballet, not in Latin Caribbean movement. Although Paolo's own style of dancing elicits the subtle isolations and posturing of his Latin Caribbean heritage, they are not a central part of the movements that are taught at the school. The similarity between Paolo's method and techniques influenced by social dance demonstrates how difficult it is to teach a lived dance in a formal setting. Given that the knowledge of change in a Latin dance is obtained from being in an actual context, a dance school in Montreal cannot be fully up to date on the alterations in salsa that emerge in actual circumstances. To facilitate the teaching of salsa in a school, this dance cannot escape a certain degree of formalization under fixed rules. The commodification of salsa transports this dance outside the realm of a street-dance style, which has the potential to evolve and transform in the concrete circumstances of a dance culture. In my interview with Paolo, he did not provide detailed information on how he stays current since he is adamant that his Caribbean heritage provides him with the expertise to teach an authentic salsa. Nevertheless, during our interview, he did show me videos of street dance styles that he uses to inspire his choreographies both in his teaching and in his performing. Besides using videos to create his dances, Paolo also travels regularly to New York and the Caribbean to keep his knowledge current.

That body isolations are not taught at Caribe could be partly attributed to the commodification of salsa throughout the city. Paolo claims that he wants to show the elegance and beauty of the "authentic" Latin Caribbean version of salsa. At the same time, he also needs to sell this dance in the Montreal context. Caribe targets the mainstream in the city rather than appealing to minority cultures such as the Latin community. For example, the company's dance troupe has performed at commercially popular events and locations such as Musique Plus, the Casino of Montreal, and the Just for Laughs Festival.

The aim of most dance schools is to teach students how to salsa in Latin clubs and to enable them to dance with various partners. Depending on the level that a student wants to reach, learning to dance takes from about six months to two years. Dance schools sell a product, and students want results. Since those taking salsa lessons are often born in Canada and Quebec, they are not well versed in the movement patterns of body isolations. For adults, who may never have had any dance training, learning to isolate various parts of the body is not easy and could require a considerable number of lessons and practice. Interest in learning Latin Caribbean kinetic patterns is not strong in the city because many Montrealers are not aware that body isolations are an integral part of salsa dancing. As many of the dance instructors in the city are Canadian-born or come from non-Caribbean Latin nations, they have not exposed their students to these movement patterns in their classes. Furthermore, a large part of the salsa dancing in the Latin clubs in the city does not include body isolations. A minority of salsa club goers who come from such parts of the Caribbean as Haiti, the Dominican Republic, Cuba, and Puerto Rico as well as from some West African nations may exhibit body isolations in their dancing. However, most of the club dancers come from Latin American and Central American nations, as well as from Canada, where body isolations are not an integral part of their dance heritages. Concentrating on how the total body moves while isolating specific parts of the body could both slow and discourage the novice dancer, who wants to learn salsa in order to be able to dance in the club setting. It is not in the best business interest of a school to focus on body isolations. After

140 ~ Chapter Three

receiving complaints from students about hip and torso separation exercises, Rita, for instance, granted her students' requests and stopped incorporating them into her salsa classes. These exercises, which students did without a partner, included extensive isolations of the hip and upper torso. According to Rita, many students found these isolations too foreign and also lewd. The most successful rendition of salsa as a marketable product is that which emphasizes footwork, turns, figures, and paired movements. To successfully "sell" the dance in the city, Caribe, for instance, does not emphasize body isolations, thereby conforming to the movement vernacular of the prevailing culture.

Dancers who have grown up with salsa or other Caribbean music styles not only exhibit body isolations, but also dance to the rhythmic phrasing of the music. As previously noted, salsa dancers need to understand the rhythm so that they can dance both with and against the clave. Very few instructors in Montreal emphasize teaching students to dance to the rhythm, a core element of the dance. Charlot, a Montreal salsa instructor, who is originally from Haiti, has found that his teaching method, which concentrates on moving to the rhythm of the music rather than only on teaching steps, turn patterns, and figures, is not as popular with clients. Furthermore, teaching students to listen and respond corporeally to the phrasing of the music is interpreted as less technical and skilled than the more popular and commercial technique of breaking the dance down into corporeal units (i.e., specific steps, figures, and turns).

According to Charlot, the only way to really dance salsa is to fully understand the rhythm in all its complexities and to learn to feel the music in the dance. "Feeling the music" is not an instinctual response that, as previously noted, has been projected onto the dance cultures of non-Western peoples; rather, it requires a deep understanding of the rhythm so that the music and the dancing body become one. Fully feeling the rhythm and expressing it with the body would be, in Caribbean culture, a sign of an expert dancer. Teaching an individual who has not been raised with Caribbean music to dance to the rhythm of salsa, feel the music in the body, and express the music corporeally is much more difficult than providing instruction in steps and turns. A focus on rhythm is similar to an emphasis on body isolations. Students who are not raised with Caribbean rhythms and dance often regard these two aspects as less important than learning steps, turns, dips, and figures. They generally want to know how to dance fairly quickly with a partner so that they can go out to clubs. Just as the acquisition of body isolations in a dance class can slow a student down, a focus on rhythm also takes time. Teaching salsa that highlights its rhythm does not sell well. As Charlot points out:

If you are teaching someone how to do the steps, that person can do the steps much faster than if you were to teach that person how to be controlled by the music. This would be thought of as less technical. I would look less educated to you as a dance teacher . . . like I am not a trained dancer. But the only person who can teach you how to dance salsa properly is somebody who can teach you how to feel the music . . . not just do the steps . . . because there are only three steps in salsa . . . because there are things to feel in between the steps when you are dancing. . . . What is important when you dance in the Caribbean or in Cuba or Puerto Rico is what you are feeling and not what you step on. It is not the beat that you step on that is important; it is what you are feeling on the step. You can either dance the step or you can dance the music.

Charlot's teaching method enables students to dance salsa in a style resembling that of the Caribbean. Nonetheless, his technique does not have commercial appeal. Although he is an excellent teacher and dancer, his method has not had a significant impact on the Montreal teaching scene. Charlot's approach stresses more the artistry of the Caribbean-based style in its lived context than those elements of the dance (i.e., steps, turns, and figures) that enable salsa to become commodified as a set of marketable units.

Salsa dance teachers have an interest in maintaining the exclusivity of their product to distinguish it from that offered at competing schools. Although some teachers are more open to the diverse styles in the city, others, such as Paolo, seek to establish their own style as the best in Montreal. The construction of difference is anchored to the commodification of the dance in the city. Linking the dance to a point outside the city facilitates the "selling" of the dance: the kind of cultural commodity that is being promoted therefore exerts a great deal of influence on how salsa is contextualized in the city. For instance, Latin music promoter, Alvaro, wants to nourish the unique style that flourishes in the Latin music and dance scene in Montreal. The highly diverse Latin population in Montreal gives rise to a wide range of Latin music; people from various backgrounds can dance to many different kinds of Latin music in any Latin music venue on any given night. According to Alvaro, this diversity itself defines the Montreal style: it stands apart from other Latin music centers, such as New York, where musical tastes are often stratified according to ethnic, racial, and cultural allegiances. He therefore opposes how some salsa teachers as well as disk jockeys and club owners promote a New York style: "But I am still having a hard time trying to convince DJs that they should push that Montreal sound more commercially because they tend to follow everything that is going on in New York. . . . But here you get a lot of promoters or clubs that promote themselves as New York

style—New York style this, New York style that. New York style dance lesson. New York ambiance."

Alvaro adds that one consequence of Montreal's diversity of Latin dances
and music is that musicians have to be able to play a variety of rhythms,
which distinguishes them from other Latin musicians, who are usually versa-
tile only in one rhythm. Speaking about a local salsa and merengue band that
he promotes, Alvaro says:

> But here, because the community is not predominantly from one area, then
> you have people from Central America and different South American coun-
> tries and some Dominicans, and I mean . . . you have people from a lot of dif-
> ferent countries [so] . . . and that is one of the successes that [the band] has had
> locally . . . you have to play salsa, you have to play merengue, you have to play
> bachata, you have to play cumbia, and you have to play boleros because the
> community is just so diverse that you want to keep everyone happy. Now what
> that is saying, musically speaking, is that many bands here are in better shape
> musically than bands that are making a lot of money in New York or in Latin
> America. Because in order to be a good musician here you have got to be ver-
> satile in about four or five different rhythms.

Rather than viewing the diversity of Latin music in Montreal as a corruption of cultural purity, Alvaro regards the effect of multicultural tastes as an
enriching force for musicians. As a Latin music promoter, Alvaro's willingness to embrace diversity in the Latin dance and music scene could be partly
linked to his desire to expand the market for Latin dance and music in the
city. Whereas certain salsa dance schools want to distinguish their dance
from others by staking out their particular style, others involved in different
sectors of the music and dance scene, especially promoters, have an interest
in maintaining its diversity and recognizing and legitimizing difference.

In Montreal, salsa dancing is both a symbol of affiliation to a specific cultural heritage for those of Latin descent and the basis for a number of businesses in the city. The commodification of salsa influences how the dance
evolves as a cultural expression within Montreal. Research that celebrates
dance as a potential site of resistance for a nation, people, or subculture is often based on the assumption that a given cultural practice is fixed and finite
and that this practice can be "owned." Analyses that view dance as an expression of a people often configure the nature of resistance in terms of a minority group's defiance of a prevailing authority. When a dance is transplanted from its "original" setting, as in the case of salsa in Montreal, it is
problematic to view dance simply as a cultural expression. My analysis of
salsa does not completely remove the political potential of dance but rather

reinscribes it to include the ways that the commodification of a practice intersects with its cultural expression.

The paradoxical nature of salsa, which both resists and succumbs to commodification, extends into the multicultural interactions that arise in the salsa dance scene. For instance, Paolo seeks to present this dance both as a heritage of the Caribbean people and as a product to be bought and sold. As a result of these two competing tensions, the salsa promoted at his school simultaneously establishes a sense of Caribbean cultural purity and adopts the dance practices of the dominant Montreal culture in order to sell the dance. Through the promotion and distribution of a cultural expression, diverse cultures interact, yielding a complex and contradictory array of relationships that convey multicultural relations in actual circumstances.

Notes

1. After the completion of my ethnographic work in 2000, I later observed that the Riviera dance troupe included more extensive body isolations in a few of their performed choreographies. For instance, at a dance event entitled "Eddie Torres: The Mambo King," held on 2 November 2002 at the Medley in Montreal, I saw a performance by the Riviera school that offered a version of the *guaguanco* in which a goup of primarily male dancers performed extensive body isolations. This dance night at the Medley featured performances by Eddie Torres from New York City as well as by various dance troupes from Montreal schools.

2. "Chacha," one of the Latin dances within ballroom, is the term used for the modified version of the *chachachá*.

3. Since I conducted my ethnographic research, the Simply Salsa school has folded. Tropical Salsa is still in business, and Salsa Celeste has expanded.

4. Rita relates her experience in Livingston in an interview: "I learned to dance the merengue in a place called Livingston. It's a black Atlantic coastal town in Guatemala. They speak Garifuna there. It's a Caribbean language. This place is really pure. It's black, black. I learned to dance merengue there. There are other dances . . . the punta. It's really gorgeous . . . a lot of hips."

5. Rita no longer teachers salsa in Montreal and presently resides in Guatemala.

6. Mais tout de suite après le style colombien, j'ai appris avec un Vénézuélien qui venait ici à la discothèque [La Palmera]. Il avait un autre style et après j'ai regardé quelqu'un de New York qui faisait un autre style après j'ai regardé quelqu'un de Porto Rico et comme ça, à un moment donné j'ai appris. J'ai maîtrisé un peu plus tous les styles. Mon style est très personnel, mais ça fait l'affaire de tout le monde parce qu'avec les styles que je fais, je peux danser avec tout le monde. Ça, c'est plutôt le style La Palmera.

7. Maintenant [1999], il y l'influence du style cubain parce qu'il est à la mode. Dans les années 80, *la salsa romantica* était le style le plus populaire. Elle a ensuite subi

l'influence de la mambo. Selon moi le style New-Yorkais c'est le style mambo mélangé avec le style cubain. C'est beau mais c'est un style plus spectaculaire. Le style que nous avons développé ici [La Palmera], étant donné que nous disposons d'un espace plus restreint, c'est un peu un style avec les pas plus réduits. C'est plutôt un style montréalais. Mais le style montréalais, ce n'est pas à cause des Montréalais mais c'est à cause des mélanges des latino-américains. On a des Haïtiens, des Cubains, des Colombiens, des Vénézuéliens à la discothèque, on a des Panamiens, on a de toutes les communautés et de tous les styles. C'est vraiment bien mélangé.

8. Moi, je suis insulté parce que j'ai une base. Je viens d'un pays antillais et j'ai grandi dans la danse antillaise. Quand je vois les gens qui font ça [enseigner la danse sans avoir une base], c'est comme une insulte. Ils insultent ma culture. La salsa vient des Caraïbes. C'est comme si quelqu'un prenait ta culture et essayait de la détruire dans un autre pays.

9. Il y a beaucoup de latins qui viennent ici de l'Amérique Centrale . . . il y a des Chiliens, les Péruviens, les Salvadoriens. Ces gens là ils ne dansent pas la salsa parce que la salsa c'est un mélange des Caraïbes.

10. Brigido Galvan, interviewed by author, 9 March 1999.

11. Tu peux faire n'importe quoi puisque dans la salsa il n'y a pas de règlements. Ce sont les blancs qui lui ont donné des règlements . . . Ce sont les blancs ici en Amérique qui lui ont donné des règlements pour faire de l'argent.

12. *Mecánico* c'est une personne qui fait une chose et c'est ça. Un professeur qui est naturel il va te faire évoluer différemment qu'une personne qui est mécanique, comme un danseur de danse de salon. C'est la danse américaine. Ça fait 80 ans . . . Si tu vois les danseurs la bas [les écoles de dance de salon], tu penses qu'ils sont des robots. Si tu vois les danseurs ici [Caribe], tu vois, qu'ils sont naturels. On a grandi dans ça [la danse latine].

13. Le *chachachá* a *son* rythme tropical, un rythme cubain qui date depuis 1956. C'était une danse populaire que tout le monde de la rue dansaient. C'est après le *son* vient le *chachachá* et c'est la façon d'annoncer ton esprit et ta personne avec la musique. Maintenant, nous [Caribe] devons montrer au public le vrai *chachachá*. Je ne sais pas si pour vous [les Nord-américains] c'est plus facile de dire chacha que *chachachá*. On a changé le nom et aussi les pas. Le *chachachá* c'est une danse qui est plus rigoureuse et qui a plus de style parce que le *chachachá* [de la Caraïbe] c'est cha-cha-cha un deux. Et tout le monde ici la danse un deux cha-cha-cha. Et quand on écoute la musique, on peut voir que vous vous êtes trompés avec la musique parce que c'est le contraire de ce que vous faites dans la danse.

CHAPTER FOUR

~

The Couple in Dance

Explaining that salsa dancing is an art form that should be recognized by mainstream American society, Serafin Corchado, an online columnist known by the pseudonym Vicente, writes: "In Latin music, a male dancer leads his partner in expression of her sensuality, to bring out elegance in movement, and to achieve an ecstasy in accomplishment of dance form" (Corchado, 2005). For people who grew up dancing to salsa rhythms, the dance's partnering structure, in which the male leads the female dancer, creates its artistry, sensuality, and pleasure. Salsa dancing has developed within a culture that regards this male and female dynamic as a "natural" and beautiful way to dance. By comparison, for dancers such as myself who did not grow up dancing with a partner but danced alone in their teenage and adult years, being guided by a male partner may feel at first like an "unnatural" imposition on the body. Since the 1980s in Quebec and Canada the dominant dance culture has been one of individual free-form expression, in which men and women move separately outside the couple configuration. The pleasure of this free-form style lies in individual expression, which enables dancers to let go and be themselves. Although dancing alone—common in the mainstream music and dance scenes of the 1980s, 1990s, and early twenty-first century—may feel "natural," expressing individuality is a part of contemporary physical culture that is both culturally and historically based. In twentieth-century North American and British popular cultures, individual freedom on the dance floor began in the 1920s and reached its zenith in the expressive cultures of the late 1960s and early 1970s.

145

Salsa, however, necessitates taking a partner into consideration. The majority of Montreal schools teach salsa strictly as a couple dance in which male and female dance patterns are distinct. Given contemporary mainstream popular dance, in which men and women move separately in a free-form style, the salsa subculture appears to be turning the clock back to a time when traditional relationships between men and women were embodied in the swirling patterns of ballroom dance. Salsa's joining of male and female into a couple creates masculine dominance, for the male always leads the dance.

The male domination entrenched within the couple dynamic of salsa prevents it from being embraced by critical research that envisions dance as a locus of empowerment for women. Dance has been heralded as a practice that enables women to assert their femininity and subvert, even if temporarily, the constraints of male domination. A recent body of literature arising from the intersection between dance studies and cultural studies looks at how the feminist ideal of women's emancipation can be located within certain dance traditions.

Salsa's incompatibility with this body of literature (see below) is rooted in its couple formation. The history of Western dance from the 1880s onward shows how the separation of coupled partners brought about increased freedom for both men and women on the dance floor. This rise in individuality eventually loosened the constraints of traditional gender roles. The link between individual expression on the dance floor and less conventional relationships between men and women is both historical and culturally based. However, the couple embrace in dance has also been revolutionary and scandalous in some historical and cultural contexts. Salsa dancing, particularly how it is promoted and taught in Montreal, is situated within recent theoretical understandings of dance and issues of gender. This dance is further positioned within the history of Western dance culture to illustrate how relationships between men and women that emerge in salsa hark back to a more traditional time. Drawing from ethnographic work, I have concluded that the male domination that characterizes how salsa is taught and promoted can be subverted but only to a limited extent. Salsa dancing's potential to subvert male control is explored in the following chapter. In salsa dance, the male dancer always leads the female. Because of this underlying male leadership, salsa is at odds with the dance cultures that feminist theorists have used to illustrate dance as a site of female autonomy. This masculine domination also contrasts with certain contemporary and past popular practices that stress women's independence on the dance floor.

When salsa dancing is part of a cultural heritage, the male and female roles are acquired informally through active participation and therefore become "naturalized." Individuals who grow up dancing to salsa do not consciously learn how to dance like a "man" or a "woman." Conversely, acquiring the dance outside a context in which it has developed requires formally learning the male and female roles. In most Montreal dance classes, this Latin dance is taught and performed primarily in pairs; gender patterns are explicitly taught in order to construct sexual differentiation. Male-female relationships are embodied within the couple arrangement, in which men and women perform prescribed and distinct movements. Most notably, male leading reinforces masculine domination and female subordination.

Moving to salsa rhythms without partners breaking physical contact is also the predominant style in Montreal clubs. When a couple performs salsa dance, male leadership is accented. Although salsa is sold and promoted as a continuously partnered style in Montreal, the dance allows separation between the sexes on the dance floor. In Cuba, for instance, the contemporary style allows for about 30 percent separation between the male and female dancers (Edie, 1999). Rita, one of Montreal's dance instructors who taught salsa dancing in the 1990s, reveals how dancing to salsa rhythms in Guatemala and Latin America does not necessarily entail the forming of couples. (As in the previous chapters, the names of interviewees are pseudonyms.) She states, "In Guatemala all my life I never thought it was important to dance with a partner. Of course, if you have a partner who dances well . . . it's a lot of fun to share. It has become the fashion here in Montreal for salsa to be a couple dance. . . . And when I arrived here [Montreal] I had my habits. I danced whenever I pleased. . . . In general, in Guatemala and lots of other South American countries, you dance alone—you dance for the pleasure of it."

Salsa dance classes are gendered spaces, with men and women usually divided into two groups to perform individual exercises before they are paired for couple practice. The actual movements of the dance are also codified as male or female: for instance, the man always starts the dance with his left foot, and the woman follows with the right. This gendered foot placement characterizes ballroom-influenced salsa more than salsa that has developed in the vernacular movement culture of salsa's numerous sites of origin. According to Ernesto, a dance teacher in Montreal, men and women who are born into a salsa culture dance with footwork rules that are less strict. Ernesto focuses less on partnering and more on how the total body moves in salsa and merengue. He insists that a man and woman can start with either foot, noting that their movements do not have to mirror each other's; the important aspect is that each dancer keeps the rhythm of the music. For the most part, however, gendered movement patterns are a trend that dominates the Montreal salsa scene.

Various corporeal arrangements produce the leading-following relation-ship in salsa. These patterns surface in diverse couple dances. Richard Dyer outlines, for instance, the leading and following patterns of paired dancing in musicals that include mirroring, mutual holding, dancing side by side, and re-lationships of dependency (Dyer, 1993: 53). These couple dynamics epito-mize how male and female dancers connect in Montreal salsa classes, in which the woman generally is taught to mirror the man's moves. The man initiates a step; the woman follows him. The woman never turns on her own but waits for the gestured signal from her male partner that she is to spin. The male dancer is responsible for twirling the female: a woman can never spin a man nor introduce a change in footwork that the man should mirror. In the basic salsa position, the couple appears to be mutually supporting each other, yet the male is still leading the dance. In this hold, the woman's right hand is in the man's left, her left hand is at his shoulder, and his right hand is at her waist (53). At times, the dancers open this grasp and move side by side. The closed hold may also be broken by dips, in which the male dancer sup-ports the female.

The guiding and leading role of the male salsa dancer is presented in di-verse ways in Montreal. Some instructors stress a heightened sense of male domination, an interpretation that assumes that the man is responsible for displaying the woman. Consequently, the male dancer is more concerned with turning and manipulating the female. Other teachers stress equal con-trol, with the two dancing more as one. The level of male domination and female subordination embodied in the dance depends on how salsa is inter-preted at the level of the body. Even though the man always guides, the dance allows the possibility of subverting the heightened sense of male dom-ination and female subordination that some of Montreal's dance teachers market and promote. In the following chapter, I show that dance theorist Ruud Vermay and some of Montreal's salsa instructors see the male dancer yielding to the female more than controlling and dominating her (Vermay, 1994: 154–55). Nonetheless, this subversion can never transgress male lead-ership in the dance since male leading is entrenched in the structure of this tradition and is an essential element of salsa when danced as a couple.

Both popular and performance dance have been proclaimed by feminist-influenced theorists as sites where women can resist stereotypical construc-tions of gendered relationships that place women in the subordinate posi-tion. Salsa dancing's reproduction of conventional gender differences at the level of movement renders this performance an unlikely site for the explo-ration of a feminist-based sense of resistance. Salsa appears to stand outside of the body of literature that reveals how dance can be a site of transgression for women. Angela McRobbie, for instance, sees the practice of women dancing alone in clubs as an act that defies the conventional male and female dynamic. The empowering potential of movement lies in the ways that dance is a sexual expression. When women move by themselves in clubs in order to experience physical sensuality as an autoerotic pleasure rather than for the goal of attracting men, their dancing challenges the stereotyped image of women as dependent on men for their fulfillment (McRobbie, 1984: 134). Expanding on McRobbie's conclusions on the political efficacy of club dancing for women, Leslie Gotfrit further elucidates how the male-dominated space of the club is transgressed when women dance alone in an alluring manner for their own enjoyment (Gotfrit, 1991: 186). Gotfrit describes a club in which women neither need to wait for men to ask them to dance, nor require a male partner to experience pleasure on the dance floor, nor yearn to meet a man to make their evening worthwhile. Maria Pini finds the form of sexuality that is embodied in rave dancing one of the transgressive elements of this culture. Looking specifically at how women experience raves, Pini concludes that the sexuality that emerges in this dancing does not have a clear sense of desire; ravers that Pini interviewed commonly described it as an "autoerotic" sensation (Pini, 1997: 119, 122). At a rave happening, which involves feelings of love produced by taking drugs such as Ecstasy and a high from dancing in a crowd, ravers exude a general sense of desire that dissolves sexual boundaries. According to Pini, the sexuality embodied in rave dancing promotes an alternative non-phallocentric representation of subjectivity. A common element unifies these authors' views of the emancipating potential of dance: they all see women as finding liberation on the dance floor by dancing alone and by redirecting their sexual desire away from the goal-oriented nature of heterosexual partnering.

The potential of performance dance to liberate women's bodies from constraining forces is also based on the abandonment of corporeal expressions that stress gender differentiation and heterosexual stereotypes in movement patterns. Modern dance developed partly as a reaction against the gendered relationships expressed in ballet (Copeland, 1997: 126). Classical ballet embodies male dominance and female subordination. When a man and woman dance together in classical ballet, the female body is transformed into a passive and ethereal spectacle that depends on the male dancer for physical support and direction. Every aspect of classical dance, such as the costumes, the movement vocabulary, the training, and the male and female partner formation in the pas de deux structure, convey this relationship between women and men as "natural" and "inborn" (Daly, 1997: 112). Ann Daly illustrates the powerless position of the female dancer and the controlling stance of the male in her description of Balanchine's choreography of *The Four Tempera-ments*: "Her partner is always the one who leads, initiates, maps out the ter-ritory, subsumes her space into his, and handles her waist, armpits and thighs. She never touches him in the same way: she does not initiate the moves" (Daly, 1987: 14). Ballet emphasizes sexual dimorphism. The male dancer's dominance over the female is emphasized by his larger size and a movement vocabulary of lifting and maneuvering the female. The male dancer's manip-ulating, guiding, and controlling stance imbues his gestures with strength and command (Novack, 1993: 43). Classical ballet conserves the gender stereo-types that stem from nineteenth-century sexual roles (43). Despite the in-credible vigor and muscularity required of a ballerina, the image of feminin-ity exemplified in classical ballet is one of fragility, sexual passivity, and an ethereal corporeality.

Early modern dancers of the 1900s, such as Isadora Duncan, Loie Fuller, and Ruth St. Denis, defied the image of womanhood that was, and continues to be, presented in classical ballet. Isadora Duncan particularly objected to the Victorian feminine ideal that was incarnated in ballet. Reacting against the embodiment of woman as frail and sexually passive, the early modern dancers created solo dances for themselves in which they projected a power-ful and self-reliant image of womanhood (Copeland, 1997: 127). The mod-ern dance movement liberated female bodies from the rigid and regulated movement vernacular of ballet and widened the terrain of female dance vo-cabulary (Dempster, 1998: 223). The founders of modern dance were prima-rily women (Copeland, 1997: 125). These dancers sought to reify a universal and natural portrayal of femininity in their choreographies (Cooper, 1997b: 139), a concept that took the form of the barefoot and uncorseted female body (31). A second generation of modern dancers, characterized by such women as Mary Wigman, Doris Humphrey, and Martha Graham, challenged how the human body is shaped, controlled, and supposedly improved through rigorous classical dance training. They provided a contrast to the highly stylized and artificial corporeal construction of ballet by creating a movement vocabulary that sought to conform to the natural movements of the female body and a primordial conception of femininity. Martha Graham's dances, for instance, project the inner being of womanhood, marked by pow-erful emotions and unconscious and libidinal forces (Dempster, 1998: 225). Although modern dancers resisted the oppressive ideology embodied in clas-sical ballet, they simultaneously reduced femininity to certain essential char-acteristics (Cooper, 1997b: 140). Their celebration of femininity as natural and emotional not only transformed it into fixed essences, but also reiterated patriarchal conceptions of the feminine (Dempster, 1998: 225). In other words, modern dance perpetuated another form of gender stereotyping.

The postmodern choreographies emerging in the 1960s defied both clas-sical and modern dance in their emphasis on a nonhierarchical and non-gendered utilization and structuring of the body, which endures in contem-porary postmodern dance (Dempster, 1998: 228). Postmodern pioneers such as Trisha Brown wanted to convey how their choreographies were products of women's minds and not simply an intuitive or instinctual extension of their bodies (Copeland, 1997: 133). This tradition focuses on gesticulation that stresses the material reality of the body itself. In the initial stage of post-modern dance, choreographers did not employ the body as a medium to rep-resent a perfected or ideal form of the inner consciousness. Postmodern training involves a period of detraining in which dancers unlearn their ha-bitual movement patterns (Dempster, 1998: 229). Consequently, the gen-dered corporealities that are taken as "natural" are deconstructed in the grounding of the postmodern dancer. Choreographer Yvonne Rainer, for in-stance, had her female dancers lift men as frequently as her male dancers hoisted women. Challenging one of the essential elements of gendered choreographic partnering (Copeland, 1997: 136) can question male-female relations that are taken as natural. In postmodern dance's rejection of gen-dered bodies, this dance tradition produces embodied images and kines-thetic experiences that consciously defy how the female body has been op-pressed by cultural ideologies.

According to Roger Copeland, feminism played a role in the emergence of both modern and postmodern dance. Modern dance expressed the femi-nist concerns of its era. Victorian puritanical ideas were linked to the repres-sion of women's bodies. The early modern dancers wanted to free women both physically and psychologically from these constraints (Copeland, 1997: 125). Postmodern dance grew out of the movement of radical feminists who viewed the sexual revolution of the 1960s and 1970s with skepticism, seeing it less as a liberation of women than as a means to make women more sexu-ally available to men. Early postmodern dance's abolishment of gender dif-ferences and voluptuous displays can be viewed as a rejection of the trans-formation of women's bodies into objects made accessible for male consumption (125).

Feminist interpretations of popular dance as a site of female transgression share a common thread with accounts of modern and postmodern dance as rooted in a desire for female liberation: for dance to be subversive, it must mark a break with conventional heterosexual partnering. The male leader-ship in salsa conflicts with configurations of dance as a privileged site for women to express their sexual equality and power. Salsa taught and promoted in Montreal both maintains gender differentiation and reinforces heterosex-ual partnering in dance. This dance creates divergent male and female roles within the couple dynamic—the sexy and submissive woman and the dominant and leading man—seemingly reinforcing culturally coded gender differences that feminists have long sought to deconstruct. Salsa's potential to be a subversive practice from a feminist perspective is certainly questionable.

The embodiment of male domination in salsa lies fundamentally in its couple formation. Since the beginning of the 1990s, there has been an increase in men leading women on the dance floor with the revival of swing, the popularity of salsa, and the growth of ballroom dancing (Thomas and Miller, 1997: 89). This burgeoning interest in couple dancing in contemporary Western societies announces a return to more conservative gender relationships in dance. Peter Buckman, for instance, suggests that part of the contemporary appeal of ballroom dancing lies in the strictly defined female and male roles of the dance (Buckman, 1978: 194). In their ethnographic work on ballroom dancing in London, England, Helen Thomas and Nicola Miller observe that gender relationships produced in the leading and following pattern echo a prefeminist era (Thomas and Miller, 1997: 95). Swing dancing's popularity as a youth movement relies partly on how the dance clearly distinguishes between the sexes (Friede, 1999: C4). As Berkeley Kaite says, "We still want boundaries and gender differences. We want to know who the boys are and who the girls are" (quoted in Friede, 1999: C4). The current revival of couple dancing is often understood in relationship to the "revolutionary" dance practices of the 1960s and 1970s. The break with the couple formation in Western social dance came about most effectively with the hippie movement of the 1970s. The freestyle dance mode of the time, in which both women and men did what they wanted, proclaimed an upheaval in gendered dance relationships that liberated the sexes from specific codes and patterns of behavior and allowed for complete corporal freedom between men and women (Polhemus, 1993: 12).

Although partner dancing is typically associated with restrictive male and female relationships, the couple formation is not inherently repressive. The gradual shift from couple to solo dancing in the twentieth century has been, nonetheless, associated with a heightened sense of individual freedom for both men and women on the dance floor. Partnering is often believed to thwart the full expression of dancers. However, the birth of closed-pair dancing in the West in the nineteenth century brought men and women physically closer, leading to less rigid and restricted relationships between the sexes. Couple dancing today is also believed to constrain male and female dancers by requiring that they conform to pre-established ritualized steps. Yet many of the couple dances of the nineteenth century broke away from the intricate and elaborate footwork of earlier dance styles that did not incorporate a closed embrace. The significance of the couple or solo framework greatly depends on the historical context in which each is practiced. Since salsa dancing in Montreal has arisen at a time when mainstream club dancing is mostly characterized by men and women moving independently outside of the couple formation, salsa appears in this context as a backward-looking tradition.

A history of Western popular dance illustrates how salsa recalls the past in its gendered patterns. Today the waltz appears to be a relic of a conservative past, yet when it appeared in the first half of the nineteenth century in the ballrooms of Western Europe, America, and Latin America, it was revolutionary (Franks, 1963: 133). Before the advent of the waltz, the ballrooms of England and America were ordered and artificial spaces (127). Ballroom etiquette in America demanded that the look, behavior, and dance practices of men and women be the same (Aldrich, 1991: 16). Nineteenth-century dances such as the cotillion and the quadrille reflected how the ballrooms were to establish social order and set standards of good behavior. Although both these dances involved couples dancing in a group formation, men and women simply held hands in an open hold. The eighteenth-century cotillion was derived from the eighteenth-century *contredanse*, which, as previously noted, was a French version of an English country dance that had been exported to France at the end of the seventeenth century (Franks, 1963: 140). The cotillion reached the United States in the middle of the eighteenth century and is an ancient precursor of modern square dancing. A modification of the *contredanse* was the quadrille, popular in the nineteenth century (140). Dance etiquette manuals of the day illustrate how the master of ceremonies in American ballrooms in the 1840s was responsible for calling out the figures of the dance, selecting the couples, and maintaining order (Aldrich, 1991: 17). The quadrille and the cotillion enabled ballroom participants to choose their dancing partners in a manner that maintained a class hierarchy. For example, an American dance manual from 1880, *Manners and Tone of Good Society*, depicts how representatives of each class would ensure that persons of different social strata were not positioned in front of each other or within the same square (Aldrich, 1991: 18). Both the cotillion and the quadrille required meticulous learning, as they involved intricate steps and sequences with a wide range of technical difficulty (Franks, 1963: 16).

The waltz marked the first time that men and women danced face-to-face in a close hold. Because of this embrace, and the rapid turning movements of the dance, the waltz was decried as a sinful and vulgar practice that would corrupt the moral sensibilities of respectable women (Franks, 1963: 129; Stephenson and Iaccarino, 1980: 14). This hold, now known as the social dance position, has exerted an influence on couple dancing since the onset of the waltz (Franks, 1963: 133). The gendered embrace of the waltz was transgressive, as it brought men and women closer, resulting in more familiar and less formal relationships between the sexes. Of course, the physical contact in the waltz was tame by today's standards: couples had to be separated enough that daylight could shine between them. Not until the beginning of the twentieth century could couples dancing variations of the "original" waltz actually come into close bodily contact (130).

The intimacy between men and women created in the waltz rendered it transgressive. The close embrace of the couple also altered the role of the male and female dancers within this paired intimacy. The waltz marks the introduction of the male lead in the world of aristocratic European dance. The man guides the turns and figures of the dance while the woman follows, surrendering completely to her partner's direction. This male lead had not been a part of the choreographies of previous forms, in which men and women who danced either independently or together moved in accordance to preordained patterns and steps (Chasteen, 2004: 124–25). This new relation between the male and female dancer needed to be outlined in manuals for those who wanted to become adept at closed-couple partnering. John Charles Chasteen provides the following example from a nineteenth-century dance manual: "The lady should allow herself to be entirely guided by her partner, without in any case endeavouring to follow her own impulse of action" (DeGarmo, 1875: 66, quoted in Chasteen, 2004: 235).

The waltz further revolutionized dance practices by breaking rules of social intercourse. Unlike previous dances, the waltz did not maintain the order of the group by ensuring that the class hierarchy was reproduced in the structure of the waltz (Aldrich, 1991: 18). Dancing masters also opposed the waltz because, like other round dances, such as the galop and the polka, it did not require considerable instruction and practice but could be learned by observation (Stephenson and Iaccarino, 1980: 14; Franks, 1963: 156). Prior to the emergence of the waltz, dance instruction taught not only the footwork but also an entire array of manners that were part of a given style (Franks, 1963: 157). Compared to such structured dances of the day as the cotillion and quadrille, the waltz appeared to be a more "natural" and "spontaneous" performance. Although the accessibility of the waltz and other round dances revolutionized dance by unleashing it from fixed rules and contrived manners, dancing masters such as Allen Dodworth hastened to codify the steps, creating correct and incorrect movements, in order to ensure "decorum, propriety and good taste" on the dance floor (Buckman, 1978: 118). Today the waltz is believed to be the quintessential couple dance in that its fixed and prescribed steps create more rigid and constrained relationships between the individual couples and the dancers in general. Nonetheless, in its day, the waltz broke barriers between the sexes and classes and heralded a more spontaneous way of dancing in Western European, American, and Latin American ballrooms.

With the advent of the waltz came other round dances that further transformed the ordered and structured atmosphere of the ballroom. The polka, which originated in Bohemia and became the rage in France, aroused more criticism than the waltz. This dance, which involved a close hold, first appeared in the United States in 1844 (Buckman, 1978: 144). At the end of the nineteenth century, dancing started to take place in dance halls geared toward a wider public than that found in the assemblies and ballrooms, which catered to the upper echelons of society. As dance become more democratic, society balls retreated to the private realms of mansions and country houses (150). Barn dances, which were popular at the end of the nineteenth century, stand as an example of the increasing spread of popular dance practices throughout all levels of society, except for the very top (151).

One of the changes that marked twentieth-century couple dances was a turning away from set steps and patterns in favor of more natural movements. An American couple dance called the Boston opened the way for a less artificial way of moving. The Boston was danced without the turned-out-feet position that had characterized social dance until its arrival in Britain in 1903. Prior to the Boston, the five turned-out positions that comprise essential elements in ballet were also the basic postures of social dance (Franks, 1963: 163). The Boston also redirected the emphasis in dance from a performance structured by a set time and tempo to an interpretation of the music on the dance floor (165).

This increased sense of individual expression on the dance floor can be partly attributed to the burgeoning influence of black music and dance on white middle-class American popular culture, which began in the 1880s with the birth of ragtime. According to Lewis Erenberg, the more natural shuffle walk that was appearing in popular American dances came from black styles. With the borrowing of more natural footwork, the emphasis on patterned feet movement, an integral part of the European-derived tradition, gave way to an increased emphasis on body movement (Erenberg, 1981: 151). A notable dance of the era, the cakewalk, broke up the turns and glides that were essential characteristics of almost every one of the dances that had come before (Buckman, 1978: 162). The cakewalk combined serious processional steps with exuberant jumps and led the way for a string of novelty dances that would mark the decades to come. The ragtime era created such "animal" dances as the crab, the kangaroo, and the horse trot. Although American blacks performed an array of animal dances that were more improvisational than those popularized in mainstream society, the animal variations that were adopted by white society had to be taught. Ragtime dances were less codified and regulated by strict rules than were previous dance forms, but there was still a "right" and "wrong" way to move the body (166). The black American animal dances that did not cross over in a "tame" form into main-stream society involved grinding the hips, and their names—the funky butt, the itch, and the grind—verbally captured the movement of the pelvis. Consequently, the Dancing Teachers Association of America refused to teach the syncopated ragtime dances, while other teachers and organizations altered them so that they were "decent" for mainstream white society. Vernon and Irene Castle, the famous husband and wife teachers who made their debut in 1911, reinterpreted these new trends in terms of the rules of good taste so that they could be deemed acceptable. The Imperial Society of Teachers of Dancing in London smoothed out the jerky movements, hops, and kicks of the 1914 American fox trot, laying the basis for the English fox trot (167).

In the 1920s it became unimportant that dancers remain with the same partners throughout the duration of a dance number. It was possible for dancers to "cut in" or change partners in the middle of such styles as the charleston, black bottom, and shimmy. According to Peter Buckman, this break with the rigid hold of the "closed-couple" stance—a hold that had begun with the waltz—allowed women to enjoy the same freedom as men on the dance floor at the level of expressive movement. The charleston, which originated with black dockworkers in South Carolina, was eventually also modified for mainstream acceptance. Although the dances of the 1920s were still performed in couples, these forms allowed individuals to enjoy the pleasure of movement without being completely dependent on a partner (Buckman, 1978: 182).

The styles of the 1930s further enhanced individual expression on the dance floor. The exuberant dance performed to swing music, known as the lindy, or jitterbug, was all the rage by 1936, especially among young people. This style introduced two innovations into couple dancing, which although novel at the time, had existed centuries before. While dancing the lindy/jitterbug, the individual dancers, particularly the male dancer, could break away from the couple and dance a solo. Black dancers had inserted an improvisational break into dances in the 1920s, but the "breakaway" became popular in mainstream dance styles with the swing era (Malone, 1996: 231). The breakaway, which had existed in Western social dancing before the seventeenth century, had been completely displaced by the "closed" position of the waltz and other round dances (Buckman, 1978: 189). The other novel feature of the lindy/jitterbug was the "air step," in which dancers literally took off from the floor. This dance move had not existed in Western dance since a sixteenth-century dance called *la volta* (189).

The solo breaks and partner changes in the dances of the 1920s and 1930s increased casualness between the male and female dancers. The strict code that women always followed men on the dance floor was interrupted by improvisational solo breaks. This departure from the continuous closed-couple position allowed dancers of both sexes more freedom by encouraging individual displays even though the popular tradition was couple dance. In particular, the lindy/jitterbug, which is essentially a partner dance, allowed room for individual expression. Both Peter Buckman and Jacqui Malone associate the insertion of a solo dance with a rise in individual freedom (Buckman, 1978: 192; Malone, 1996: 231). From today's perspective, the lindy/jitterbug would be viewed as a couple dance, yet the swing dances signaled an increase in individual expression on the dance floors. However, there was a backlash against the frenetic dances of the 1920s and 1930s. According to Peter Buckman, in 1924 the Imperial Society of Teachers of Dancing standardized dances such as the waltz and fox trot to resist what they considered the anarchic behavior of young people on the dance floor (Buckman, 1978: 194). The popularity of ballroom dancing, which began in the 1930s and continues today, could partly be attributed to a desire to return to well-defined gender roles, in which the male leads the female through the dance (194).

The informality and autonomy that both men and women experienced with the lindy/jitterbug anticipated the even greater liberation that dancers would enjoy with the advent of jive and rock dances of the 1950s and 1960s. Prior to the rock of the 1950s, American popular dance had been marked by a series of novelty genres, many of which were Latin American. Some of these dances were the samba, introduced in 1939, and the mambo, the chacha, and the merengue, of the mid-1950s. Although these styles were commonly danced with a partner, the chacha, for instance, was a couple dance in which contact between partners was infrequent. Both dancers could take pleasure in movements of the chacha on their own (Buckman, 1978: 199–200). In the 1950s, rock styles burst out of the couple formation by emphasizing movement as a group rather than dancing with a particular person (212). Rock and roll dance, which stemmed from the complex and intricate forms of the swing era, combined improvisation and prescribed steps that were continuously evolving. One of the group dances of this era was the madison, which was performed in a line. In other styles of this era, such as the jet, the locomotion, and the choochoo, individuals danced in gangs (213).

The twist of the 1960s is often believed to be the dance that most strikingly characterizes the move away from the fixed patterns of couple dancing to individual expression. According to Jim Dawson, the twist marks the first break with the patterns of leading and following that had characterized American dance (Dawson, 1995: xiii). Don McDonagh asserts that the twist represents the first time since the charleston that dancers could perform with a partner while being completely independent of one another. Couples dancing the twist neither touch nor rely on each other to complement their individual steps (McDonagh, 1979: 94). According to Buckman, however, the twist was not the first individual style; most of the dances of the rock era that preceded it were individual genres (Buckman, 1978: 217). The hip-swivelling motion of the twist produced copycat dances such as the shake, the hitchhike, the monkey, the swim, and the skate (217). During the 1960s, the smooth ballroom couple dances, such as the waltz, fox trot, rumba, and samba, almost disappeared (McDonagh, 1979: 95). The individual expression and hip movement of the twist as well as its mimics are heralded with liberating dancers, specifically white Americans, from the bodily restraint that characterizes so many European-derived dances (Dawson, 1995: xii).

By the late 1960s, rhythmic movements of the body had completely replaced fixed and preordained steps. Dances stopped being named, and the continuous series of dance crazes that had proliferated in American popular culture ended. Soul music, for instance, which became popular during this period, had very few distinct dances. Dance styles of the late 1960s are characterized by the wild and loose expressions of go-go dancers and by the freeform bodily movements of the hippies (Straw, 2001: 164). At Woodstock in 1969, people danced without a floor, partners, or prescribed steps (McDonagh, 1979: 103). In hippie dancing, the man neither asks the woman to dance nor controls the rhythm and pace of the movements. According to Ted Polhemus, hippie dance culture revolutionized gender equality on the dance floor (Polhemus, 1993: 12).

Men and women returned to couple dancing with the disco craze of the 1970s. Disco brought back the "social dance position," the closed hold that characterizes ballroom dance, as well as fixed dance steps. Moving to disco music entailed once more that the man lead and the woman follow. This reprise of couple dancing is often viewed as a conservative impulse: according to Will Straw, all the facets of disco club culture—such as the prescribed steps and stylized figures of the dances, the dressy outfits, and the orchestrated music—echoed, for many, the nightlife of the cabarets and supper clubs of the 1930s and 1940s (Straw, 2001: 167). Ted Polhemus laments that disco reintroduced male domination to the dance floor; the man asks the woman to dance and controls the style and pace of the disco moves (Polhe-mus, 1993: 178). Not all styles, however, involved continuous dancing in the closed couple position. The hustle, for instance, allowed for some solo breaks (McDonagh, 1979: 112). Although disco meant conforming to certain rules and regulations that confined the practices of individuals within boundaries, at the same time, the heterogeneous nature of the disco clubs broke down some barriers. These clubs brought together individuals from diverse social backgrounds and lifestyles, such as suburban heterosexuals, inner-city homo-sexuals, and young black urban professionals (Straw, 2001: 167). Perhaps be-cause disco allowed actual physical contact at a time when contact dancing was virtually extinct, the coupling on the dance floor incited the mixing of diverse groups in clubs.

Rock and punk fans of the late 1970s decried disco music and dancing. Couple dancing certainly did not have a place in these two musical cultures. Punk dancing, for instance, had virtually no touching on the dance floor. One dance, the pose, at times allowed two people to move together in a man-ner resembling couple dancing but was more often performed by same sex partners without physical contact. One participant assumed the pose of a fashion model while the other crouched as if to take a photograph (Hebdige, 1979: 108-9). The pose was more a parody of paired dancing. Punk dancing generally defies the commonly held view that dance is a social activity serv-ing as a courtship ritual in heterosexual romance.

Since the early 1980s, a proliferation of dance music styles have even stemmed from those musical cultures that traditionally disdained dance mu-sic. Punk branched into various forms that had danceable styles, such as syn-thesizer pop and a revival of ska music. Even though rock fans of the 1970s vehemently distinguished rock from dance music, by the beginning of the 1980s a marriage between rock and dance had occurred, resulting in the emergence of "Dance-Oriented Rock" (Straw, 2001: 170). Disco supposedly died in 1979, and the dance club clientele splintered off into various musical cultures, such as the Hi-NRG sound of gay dance clubs, electro-funk, British synth pop, Eurodisco, and rap (170). The style in these clubs was individual free-form expression. While disco had brought together people of diverse racial groups, sexual orientations, and classes, the fans of the various musical styles of the early 1980s were stratified. During this period, various African American styles, such as rap and hip-hop, became associated with black American culture. Hip-hop has more stylized and ritualized patterns than the free-form expression of the white dance culture but is still a solo bodily per-formance. The dancing that occurred in rock clubs in the 1980s contrasts with couple dancing as well as with the elaborate and exuberant steps and figures of disco dancing. Controlled movements and an unspoken rule of no physical contact between the dancers characterized rock dancing (171). House music's arrival on the dance music scene in the mid-1980s laid the foundation for the widespread dance movement of rave culture (171). Rave, which started as a massive dance culture in Britain, did not become popular in North America until 1992 or 1993 (173–74). Rave dancing is characterized by free-form individual expression.

As already noted, since the mid-1980s salsa dancing has become popular in the dance music scene in Montreal and elsewhere in Canada as well as in cities in the United States, Australia, and Europe. Given that Latinos will be the largest minority group in the United States in the twenty-first century (Mendieta, 2000: 45), interest in Latin music should continue to grow. Salsa dancing and Latin clubs diverge greatly from the dance music scene that has developed in North America since the 1980s. Since couple dancing predominates in salsa clubs, this practice appears outdated compared to the free-form dance styles that have characterized dance clubs since the beginning of the 1980s. At the same time, salsa clubs are reminiscent of the disco era, when diverse groups of people came together on the dance floor. As previously noted, the clientele of Latin clubs in Montreal comprise immigrants of both Latin and non-Latin descent as well as Canadian-born individuals from diverse ethnic backgrounds. Salsa clubs cross the barriers of ethnicity, race, and class but not of sexual orientation: these Latin clubs are definite heterosexual spaces. Although salsa clubs may appear conservative because they emphasize couple dancing in which the female follows the male lead, they are also transgressive, as they permit diverse groups to mix.

The intimacy that couples enjoy on salsa club dance floors gives the dance its supposedly "exotic" flavor. Although salsa is often considered a foreign Latin Caribbean expression, the coupling structure of today's salsa stems from European dance influences within the Caribbean. The Cuban dances that developed with the Spanish settlement of Cuba beginning in 1509 were variations from Andalucia and the Canary Islands (Daniel, 1995: 32). The sixteenth- and seventeenth-century forms known as the *chaconas* and *zarabandas* were sensual styles that nonetheless maintained separation between men and women. Dancing without touch stems from the African influence in Cuba: the African tradition permitted the male to enact a pursuit of the female and allowed them brief moments of closeness, but it did not involve holding each other or moving together in a closed position (33). According to Léopald Sédar Senghor, "The African dance disdains bodily contact" (Senghor, 1956: 33, quoted in Stearns and Stearns, 1968: 12). At this time, African dance mores considered couple dancing unacceptable: the separation of men and women was an African element in these dances that came from both Africa and Spain. As previously noted, before coming to the Americas, the Spanish culture mixed with North African culture; Spanish music and dance had already incorporated African aspects (Daniel, 1995: 32).

Partner dancing in Cuba, the birthplace of contemporary salsa, derived from European set dances. As previously mentioned, to escape the 1791 slave rebellion in Haiti, French colonial families from Haiti and their slaves fled to Cuba at the end of the eighteenth century, taking with them the *contredanse*, which became known as the *contradanza* (Daniel, 1995: 38). The *contredanse* was not a closed-couple dance but did allow for men and women to hold one another. According to Daniel, "The *contradanza*, like the minuet and quadrille, used passing and turning formulas that led couples in line and circle formations, usually with bows and greetings" (38). In the middle of the nineteenth century, the Cuban culture incorporated other European dances, such as the quadrille and the lancer (Szwed and Marks, 1988: 31). Eventually, the European *contredanse* and its Cuban version, the *contradanza*, along with the other European styles evolved into a creolized dance: the *danza*, which emerged in the mid-1800s (31). The *danza* marks the first time in the salons and ballrooms of Cuba that couples danced in the closed social dance position (Balbuena, 2003: 28). The *danza*, therefore, enabled couples to touch throughout the dance and to employ individual couple floor patterns (Daniel, 1995: 38). The change in choreography in Cuban dance was a result of the widespread influence of the waltz, which brought the dancing couple in nineteenth-century Europe, America, and the New World together in a close embrace. In its incorporation of a hip accentuation triggered by a gliding or sliding step, the *danza* differed from other European couple dances such as the waltz and the polka (39). A slower and subtler version of the *danza* was the *danzón*, also a couple dance enjoyed by the upper strata of society in nineteenth-century salons.

In the middle of the nineteenth century, the *son* developed from an originally rural dance that incorporated styles of the urban salons. The *son* combined the vigor and ardor of Cuban rural workers with the sensuality, intimacy, grace, and rhythm of the salons (Daniel, 1995: 40). At the beginning of the twentieth century, the *son* opened the close partnering of the previous ball and salon dances and allowed couples to alternate between the closed social dance position and the independent but still closely connected partnering. What is known as salsa today, as previously noted, has its roots in *son* music and dance. According to Yvonne Daniel, such twentieth-century dances as the mambo, *chachachá*, and *casino* are derived from the *son*. John F. Szwed and Morton Marks claim that a mambo section was added to the *danzón*, and since the *chachachá* was born from the mambo, they argue that both the mambo and *chachachá* have roots going back to the *contradanza* variations, which stem from the European set dance, the *contredanse*. Szwed and Marks reveal how the *danzón*, a derivative of the *contradanza*, intersects with the *son* dance and music complex (Szwed and Marks, 1988: 30–31). Contemporary salsa has consequently developed from various Cuban traditions whose partnering arrangement is traceable to the European presence in Cuba.

In Montreal, salsa is often framed as an exotic dance practice; its couple formation and prescribed steps give it a foreign veneer. Nonetheless, these elements stem from nineteenth-century European culture that influenced the Caribbean. With the male leading the dance, salsa reawakens relationships between men and women that hark back to prefeminist times. In Montreal, salsa is primarily taught and danced as a couple dance. In cities in Europe, Australia, and North America where salsa is popular it is generally also promoted as a couple dance. This insistence on heterosexual partnering goes against the historical tide of Western popular dance, in which the partner structure slowly gave way to individual free-form expression, allowing both men and women the autonomy to enjoy the pleasure of dancing on their own. Salsa's emphasis on male leadership in the dance keeps the practice firmly anchored to gender relationships in which women are dependent on men and in which men are responsible for women. Salsa dancing cannot be easily configured within feminist perspectives on dance as a site of liberation for women. The Latin tradition appears outdated in these terms. Nonetheless, salsa is progressive in its potential to create multicultural connections. As previously illustrated, the contact element of this dance allows individuals from various cultural and ethnic backgrounds to mingle in the city's schools and clubs. Although after the 1980s many music and dance subcultures became stratified along lines of race and ethnicity, salsa in Montreal embraces people from a wide spectrum of backgrounds.

CHAPTER FIVE

~

Commodifying the Gendered Embrace

It is not surprising that the 1980s revival of couple dancing has emerged in the "foreign" Latin dances of salsa, merengue, *bachata,* and tango as well as in trends such as ballroom and swing that echo past eras. These styles incorporate a male-female dynamic that is considered outmoded: it is the responsibility of the male to lead his female partner through the steps, dips, and whirls of these dances. Throughout my ethnographic work in Montreal's clubs and schools, I was constantly struck by the masculine domination that is reproduced through the movements of salsa and in the scene as a whole. Montrealers of both Latin and non-Latin descent with whom I spoke in either formal interviews or informal discussions often criticized salsa and the world that surrounds it for being sexist and macho. Indeed, machismo is rooted in salsa. The image of the violent gangster and narcissistic dandy depicted in the lyrics of such songwriters as Willie Colón and Reuben Blades in the late 1960s and 1970s perpetuated the tradition of machismo, which José Arteaga Rodríguez (1988) claims can be found in old Cuban songs (Manuel, 1998: 38). However, configuring salsa simply as part of machismo culture does not address the complexity of this dance at the level of movement. Reducing the salsa world to a male-dominated sphere homogenizes the diversity of individuals involved in creating this scene. Salsa instructors present the male and female relationship in the dance in diverse ways. How dancers express the steps, turns, and stylized figures of salsa with their bodies has the potential to both maintain and subvert masculine dominance. The masculine leadership in the different dance styles that are taught is revealed as the dance is performed and also in how salsa schools and instructors market the dance as a cultural commodity.

The unequal relationship between the male and female dancers in the salsa coupling incarnates gender dynamics that stand apart from the wider social context. Since the Quiet Revolution in Quebec, which lasted from 1960 to 1966, the province has sought, in both legislation and practice, equality between men and women. Women may "submissively" follow the male dancer's lead in salsa, but they also direct the production and distribution of the dance in the city. At the same time that many instructors promote salsa as a dance privileging masculine authority, female instructors take a leading role in teaching and promoting salsa in Montreal. The salsa dance scene mainly comprises male instructors who have immigrated to Montreal from Latin American and Caribbean nations and female instructors raised in Quebec or, to a lesser degree, in other parts of Canada. The females who lead the salsa dance lessons have not immigrated to Canada from Latin nations. Women immigrants of Latin American and Caribbean descent do not have a prominent place within the salsa teaching scene. Therefore, much depends on perspective: male domination is reinforced and maintained within the dance itself, yet the teaching and promotion of salsa is under a considerable amount of female leadership. The production of the dance is accompanied by perhaps another form of control: the possible exclusion of immigrant women of Latin descent from active roles in teaching and promotion. This topic is explored in relationship to literature that addresses how gender affects these women and the history of women in Quebec. The intricacies of gender roles play out both in the dance and in its role as a commodity that is promoted, bought, and sold.

My participant observation in Montreal dance schools and clubs and my in-depth interviews with salsa instructors revealed several ways that male and female partnering in salsa is conceptualized and reproduced at the level of movement. The constructions of "masculinity" and "femininity" in dance can be understood from various perspectives. Although the fact that men lead in salsa remains an unchanging characteristic of this dance, how salsa produces male and female identities does not correspond to fixed essences. Consequently, the subversive potential of salsa dancing in Montreal lies in how different modes of masculinity and femininity are both produced and promoted by teachers in order to sell the dance. Most teachers do not consciously try to subvert cultural constructions of gender by demonstrating how identity is artificially fashioned. Nonetheless, through their teaching and promotion of gender identity as a performance, salsa dancers in Montreal inadvertently show that sexual identities are cultural constructions. The following statement by Janet Wolff about the transgressive potential of post-modern dance is applicable, albeit to a limited extent, to the creation of gender relationships in the production of salsa in Montreal: "What this means is that dance can only be subversive when it questions and exposes the construction of the body in culture" (Wolff, 1997: 96). The teaching of male and female identities in salsa dance classes shows how gender identities are contrived, but unlike the intellectual focus of postmodern dance, most salsa instructors are not interested in objections to stereotyped gender fabrications in their classes. My concern with uncovering and analyzing asymmetrical relationships between men and women in salsa did not seem to be of primary interest to most salsa club goers. This issue brings to mind a comment made by Helen Thomas and Nicola Miller regarding their ethnographic work on ballroom dancing and the issue of gender relationships in the dance. Remarking that one of the women interviewed was unperturbed by the different roles that women and men had in ballroom dance, they write, "It is clear, however, that it is *we* rather than she who are concerned about the relative importance of the man and woman who form the couple" (Thomas and Miller, 1997: 107).

Most people view the leading and following in salsa as simply part of the rules of the dance. They are dispassionate about the male domination and female submissiveness that they recreate as they perform steps and turns. Nonetheless, salsa dance provides a concrete example of how gender identities can be formed and fashioned and how, through repeated performance, they can pass for "natural" differences between men and women. The footwork, stylized figures, and bodily gestures in Montreal salsa classes are taught as those of a man or a woman. These gendered patterns are reiterated and practiced to such an extent that they become automatic and may ultimately be experienced by the dancers themselves and those observing their movements as "natural" corporeal expressions. This exploration of the production of the gendered body in salsa dancing draws on a feminist postmodern perspective that posits embodiment not as a fixed and natural given but as a construction that is continuously open to flux and therefore a site of possibility (Shildrick and Price, 1999: 2). Feminist postmodernism's involvement with issues of the body differs from the two predominant ways that corporeality has been configured within feminism since the beginning of the movement. As woman's supposedly "inferior" status has been linked to her body, a great deal of early feminist thought rejected the importance of the female body and focused instead on intellectual pursuits. Recently, however, contemporary feminists such as Luce Irigaray have recovered the body as the substance of what comprises being female (3). Concern with how the physicality of the body is mediated by context, such that the body's materiality is never fixed and solid but always multiple and fluid, appears in the writings of such theorists as Elizabeth Grosz and Judith Butler. The importance that feminist postmodern writers give to corporeal concerns developed partly as a reaction to the philosophies of poststructuralism and postmodernism, which have been criticized for a masculinist bias in their indifference to concerns of materiality (6).

Judith Butler's theory of performance might address the process by which gendered moves are repeated by men and women in dance classes in order to create the "male" and "female" dancers. Butler elucidates how performances of the body enacted through repeated corporeal acts and gestures produce distinct sexes, which by virtue of reiteration create identities that can be both fixed and fluid (Butler, 1990). Her work echoes Michel Foucault's concept of the ways that various practices discipline the body and, in turn, produce bodies. According to Foucault, forms of sexuality that did not conform to the "economy of reproduction" were cast out as early as 1877 and considered perverse and unnatural (Foucault, 1978: 154). The division of sexuality into two discrete and unified categories conceals the power structure of the "economy of reproduction." Foucault states that "the notion of 'sex' made it possible to group together, in an artificial unity, anatomical elements, biological functions, conducts, sensations, and pleasures and it enabled one to make use of this fictitious unity as a causal principle" (154). Adapting Michel Foucault's theory, Judith Butler claims that the performance of masculinity and femininity, which is considered natural, conforms to the dictates of heterosexual hegemony or compulsory heterosexuality, a term first coined by Adrienne Rich. The system of compulsory heterosexuality is both produced and kept hidden through the creation of bodies as distinct sexes with "natural" demeanors and "natural" heterosexual habits and temperaments (Butler, 1988: 524).

The ideas of postmodern feminists such as Judith Butler intersect with the theoretical perspectives of Foucault in that power is viewed as a productive force that operates at the microlevel in everyday practice. In the *History of Sexuality* (1978) Foucault illustrates that strategies to repress sexual expression took the form of prohibition, censorship, and nonrecognition. Rather than controlling sexuality, these approaches produced new discourses on sexuality by men of authority, which in turn gave rise to new forms of oppression (Cousins and Hursain, 1984: 204–7). Discourses that outlined permitted and forbidden sexual expression produced the "deviant," "homosexual," and "normal" adult (207).

Power is at work in the creation of distinct gender identities. Butler's understanding of the construction of gender as a stylized repetition of acts is vividly demonstrated by the fact that salsa's male and female movements are learned through the repeated practice of contrived dance moves. Gender is brought into being through the stylization of the body and consequently must be comprehended as the manner in which varied corporeal gestures, movements, and performances institute the deceptive appearance of a conforming gendered identity (Butler, 1988: 270). Gender is not a fact that refers either to an actual essence or to an ideal. Rather, the repeated corporealities that constitute gender itself create the notion of gender; without these performances there would not be gender (273). As Judith Butler states, "Gender is, thus, a construction that regularly conceals its genesis" (273). The unvoiced consensus to enact, institute, and maintain separate and binary genders as "cultural fictions" is shrouded by the very credibility of this consensus, which does not acknowledge the fabrication of gendered distinctions (273). Gender, therefore, is neither a fixed identity nor a source of agency creating specific acts but an identity that is historically constituted (273). Butler adopts Simone de Beauvoir's distinction between sex as a biological "facticity" and gender as the cultural understanding or significance of that "facticity" (273). To be female is to become a woman and to force the body to abide by a historical idea of what constitutes "womanhood" (273). Butler believes that the body becomes its gender through a succession of acts, which are renewed, reworked, and reinforced through time. Nevertheless, the body is not merely a passive recipient of its identity. Sexual identities are neither completely determined nor arbitrary but function within the polarities of determination and free will. When men and women perform their sex according to heterosexual criteria of natural and ideal sexual behavior and through adherence to gender norms, each individual is participating in the production of sexual stereotypes (Butler, 1990: 136). Because identity is constructed through the stylized repetition of acts, Butler claims that the performative nature of identity bears the seeds of subversion of heterosexual conformity, for it is possible to perform one's identity differently within this framework of gender construction (142–49).

Although Butler deals exclusively with how identity continuously shifts, she does not address how the body assumes, creates, and negotiates the potential instability of gender (Cooper, 1997a: 10). Notions of cultural construction such as Butler's theory do not take into account the materiality of the body in the embodiment of gender identity. Cultural construction often assumes that the corporeal is a tabula rasa whose image is fashioned and formed by society's conceptions: it does not address the body's physical involvement with the world. A clear division between somatic identity and cultural identity cannot be cleanly forged. Cultural identity may not be exactly the same as somatic identity, but as Ann Cooper Albright states, "Yet neither is a somatic identity any more 'real' or essential than a social one simply because it is anchored in the body" (12). Both cultural and somatic identities are intertwined through the process of what is known as experience. In dance both these cultural and somatic spheres are interconnected (12). This analysis of how students assume their gender identities in dance and how teachers promote them illustrates how gender distinctions are mapped onto the dancing body to the extent that the dancer's materiality itself is merely a passive recipient of a cultural hegemony that supports male domination and female subordination. At the same time, how the dancing body negotiates and produces these patterns can alter the meanings and cultural identities that are produced. Dancers physically incarnate salsa in corporeal movement, affecting how bodies create dominant and submissive moves. The teaching of masculine and feminine movements is an aspect of salsa dance that is bought and sold. How these identities become a part of the market economy must be viewed through the filter of salsa as a cultural commodity in Montreal. The ethnographic account of how gender identities are construed, contested, and negotiated in Montreal salsa dance schools reveals the interplay between the materiality of the body and cultural notions of gendered identity in the concrete site of experience.

Before requesting an interview with an instructor of dance lessons at a studio or Latin club, I took at least one salsa course with the instructor, which consisted of eight to twelve ninety-minute sessions. Although I informed the instructor that I was researching salsa dancing early in my participant observation, I waited until after the course had ended before scheduling an interview. I chose this method so that I could observe the male and female dynamic being established in each class. Since I had already been exposed to the teaching methodology and gender relationships promoted at the school prior to conducting interviews, I was better able to interpret answers and comments made by my interviewees. I attended classes and conducted interviews for four consecutives summers (May to September) from 1996 to 2000. I interviewed twelve dance teachers: seven men and five women. My analysis is also informed by participant observation in the city's dance clubs and by numerous interviews with individuals involved in the Montreal salsa scene, such as community radio disk jockeys, club disk jockeys, music promoters, musicians, and club owners.

This ethnographic work reveals two predominant ways to frame the relationships between men and women that arise through the leading and following arrangement within salsa. Both the man and the woman can find fulfillment on the dance floor by moving together as one, which mediates the predominant position of the male dancer, or they can jointly yield to masculine dominance, sharing in the enjoyment of this power dynamic. The two models of heterosexuality that Richard Dyer identifies in the couple dances of the musical are analogous to the two prevailing ways that Montreal dance teachers interpret gender differences in salsa. He cites the "Jane Austen model," in which male and female partners achieve equality and joy in dance through the blend of their opposite roles. On the other hand, the pleasure that dancers experience in what Dyer refers to as the "Barbara Cartland model" lies in the performance of inequality. The woman revels in her relinquishment of power to the male dancer, who in turn luxuriates in his mastery over her (Dyer, 1993: 49). This link between couple dances performed in musical films and popular salsa dance practices is apparent since the prevalence of couple dancing in musicals, rather than group choreography, helped to develop and maintain the popularity of social dancing (Straw, 2001: 162).

The majority of salsa teachers in Montreal do not present the relationship between men and women as a power play in which the female surrenders to male control. The main proponents of this view of gender relationships in salsa are Paolo of Caribe and Marcus of Exclusive Salsa. However, Caribe's interpretation of salsa as a play of forces makes it a prevailing conception, even though only a minority of dance schools maintain it. As one of the city's largest Latin dance schools, Caribe[1] has influenced attitudes about what constitutes salsa dancing. In these two schools, the leading capacity of the male salsa dancer is not confined to the structure of the dance: male leadership also underlies how salsa is taught. Both schools stress teaching men how to guide but do not emphasize how women should respond to the lead in order to make the leading and following pattern successful. During two sessions of salsa lessons at both schools, I was never explicitly taught how to follow. At Exclusive Salsa, Marcus was my instructor; at Caribe, Nancy and Richard were my teachers. According to Paolo, he trained both these instructors. The leading and following dynamic of the dance involves the man applying a light pressure that communicates to the woman which direction to take. The woman can respond to the male lead only if she holds her body and arms in a way that allows her to slightly resist the pressure that she feels when she is being guided; however, this resistance is not overtly taught. During my classes at Caribe, I asked the instructor, Richard, several times to explain how I should react to the male lead. He answered, quite simply, that I would just feel his lead. Consequently, the following by the female is taken as a "natural" given: it needs to be neither taught nor learned. By virtue of being female, a woman is supposed to automatically understand her following role in the dance.

Because of this male leadership, both Marcus and Paolo believe that men should teach salsa. Marcus argues that a woman cannot teach salsa at all because the male assistant required for her to demonstrate the couple formation of the dance will find himself in a contradictory position: he will guide the dance because he is male and, at the same time, be led because the female instructor is in charge of the class. Paolo is of the opinion that only a male dancer can teach salsa at the higher levels. He says, "A woman can teach a man at the beginner level, but in order for the man to evolve as a dancer, he needs a male teacher . . . because there is not a woman that feels what I feel. Even if she is a good instructor, she will never be able to develop a man's dancing ability like a male teacher will be able to" (my translation).[2] Although both men believe that a man must teach the masculine role to the male dancer, they see no problem in a man teaching a woman how to dance.

Male leadership in the structure of salsa also carries into the male-female dynamic created in the dance classes. At Caribe, when the couple dance section of the class began, only male students were given the "right" to choose their dance partners. "Men go find a woman," Nancy would announce. At Exclusive Salsa, the male student bore the entire responsibility for the success of the couple dance: if something went wrong, it was always his fault. Prefeminist relationships are produced in these dance classes. The man chooses the woman with whom he wants to dance, while the woman waits to be picked. As the leader of the dance, the man is accountable for its success or failure. The woman is dependent on him. Nonetheless, since women and men take salsa lessons primarily for the pleasure that they experience from this practice, both sexes appear to enjoy this gendered dynamic in which male leadership is emphasized.

Caribe specifically teaches male and female moves in the couple dance, thus promoting a stereotyped portrayal of heterosexuality. Besides giving lessons in the gendered movements embedded in the structure of the dance, this school also teaches male and female gestures in addition to the steps and turns of the dance. For example, women are shown how to project a "sexy" look by slowly caressing their hair, shoulders, and upper bodies. Men are taught to convey a "manly" and "forceful" stance by isolating and shaking their upper bodies in a shimmy-like move.[3] In addition, the school intends to offer classes providing specialized instruction in these male and female corporealities. These classes would also be segregated by gender.[4]

The heightened portrayal of heterosexuality that is promoted at Caribe resembles the depictions of masculinity and femininity in the Latin side of competitive ballroom dance, also referred to as competitive Latin American dance. Ruud Vermay's work on Latin American dance exposes how the exaggerated sense of masculinity and femininity conveyed at Caribe resembles Latin dance that has arisen from the European-derived ballroom tradition more than it does Latin dances that have emerged in lived Latin American contexts. Vermay argues that competitive Latin American dance embodies a contrived and extreme image of heterosexuality. In training to compete in the Latin American dance competitions, female dancers are taught to be sexy and feminine. Male dancers emulate a macho, masculine, and butch demeanor. The dancers forge these stereotyped gender distinctions through overstated choreographed gestures, excessive facial expressions, and overdone costumes (Vermay, 1994: 58). Performances stress images such as a "dynamic sex kitten," "a high-class prostitute," "a sophisticated romantic," "an animalistic undulating look," and "a gypsy look" (58, 62).

These physical incarnations of stereotypes are statements of excessive masculinity and femininity that are added to the dancer's body as adornments, as opposed to being embodied in the structure of the dance. This division between the dancing body and hyperbolic gestures reveals how form and content become separate in competitive Latin American dance. Form is considered to be technique, and content is regarded as expressions. Dancers learn their footwork first and then attempt to include the gestures and facial expressions (Vermay, 1994: 63). Ruud Vermay claims that in Latin dances that are part of a lived culture, which he terms "ethnic Latin dances," there is no distinction between form and content. He argues that these two elements cannot really be disconnected in dance: "Form and content cannot be separated. As you cannot be separated from your leg, the dance cannot be separated from its content" (62). In other words, since dance involves the whole body, a gesture cannot be divorced from the movements of the dancing body: the two are always interconnected. The distinction between form and content in competitive Latin American dance has developed in order to convey an exaggerated sense of masculinity and femininity. Vermay considers this desire to portray a heightened heterosexual narrative in the dance a misreading of how the male-female partnership should function in both the teaching and embodiment of Latin American dance (96). He contends that a man and woman do not need to exaggerate their maleness and femaleness, for these gender distinctions are already entrenched in the structure of the dance. Simply concentrating on the movements of the dance will exhibit a male and female dynamic that is both sufficient and beautiful. According to Ruud Vermay, when Latin dances are performed in their sites of origin outside the ballroom dance tradition, the relationship between the male and female is produced in the dance through its structure and movement alone. Consequently, Vermay claims that exaggerated masculinity and femininity in Latin American dance are traits derived from the ballroom dance tradition, not from dances that have emerged in a context. The portrayals of Latin femininity and masculinity in ballroom dance illustrate how Latin culture is stereotyped, perhaps even made offensive, by this western European–derived dance tradition. The pantomimic and potentially racist performance of Latin American dance also becomes apparent in how dancers cover their faces with makeup to appear darker. Juliet McMains argues that the "darkening" of Latin dancers evokes the racist performance of blackface minstrelsy (McMains, 2001/02: 55). Although the male and female gestures that are added to the steps and turns of the salsa taught at Caribe are not as inflated and excessive as those in competitive Latin American dance, the fact that gesture is added to movement in this dance school brings the Caribe dance method closer to the Latin side of ballroom dance.

Another heterosexual narrative that conveys inequality between the sexes is a visual display of the female body being manipulated by the male dancer. This demonstration of feminine passivity through spectacle is found in competitive Latin American dance and at some dance schools in Montreal. Seeking more equality between men and women in Latin dance, Ruud Vermay decries the objectification of the female form: "To some, indeed many people, the portrayal of women as mere objects of sexual desire, thrown around by men, treated as men's pleasure is wholly distasteful today. It still strikes me as incredible that during the final heat of a competition the 'announcer' can ask the audience to show its appreciation of a female competitor's look (never a male's) by applauding accordingly when [her] number is called" (Vermay, 1994: 99).

Various Montreal dance teachers promote a dance style that focuses on the male dancer using turns to display the woman, thereby transforming her into an object of spectacle. The male concentrates on maneuvring the female and consequently dances less; his body is not exhibited to the same extent as the woman's. The man's leading facilitates displaying the woman's body. This focus on feminine spectacle is exemplified by the dance styles promoted at Caribe and Exclusive Salsa. For instance, Marcus views the exhibition of the female dancer as an element of the dance that balances out the male leadership, as women derive pleasure from being led through steps and spins that

transform the female form into an object of beauty to be flaunted and exhibited. He says, "There always has to be someone who follows. That is not sexist. But sometimes, they say we [Latin men] are macho, and at home, it's the
man . . . but if we look at it from another angle, we see that the woman is the
spectacle of the dance. It is the man who displays the woman. The man
makes the woman move. Then it's the woman who is displayed. And it's the
woman who always follows" (my translation).[5]

There is a certain degree of truth in what Marcus says. Many female salsa
dancers luxuriate in being observed and admired as the male dancers display
their bodies. Many women revel in how their dancing enables them to be ap-
preciated and desired. The overt objectification of the female form is one element that draws both women and men to salsa clubs and schools. Both in
clubs and in dance classes, some women actively participate in the meta-
morphosis of their bodies into objects of spectacle. They dress in alluring and
revealing clothes that draw attention to their legs, breasts, and navels. In
contrast, men's bodies are usually completely covered. Not all schools seem
to create an atmosphere where women dress in an alluring manner. Proponents of the politics of pleasure may argue that female salsa dancers are not
simply at the mercy of the male gaze when their bodies are exhibited, but also
able to obtain power as the gesticulations of the dance and their enticing at-
tire mold them into objects of male desire. Nonetheless, the power that
women might attain in salsa never transgresses the male leadership in the
dance. Jane Cowan illustrates that any supremacy that women attain in the
dance is always circumscribed by masculine control. Referring to the dance
culture of Sohos, Greece, Cowan writes, "In my view, any sexual or gender
complementarity—like women's powers generally—that may be observed in
particular sites and moments must always be seen in the context of a broader
asymmetry of male dominance and of the androcentric and patriarchal institutions through which it is manifested" (Cowan, 1990: 10–11).

The emphasis on the visual display of the female body that characterizes
Western classical ballet intersects with how certain dance instructors stress
the exhibition of women's bodies. In the nineteenth century, the movement
patterns of the male ballet dancer decreased, as his function was reduced to
manipulating the female, whose body was increasingly transformed into a
spectacle through the popularity of pointe work and the ethereal ideal of
the female form (Copeland, 1997: 130). The male dancer's role is to exhibit the
female in a dance genre that hyperbolizes the visual, especially through
the turned-out position of the legs (130). Classical ballet further accentuates
the visual above the other senses. Modern dance's rupture with classical ballet
partly stems from modern dance's heightening of the tactile and kinesthetic

experience of movement and its downplaying of the visual emphasis of ballet (134). Using Balanchine's choreographic construction of the ballerina in *The Four Temperments*, Ann Daly denounces how his work transforms the female body into an object of pleasure for the male gaze. The dancer, rendered ethereal and frail by her pointe shoes and her lithe frame, is supported and lifted by the male dancer. This dynamic of female subordination and male dominance transforms the ballerina into something to be looked at, or an object of the male gaze, a concept borrowed from Laura Mulvey's psychoanalytical readings of the visual display of women in cinematic representation (Daly, 1987: 10). According to Mulvey, classical American cinema inevitably "masculinizes" the spectator, regardless of the actual sex of the real moviegoers. In cinema the female body is transformed into an image to be stared at, something valued for what Mulvey coins its "to-be-looked-at-ness;" the exhibition of a woman's body transforms her into a passive object of desire (Mulvey, 1975: 11). Mulvey's influential work has been criticized for emphasizing female passivity and not recognizing the agency of the female viewer. Mary Ann Doane, for instance, challenges Mulvey's assumption of masculinization, which does not allow for an active female spectatorship (Doane, 1982: 3–4).

In a similar criticism, Stephanie Jordan and Helen Thomas dispute Ann Daly's understanding in *The Four Temperments* of how a ballerina surrenders to the power of the male, arguing that the female is more than simply a passive, ethereal creature manipulated by the male dancer. They refigure, for instance, Daly's interpretation of the "drag step," in which she claims "the man literally carries the ballerina on his back" (Jordan and Thomas, 1998: 247; Daly, 1987: 9). Jordan and Thomas propose this step as a means by which the female dancer increases the movement of the male by "clinging aggressively to his back" (Jordan and Thomas, 1998: 247).

Returning to the exhibition of the female in salsa, it is perhaps possible to grant the female dancer a certain degree of power rather than reducing her to a passive object of the male gaze. Through her dress and movements, the female dancer participates in her transformation into a spectacle. Any subversive potential in feminine display brought about by a rereading of passivity as partly produced by the female dancer herself is always mediated by the issue of male leadership at the core of salsa dancing, particularly in the teaching styles of those Montreal dance instructors who emphasize masculine control.

Just as Stephanie Jordan and Helen Thomas argue that the female classical ballet dancer influences the controlling movements of the male dancer, it is possible to view the woman resisting the male lead in salsa dancing as the woman facilitating male leading. In this sense, the female is not a passive agent but actively contributes to masculine control in the dance. Nonetheless, instructors who stress male domination in salsa dancing choose to portray it in this light partly to sell the dance. Although Paolo and Marcus strongly believe that male leadership is central to the dance, this emphasis may be linked to the commodification of salsa in Montreal. Salsa's appeal might be located in the gendered power play—that is, people might be drawn to salsa dancing *because* it allows for male dominance and female submission. Caribe's allure, for instance, could be its emphasis on male control in the dance. Speaking of how the female follows the male lead in salsa, Paolo claims that this dynamic is simply part of life: "You know why because in life, there is always someone who leads even in a company. There is always a head. There cannot be two heads. If not, it does not work. In dance as in life there is always one person who respects the other" (my translation).[6] Paolo's unabashedly sexist stance on salsa characterizes the teaching style at the school.

Despite the blatant inequality between the sexes that is promoted at Caribe, this school is highly successful. The question begs to be asked: why are both men and women willing to engage in an activity that openly encourages male domination? Paolo suggests that Montreal men and women are attracted by the dance's performance of masculinity: "The dance is very sensual. Therefore, there is a lot of communication. It is a way to speak. When you touch someone, you make her turn and you make her dance. Therefore the woman feels the masculinity of the man in the dance. This we have lost here in North America" (my translation).[7] Explaining how masculinity is conveyed in the dance, he adds, "It is us [men] who lead. It is us who decide when the girl will turn in all Latin dances. In merengue, in all of them. So the girl feels more protected in the dance than she feels now" (my translation).[8] The relationship between the sexes in Paolo's vision of salsa evokes a time before the ideology of feminism pervaded the popular imagination. Men are given more responsibilities than the female, but at the same time they are expected to take care of and to protect women.

This interest by Montrealers in learning a salsa style that privileges masculinity could be partially motivated by a desire to return to a prefeminist male-female dynamic. Since the Quiet Revolution, Quebec society has made great strides toward creating equality between men and women at the level of legislature. Why is gender inequality condoned and even relished in salsa dancing? Montrealers might be more willing to engage in these "illicit" relationships in what is considered a "foreign" cultural practice. Salsa is commonly associated with Latin stereotypes that pervade the imagination: the macho forceful male and the sexy enticing female. Schools earnestly present this gendered narrative of heightened male domination simply as part of the "rules" of the dance. Consequently, Montrealers who take dance lessons are given license to enjoy the pleasures of the male-female power play without questioning its sexist implications. Although salsa students may feel reticent about enacting exaggerated masculine or feminine stereotypes in other areas of their lives, they may feel justified in doing so in salsa since their performance of these gendered distinctions is simply part of the rules of the dance.

Translating the male-female relationship embodied in the dance into a set of regulations transforms this gendered connection into a commodity that can be bought and sold. Schools such as Caribe and Exclusive Salsa promote heightened male domination because this depiction of salsa conforms to their vision of the dance. At the same time, there is a market for their understanding of salsa. As taught by Paolo and Marcus, salsa allows Montrealers to escape the discourse of male and female equality that permeates mainstream society because it provides a safe and rule-governed sphere where they can perform (and enjoy their desire to experience) more traditional gender relationships. As this "return" to conventional gender roles occurs in the "foreign" and "exotic" space of the salsa class and Latin club dance floor, salsa's male-female dynamic can be regarded as distinct from that of everyday life, in which the gender imbalance between the sexes may be more ambiguous and fluid. The version of salsa that stresses male domination concretizes pronounced gender inequality as a formalized ritual.

A conversation that I had during my participant observation at one of the city's Latin dance clubs elucidates how salsa for some of its dancers can be divorced from daily life. One evening, at the club La Palmera, I chanced to meet a woman who works as an administrator at the university where I then taught. All evening, men asked her to dance, and I could tell by the ease that she exuded dancing with a variety of partners that she was an excellent dancer who had been on salsa club floors for a number of years. Before leaving, she asked that I not tell anyone at work that I had seen her at a salsa club. Of course, I have always kept her secret. Her desire to keep her salsa life hidden, however, poignantly illustrates how for some club goers, Latin dancing is an illicit activity that stands apart from the daily routine of work and perhaps of family life.

In contrast to the heightened sense of masculinity conveyed in the teaching and promotion of salsa noted above, a number of the city's dance teachers view the leading and following pattern of salsa as a complementary relationship between the sexes. The instructors who impart this dynamic to the dance teach salsa in a manner that emphasizes both the female and male involvement. For instance, in addition to teaching men how to lead, Carlos of Salsa Celeste also teaches women how to follow. The main proponent of the balanced relationship is Daphne of Riviera, who feels that for salsa to be a successful dance, there must be a sense of equality between the sexes. People must take into account their dancing partners: Daphne points out that both male and female may try to control the dance by not adapting to the needs of their partners, behavior that undermines its success. Commenting on the leading and following pattern in the dance, Daphne says:

> When a man is leading and a woman is following, I see it as a balance and not as an inferiority or a superiority . . . I think, as they say, it takes two to tango. So if you are relying on each other, there has got to be equality. Right. You need each other. Right there, it's clear. It could be fair. I also think that certain men dance with equal lead. And what I mean by that is they will lead and will take into consideration what will be best for their partner. And there are others that will roughly push you and not care or think about where you will end up. What is important is that they look good on the dance floor. Then I feel it could be a little macho on their part. But that is very individual. It changes from one male to the other. Just like you can have the opposite. You can have a woman leading herself, totally not caring what the guy is interested in doing and just making sure she looks good. It can work both ways.

Most of the female teachers in the city share Daphne's understanding of salsa as a dance that establishes equality and balance between men and women despite their different roles. Given that many female dancers teach salsa, it would seem that they want to market it as a practice in which the woman is not completely subordinate. Through their teaching of the dance, female instructors in Montreal contradict those male instructors of Latin descent who hold that a woman is less capable of teaching salsa than a man. Although some male dance instructors believe that men are more qualified to teach salsa, not all share this view. In an interview, Gustavo of Salsa Brava, for instance, insists that there is no distinction between male and female instructors: "There is not any difference if it is a man or a woman who teaches salsa. Because just as a woman can learn to lead and learn the steps of the male dancer, a man can also learn the female steps to show them the moves that the female dancers should do. There is not any difference" (my translation).[9]

Daphne believes that she can better teach a man how to lead than can a male instructor precisely because she is a woman. She bases her claim on the premise that, as a female salsa dancer, she has experienced many different kinds of male leads and is therefore more adept at interpreting a male student's leading style than a male teacher, who only knows his own style. Men never (or extremely rarely) dance salsa with other men in hetereosexual contexts and therefore, unlike a female dancer, cannot experience different male techniques.[10] In Montreal's salsa clubs in the 1990s, specifically those such as Casa Nacho that cater to clientele of Latin descent, it was not uncommon to see two women dance salsa as a closed couple dance. Indeed, women more readily dance salsa with other women. In dance classes, for instance, the female teacher may pair with a female student to demonstrate a step or turn; the instructor leads the dance in these cases. As women feel more at ease dancing with same sex partners than do men in the Latin dance scene, a female teacher has greater knowledge of the diverse ways that men and women interpret the movements of salsa. Since all the female dance instructors in the city, with the exception of Rita, were born in Canada, they cannot claim a "right" to teach salsa based on their Latin heritage. Consequently, their legitimacy as salsa teachers is founded on their versatility in interpreting both the male and female parts of the dance. Most of the schools headed by women downplay male domination and stress equality on the dance floor. Also a few male teachers of Latin descent, most notably Gustavo, do not emphasize masculine control in their teaching and dance style. Selling salsa as a dance that encourages a complementary relationship between the sexes gives women a more active place in a practice that has male leadership at its core.

A style that allows for greater equality between the sexes more closely resembles how salsa is experienced when it is part of the cultural heritage of a people. Rita, who grew up dancing to salsa rhythms, shares the view that equal partnering is an integral part of the dance. Nevertheless, this perspective is not universal. Cuban salsa dancing, for instance, is often characterized as male dominant. The following online description of a *casino* in Cuba illustrates masculine predominance:

> When the music is right the men get going. Wow. Starting with the women, they go into a competitive macho routine that gets rivulets of sweat running down their backs. Their bodies are so fluid it is like water; their footwork is weighted, afro-funky, their energy is frightening. And then, the women are pulled in to join a casino circle and we are spun, dragged and half thrown between them at bewildering speeds. The air is punctuated by shouts from the men and squeals from the women—usually when we are caught out by unexpected high kicks from the men or directed in a way that is not entirely polite. ("Our Mag in Havana," 1 April 1999)

Based on observations of Cuban dance in Europe, another website devoted to documenting diverse salsa styles describes the Cuban style as a dance that restricts women:

I would say that at least 30% of Cuban style is being danced solo, depending on the song and its rhythms. If there is a tremendous amount of percussion, the woman can shine with her incredibly beautiful and rhythmic body movements. In fact, partner dancing the Cuban style is so restricting to the woman, that I found many of the women could not wait to dance solo for a while. (Edie, 1999)

According to Bárbara Balbuena, the role of the male dancer in the *casino* in Cuba has become less predominant than it was during the 1970s and 1980s (Balbuena, 2003: 100). The female today has a more central role in dance, particularly during the *despelote* (100), or "hot" sections, of the *casino*, inspired by the climatic moments in the *sonero-salsero* compositions, referred to as *bomba* or *timba* by Cuban musicians. During the *despelote*, the couple hold is loosened, and male and female can perform individually with frenetic and impassioned body isolations (93, 95). Cuban women can also improvise on their own without necessarily repeating the movements of their male partners. Furthermore, the female dancers in Cuba today learn how to turn their dancing partners, a role usually delegated to the male. Despite these evolutions, men still direct the *casino* when it is danced in the circle formation (*la rueda*) or in rows of couples (*filas de parejas*). And the male continues to lead the dance when it is performed in a couple (100).

Even though the male dancer always leads the couple in lived Latin contexts such as Cuba, the actual technique that characterizes the "male lead" seems to allow for a certain degree of equality at the level of movement when salsa is part of the cultural heritage of a people. I base this on my observations of salsa dancers in Montreal's clubs, interviews with instructors, and Ruud Vermay's understanding of the "ethnic" sources of contemporary Latin dance, which are part of the ballroom tradition. He configures the "equality" created between the male and female as produced by the shared exchange of energy flow between two dancing bodies. Consequently, leading and following are broached from inside the dance as a system of movements. Vermay argues that contemporary Latin dances in the ballroom tradition—samba, cha-cha, rumba, and *paso doble*—should return to their "ethnic" sources to revitalize their present interpretation in competitive dance. Vermay's conceptualization of the leading and following pattern in the "ethnic" sources of these dances connects to how salsa can be performed in lived circumstances and, to a lesser extent, to how the dance is taught in Montreal. Although Ruud Vermay does not refer to salsa in particular, his understanding of Latin dance is relevant to the Montreal dance scene because it pertains to the roots of salsa. (As noted in chapter 3, the rumba that was integrated and modified in ballroom dance is actually the *son*, the precursor of today's salsa; the *chachachá*, its name changed to chacha in Latin dance, is derived from the *danzón*, another of salsa's predecessors.)

Speaking about accomplished male-female partnering in Latin dances, Vermay identifies a quality that these dances have in common: the effusion of energy shared equally by male and female dancers notwithstanding the male's leading. Ruud Vermay writes, "In Latin dance, despite the emphasis on the notion of the 'male lead,' successful partnering is the result of the equal flow of energy between two people, two people dancing *with* each other. If the energy flow is unequal, manipulation results. The manipulator dances *at* the partner, the manipulated dances *for* the partner" (Vermay, 1994: 150, emphasis in the original). The transmission of energy between the dancers allows for communication between them so that the woman can respond to the male's lead. This energy is distributed by the male dancer applying a light pressure with his hands, arms, and body, which the female responds to by slightly resisting the tension of the male. As Vermay expounds, "The sharing of energy, the passing of tension to one another and the reception of this tension from one another, is a highly sensitive function which requires acute understanding if it is to be effectively and subtly mastered" (150). Gustavo identifies the male-female dynamic in salsa as a sharing of energy:

> When I speak of listening, as I said before, it's about a certain physical tension so that the dancer can be attentive. And the guy must give the necessary pressure so that the girl does what is wanted of her. When we say afterwards that there was a feeling between them and understanding . . . we are speaking here of feeling and understanding . . . it's exactly this energy that I was talking about before. For the man and the woman, it gives the desire to move and it gives the desire to dance. When we are two, we need this energy that circulates between the two bodies. In order for this energy to circulate, the woman and the man must resist a little in the dance. If one of their arms is too stiff, too straight, this will be felt. The partner will feel that the arm is too straight. And if it is too loose, that is felt also as though one were dancing without a partner. As if the dance was being danced alone. Then, rightly so, we need this little tension between the two so that the energy circulates between the two bodies. And the communication and the leading comes from that [tension]. (My translation)[11]

The "equal" relationship between the male and female dancer is carried through this shared exchange of energy. Most of the Montreal salsa instructors who teach leading and following patterns based on tension and resistance stress that these movements stem from hand and arm moves. According to Ruud Vermay, to ensure a balanced energy flow between two dancers, their entire bodies must be involved in the dance. Most Montreal salsa dance teachers do not teach their students to move the entire body in dance; they focus on the feet, the arms, and the hips as though these were separate from the total dancing body. Vermay identifies this emphasis on specific body parts as characteristic of Latin dance within the ballroom tradition. He argues that the preoccupation with steps and techniques leads to an understanding of dance as comprising movements of specific body parts rather than the total body. He says, "It appears as though our preoccupation with steps and technique has resulted in dancers treating these as the *text* of the dance and ignoring the *subtext*, i.e., what is inherently there by virtue of the fact that the dancers are not arms, legs and feet, but human beings moving with all the implied associations of human movement" (Vermay, 1994: 90). Dance requires total body engagement with the rhythms of the music: "It must be remembered that the whole body from top to toe is always active in dance whether in motion or in stillness" (103). Dancers feel and sense their partners as extensions of themselves when their entire bodies are engaged in the exchange of energy between them (152). Male leading becomes less about dominance and control and more about merging with and yielding to the other (154–55). For instance, when there is no equal flow of energy between male and female dancers because their whole bodies are not actively involved, as the male dancer pulls the woman, he pulls only her arm, not her entire body. This breaks the transfer of energy, making the movement look jolted and forced. The masculine position of leading becomes one of contending and fighting. On the other hand, if both the man and woman interpret the rhythms of salsa with their bodies as a whole, when the male dancer pulls the woman's arm, she will respond to the tension with her entire body. The total body moving in dance also creates his action of drawing the woman's arm. The movements of the dance are truly controlled when the flow of energy between the dancers remains fluid. Viewed from the perspective of body dynamics, accomplished male leading does not apply strength and force but concedes to gravity and the woman's energy: "In other words, yielding and merging *is* control" (154, emphasis in the original). This analysis of male leadership in couple dancing somewhat subverts the concept of "masculinity" as dominance founded on force and command.

The flow of equal energy between the dancers is not a central concern of the majority of dance schools in Montreal. Teaching couples to share their energy on the floor is difficult and requires extensive training that is not part of salsa dance instruction in the city. The dance schools need to sell the dance successfully. If they concentrate too much on elements of the dance that require more comprehensive training, novice dancers will become discouraged. The elements that a novice dancer would find difficult to acquire are an integral part of the dance for people who grew up dancing to the salsa rhythms. The total body expresses the rhythms of the music; leading the dance demands the entire physicality of the male dancer. The following description captures the feeling of dancing with a man who has grown up with salsa in Cuba:

> Dancing with a man who has been dancing all his life is as easy as sitting in an armchair. Not for the incessant spins and turns we are used to; they are totally relaxed, listening to the music and playing with it; focusing on expressing the rhythm with every part of the body: torso, belly, pelvis, arms, feet—nothing is out of sync; when they turn they don't use their arms alone. The whole body directs the woman to turn at the desired speed; it is impossible for her to move in any other direction. ("Our Mag in Havana," 1 April 1999)

These observations of Cuban dancing, made by a woman from the United Kingdom, show how the man in the Caribbean context leads his female partner using his entire body. In the Caribbean, the male not only dances with "every part of the body," but also moves as much as his female partner. Generally, the man's role in salsa, in Western contexts, which is the case in Montreal, is to turn and direct the female so that her beauty is displayed. Hence the woman dances more than her male partner. According to Montreal salsa instructor, Charlot, the relationship created between the male and female in salsa in the tropical culture enables both dancers to move extensively on the dance floor, thus allowing both to fully express themselves. Charlot uses the term "tropical culture" to refer to a culture either in the Caribbean or in a Latin American context that has been influenced by the Caribbean. The male's leading role incites the woman to fully experience her emotions and spirit so that the male dancer can also attain a high level of emotional and spiritual fulfillment. For Charlot, the male lead does not restrict or control the female; rather, the male dancer challenges his female partner to fully express herself physically, spiritually, and emotionally. Salsa in the tropical culture is not about exhibition and display and about trying to look good on the dance floor. The impulse is directed inward and is more concerned with expressing emotions and spirit through movement. The dominance of the male dancer is somewhat diminished in Charlot's understanding of salsa in Caribbean or Caribbean-influenced contexts:

> In the tropical culture, if I am dancing with you, I am motivating you. In the Western culture, the girl tends to dance more. [Girls] are more sensual with their bodies. The guys do mostly the leading and fast footwork. They are like pimps because the guy is the frame and the lady is the flower. So the man is like a pimp and the lady is doing most of the work which is different in the

tropical culture from the Caribbean. In the tropical culture from the Caribbean or South America, if I am dancing with you it is almost like I am motivating you by competing with you on the dance floor. While I am dancing, I am instigating you to reach a higher feeling in terms of letting yourself go on the dance floor . . . that is the tropical culture. The man in the tropical culture has to be as good if not better than the woman. But here [in Montreal] the man is a mere king pimp leading the lady to do dance figures and once in a while, he does a little flip or some turns and some footwork . . . fast, fast, fast. Even if I don't speak, when I am dancing my body language is saying, "show me what you got." I have to instigate you to get to a higher feeling and that will instigate me to be even better, to reach a higher feeling myself, too.

In this understanding of salsa in the tropical context, the male and female dancers are in a sense "competing" on the dance floor. And in this "competition" to outdo one another for the sake of the dance and to reach a high level of emotional and spiritual fulfillment, both male and female dancers are equal partners.

Despite the possibility of subverting masculine dominance when male leadership becomes either more about yielding to the female dancer than about controlling her or more about challenging her to incite the male to perform than about directing her performance, there is no denying that the male dancer still leads the female in salsa. Although women may follow the male in the dance itself, they are influential in teaching and promoting salsa in Montreal: female dancers have managed the city's two largest dance schools. Daphne is the owner and director of Riviera, and Nancy was the director of Caribe when I was conducting my ethnographic research. The commodification of salsa dancing in Montreal allows for the "dominance" of only certain women, specifically Quebecois and Canadian women, here defined either as those born in Quebec or Canada or as immigrant women who identify themselves as Quebecois or Canadian. With the exception of Rita, few immigrant women of Latin descent have played a dominant role in the salsa dance scene. Of the five female salsa dancers interviewed, only one was raised in a Latin country; all the others but one were raised in Quebec, and she is from Manitoba. All had learned to dance to salsa rhythms in Montreal before they started teaching. A few women of Latin descent assist male teachers who are their fathers or brothers. These women do not take leading roles in the dance school but stand behind the Latin male instructors, who are the central figures.[12] Yet there are Canadian-born women who are leaders in the Montreal scene.[13] In discussing the influential role that women play in producing and maintaining salsa in the city, only a specific group of women is actually represented.

The idea that women should not be viewed as a category without such determinants as class, race, age, ethnic background, and sexual orientation was voiced by African American feminists in the United States who addressed how race and class affect a woman's position in the American context. They spoke out against "white-washing," which they saw occurring in the white, middle-class, academic American feminism of the late 1960s and 1970s. Such writers as Frances Beal, Audre Lorde, Cora Kaplan, bell hooks, and the Combahee River Collective argue that both the historical and contemporary reality of black women stands in sharp contrast to the experience of white middle-class women. Their observations and criticisms have furthered feminism to take into account the differences among women and to resist conceptualizing "women" as a monolithic category. Although the idea that the category "woman" does not exist as such is commonplace in contemporary feminist thought, this academic field is indebted to the early contribution made by African American feminists. During my ethnographic work in the Montreal salsa scene, I became aware that immigrant women of Latin descent were not actively involved in teaching and promoting this dance. My inclination to interpret this dearth as a meaningful finding has been influenced by the insight of African American feminist scholars that not all women, by virtue of being the same sex, share similar experiences in a society.

My interviews with most of the male salsa dance teachers of Latin descent did not provide much insight into why so few women of Latin descent play an active role in teaching the dance. The majority of dance instructors could not find a reason for this discrepancy. Oscar of Salsa Plus ventured as a possible reason that Latin women tend to have children in their late teens and early twenties, whereas many Quebecois women delay motherhood until after thirty. Consequently, Latin women are not as "free" as Quebecois women to go out dancing and be part of a nighttime club scene. Commenting on the differences between Latin and Quebecois women, Oscar says: "Latin American women have many children and therefore they go out less. Quebecois women have fewer children and therefore they go out more. Latin American women do dance a lot. There are a lot of good female dancers who have not been discovered. [But] they are not in Latin clubs" (my translation).[14] Paolo of Caribe questioned whether Latin women in the city have the ability to teach: "You know, in business, there are many ways to make money. But, if we speak of reality, the truth is the truth. Therefore, there are girls who move well, but that does not mean that they are good instructors or that they know how to dance" (my translation).[15]

Female dance instructors seemed less hesitant to suggest reasons for this discrepancy. Daphne offered the following explanation for the lack of Latin immigrant female representation in Montreal's salsa scene:

> Well, I will tell you something about Latin culture. They don't promote or would approve of their daughters becoming dance teachers. You kind of . . . how can I say . . . you know . . . it's not a great job. . . . And I don't know, that culture is a little macho. It is based on, well, men can do certain things, but women can't, so I think that is another reason. But, then again, with myself being of a [Mediterranean] background. You know a [Mediterranean] background is not any different. You know. It is the same thing. There is machoism. And at the same time, females are not supposed to be doing this. But having grown up here, having had certain experiences, my attitude is different. You know. So I don't know. Maybe there is a need to have more Latin female teachers. I know of some. Rita is around [teaching in Montreal]. I know there are more in New York than there are here . . . female teachers, and there is a couple in Toronto that I know of. But the thing is . . . I think it is just the basic cultural mentality [that] men can do things, but women really shouldn't.

Catherine, a dance teacher and the owner of Simply Salsa, provides further reasons why women, in general, may feel excluded from teaching the dance:

> As a woman, it is pretty hard to teach dancing because a lot of the dancing is male-dominated. In the dancing itself, it is basically the male who takes the woman. In Latin dancing, it is usually the men who lead the women into the salsa and merengue dance. That is probably why . . . most people . . . I think it would be probably less appealing for a man to take lessons from a woman . . . teaching him how to dominate the woman when she is a woman . . . I think that causes some sort of problem for the clientele . . . I don't think that there are a lot of women out there who have the time, as well, to put into a dance school.

Montreal salsa instructor Charlot, who is of Haitian descent, confided that often men from the Caribbean and Latin America immigrate and as a consequence enjoy new freedoms. Yet they do not always want the immigrant women from their native country to share this same liberty. Rita likewise disclosed that men from her country of origin often allow women born in Canada and Quebec freedoms that they do not "permit" women from their home country. As one of the first salsa dance teachers in the city and the first female teacher of Latin descent, she experienced considerable hostility from some of the male salsa teachers of Latin descent.

These insights into the lack of Latin immigrant female dance teachers assembled from interviews and informal discussions paint only a sketchy and scattered picture of the reasons behind the dearth of Latin women in the dance world. Some of the explanations offered are as follows: Latin immigrant women are deprived of certain freedoms granted to men; teaching salsa and living the club life are more acceptable practices for Latin men than for Latin women; Canadian and Quebecois women may feel more at liberty to become active in Montreal's salsa dance world; Latin men may be more accepting of a Canadian or Quebecois woman teaching salsa than they would be of an immigrant woman of Latin descent doing so; the priority of women who were raised in Latin countries is raising children and having a family, which takes them out of the public sphere of the nightclub. There is a key problem in drawing these conclusions at the conceptual level: Latin attitudes and cultural practices concerning the relationship between men and women are perceived as absolute and monolithic despite the diversity that characterizes the Latin population in Montreal.

Frances Aparicio's perspective on salsa music and the issue of gender illustrates how a patriarchal hegemony frames the relationship between Puerto Rican men and women in the United States. The various musical dimensions of salsa—its lyrical compositions, its performance, and the production of the music—systematically exclude women: in fact, this musical sphere profoundly oppresses them. Aparicio writes, "Salsa's repertoire is clearly marked by male voices that systematically privilege a masculinist perspective, a patriarchal ideology, and thus a phallocentric discourse" (Aparicio, 1998: 123). The patriarchy in salsa is part of a wider characteristic of Latin society. She claims that Anglo-American women find themselves in a different situation in their relationship to men than do U.S. Latinas and Latin American women, asserting that many Latin women still face a great deal of "outright conflict and even physical violence" (168). Aparicio argues that there have been so few successful female salsa singers partly because the venues where musicians perform and practice (i.e., clubs, jam sessions, and cast parties) are not considered acceptable for decent Latin women and also because the lifestyle of a musician, particularly touring, is not regarded as suitable for a woman (173).

Vernon Boggs shares the opinion that women are discouraged from participating in the production of salsa music. The negative light that was cast on African-derived music in Cuba prior to the Communist reforms kept many women out of the music-producing domain. Association with the music world could ruin a woman's reputation. Nevertheless, a number of female salsa singers, such as Celia Cruz, famous since the 1950s, and Lupe Victoria Yoli, known as the "Queen of Latin Soul" in salsa's heyday years in New York, managed to penetrate the male-dominated barriers. Even today, women enter the world of music primarily as singers, not as musicians. The musical realm of salsa is an exclusionary men's club to which women do not have access (Boggs, 1992b: 112–18).[16]

Frances Aparicio's understanding of the relationship between men and women seems at times too rigid since she does not allow for much female subversion of the forces of patriarchy. Nonetheless, her belief that a strong patriarchy governs the lives of Latin women is echoed somewhat in attitudes and beliefs that I documented during in-depth interviews and informal discussions with Montrealers involved in the dance scene. In dealing with ethnographic findings that revealed essential qualities underlying Latin culture, I found myself faced with the problem of how to come to terms with "Latin" culture when it originates with individuals from Latin American, Central American, and Caribbean nations as well as from Quebec and when it is so stereotyped and essentialist that it homogenizes the plurality of Latin cultures. Embracing an essentialist understanding of identity and culture also sharply contrasts with the postmodern-based framework that has been employed to map the enactment of masculinity and femininity in teaching and promoting the dance in Montreal salsa schools. The relationship between the sexes that is produced in the couple dance stresses how the masculinity or femininity that is embodied through the repetition of certain movements does not refer to an original essence but is constructed. Consequently, heterosexual relationships are unstable and multidimensional.

Are essentialism and constructivism always at odds at the theoretical level? According to Diana Fuss, essentialism lurks within constructivism. Referring particularly to the writings of Jacques Derrida, Fuss claims that "any radical constructionism can only be built on the foundations of a hidden essentialism" (Fuss, 1989: 12–13). In particular, the idea of contradiction, or "difference," in Derridian logic surfaces as the given, or "essence," of deconstruction. Contradiction is at the center of deconstruction and is the prerequisite for its operation (18). Furthermore, Fuss reveals that the claim that essentialism is always reactionary is essentialist, as it assumes that essentialism has an essence (21). Moreover, she argues that Derrida himself would agree that a given theory can never completely transgress metaphysics. As Western metaphysics is based on the binary opposition between essence and accident, essentialism will always emerge (13). As social constructivism cannot escape essentialism, it is possible to speak about an essentialist deconstruction.

When essentialism and deconstruction are combined, the function of essentialism is radically altered. Traditionally, feminists have opposed essentialism because it has been used to explain social conditions in terms of biological givens. However, incorporating essentialism into a deconstructionist stance cannot serve the purpose of maintaining universal essences, for deconstruction illustrates how all concepts, including essences, are historically contingent. Fuss draws a distinction between falling into essentialism and deploying it strategically. Falling into essentialism would entail a return to universal categories, whereas deploying essentialism strategically would preserve certain "essences" in the interest of those who have a political investment in their maintenance while simultaneously recognizing that these essences are merely constructs (20). Fuss herself, for instance, incorporates the arguments of Henry Louis Gates, Jr., Anthony Appiah, and Houston A. Baker, Jr., to arrive at an essentialist-constructionist approach to race. She brings into her discussion Baker's claim that the category of race must be retained as a political category to safeguard race from those who wish to silence its political voice. In a theoretical debate between Appiah and Baker, Appiah argues that the term "race," as used in biological discourses, should be eradicated, whereas Baker seeks to retain it as a political term in literary and critical discourses. Fuss reconciles these two stands by proposing that race can persevere as a political category while recognizing that it is a biological fiction. The term "race" must be maintained as a political category to stake a position from which to address the material effects of racial differentiation. As Fuss says, "To say that 'race' is a biological fiction is not to deny that it has real material effects in the world; nor is it to suggest that 'race' should disappear from our critical vocabularies" (91–92).

Diane Fuss combines essentialism and social constructivism to come to terms with the supposed incompatibility that exists between a postmodern understanding of identity as a construction that does not refer to fixed essences and the fact that in everyday life identity categories such as race, gender, and class have real effects on the lives of men and women. How Fuss mediates the workings of identity at the level of theory and practice can be incorporated into the gender dynamics at play in the Montreal salsa dance scene. The contrived forging of dance students into male and female players illustrates how gender differences are molded and fashioned. Despite being a mutable fabrication that does not refer to fixed essence, gender nonetheless has a real impact. The material effects of gender differences can be maintained by the legal and state apparatus, or they can be produced in a Foucauldian sense through the microprocesses of power in various facets of everyday life, even in the realm of such pleasurable activities as dance. The absence of Latin women in Montreal's salsa scene could certainly be, as Daphne suggests, related to how gender issues differently affect the lives of immigrant women and women born in Canada and Quebec. As part of the Latin diaspora, Latin American women may have to face a gendered reality that differs from that of women born in Quebec. James Clifford comments on the ways that gender affects the lives of women who have migrated from their place of origin: "Life for women in diasporic situations can be doubly painful—struggling with the material and spiritual insecurities of exile, with the demands of family and work, and with the claims of old and new patriarchies" (Clifford, 1994: 314).

Literature that analyzes how the lives of Latin American and Caribbean women are affected by migration to the United States and Canada reveals that these women often feel compelled to conform to the gendered ideology of their country of origin while living in the new country. Research on Latin American and Caribbean women in the United States and, to a lesser degree, in Canada has arisen because the vast majority of immigrants from Latin America and the Caribbean have migrated to these two nations (Acosta-Belén and Bose, 1993: 109). The study of women immigrants from Latin America and the Caribbean is a relatively new area of inquiry; previously, male immigrants were the primary concern. Nonetheless, the male bias continued in the research of the 1970s and 1980s (103). Nancy Foner and Patricia R. Pessar are two anthropologists who explore how gender affects the lives of Caribbean and Latin American women in American cities. Reference is made only to the work of these two writers because their research is the most relevant to the salsa dance scene in Montreal.[17] Both scholars argue that while immigrant women may behave in accordance with gendered patterns from their country of origin, their understanding of their position as women is also transformed by prevailing gendered attitudes and practices in the United States. These authors look primarily at the situation of working-class Latin American and Caribbean women, although Nancy Foner at times refers to women from various classes. Most of the immigrants from Latin America and the Caribbean who migrate to Montreal are in low socio-economic income brackets (Beaulieu and Concha, 1988: 127-28).

Research on immigrant women in New York provides an understanding of the issue of gender and migration that can be applied to the situation of women in Montreal. The lives of immigrant women are both improved and constrained by their migration to New York. Women who have immigrated are still affected by the traditional and patriarchal gendered codes and practices of their countries of origin in Latin America and the Caribbean (Foner, 1999: 96). They also, however, gain certain advantages through the migration process. Citing specific examples of immigrant women from such countries as the Dominican Republic and El Salvador, Nancy Foner discusses how these women can feel a greater sense of equality with their husbands in their home environment in New York than they could in their country of origin, where most did not do paid work (Foner, 1998: 9–10). In the 1990s only 15 percent of women were in the labor force in the Dominican Republic (Foner, 1999: 102). Referring to observations made by Patricia Pessar, Foner outlines how working in New York and acquiring a salary offers Dominican women a means of gaining more equality with their husbands because they can contribute to the household income. As a result, these women are less economically dependent on men (Pessar, 1984 and 1995: 44, cited in Foner, 1999: 102). Because women work outside the home, Latin American and Caribbean men may be more inclined to help their wives in the home than they would be in their countries of origin (103). Immigrant women are more apt to make demands on their husbands for help in the domestic sphere than they would in their home countries because the "dominant norms" of the United States condone and support husbands' assisting their wives in the home (Foner, 1998: 13; Foner, 1999: 104). Further, they have access to economic support if the marriage breaks down and to welfare and legal help in the event of serious spousal abuse (Foner, 1998: 16).

Nonetheless, male involvement in the home and the greater equality that immigrant women may feel in New York does not constitute a dramatic change in the male-female domestic dynamic, in which the woman's position is that of primary caretaker of the home and the children. Foner states, "Indeed, Latin American and Caribbean women strongly identify as wives and mothers and they like being in charge of the domestic domain" (Foner, 1999: 104). Despite alterations in the domestic and work situation of immigrant women in New York, premigration patterns continue to exert an influence on the lives of immigrant women, and their impact can be constraining. Immigrant women of all social classes are primarily responsible for the care of the home and the children. Therefore, after a day of working outside the home, they are expected to continue working in the home—cleaning, cooking, and washing. Although the domestic and family responsibilities of women are commonly viewed as a burden, Patricia Pessar argues that this perception could stem from middle-class feminists' characterizations of working-class women. Some immigrant women do not want to forgo their role as the primary domestic worker in the home, seeing it both as a positive way to create a home and care for a family and as marking a break from the pressures and coldness of the work environment outside the home (Pessar, 1995: 37). Certain immigrant women may also perceive their responsibility to create a home as liberation from the burden of paid labor, which often involves long hours and physically demanding work conditions. Nonetheless, these women do find themselves working, often more than their husbands. Unlike most men, women labor both inside and outside the home. Immigrant women may be tied to a patriarchal gender code, which defines womanhood in terms of her work in the home and devotion to her family. As Nancy Foner states, "Moreover, despite changes in women's status in New York, premigration gender role patterns and ideologies do not fade away; they continue to affect the lives of migrant women, often in ways that constrain and limit them" (Foner, 1999: 105).

American-based research on women and migration is applied to the situation in Montreal because almost all inquiry on this topic is based in the United States. However, work by Deirdre Meintel, Micheline Labelle, Genevieve Turcotte, and Marianne Kempineers (Labelle et al., 1987; Meintel et al., 1987) provides insight into the Canadian situation. The authors investigate the lives of immigrant women of Portuguese, Greek, Haitian, and Colombian descent working in the labor market in manufacturing and service occupations. Even though immigrant women may have worked both in and out of the home in their country of origin, negotiating these two work realms is more burdensome in the Canadian context. Domestic work could possibly be better integrated into the work life of immigrant women in their country of origin. Many of the immigrant women that the researchers interviewed, for instance, had worked for family businesses before coming to Canada. Furthermore, distances between workplaces and homes were less in their country of origin (Meintel et al., 1987: 280). Nonetheless, immigration has changed the attitudes and practices of men in the home. A number of women interviewed pointed out that their husbands help them at home, whereas in their home country male participation in the domestic realm is not a reality. As one woman says: "I tell you sincerely, if I had stayed in Colombia, I wouldn't have a husband today. In Colombia, like everywhere in Latin America, the man wants to be king at home. So anything to do with laundry, ironing, sewing, cooking, they don't know about it. Whereas here, everyone has to collaborate. . . . If the husband gets home from work first, he makes supper. . . . My children have been raised this way too: they are all able to cook, iron; they do everything" (288).

Even though some immigrant women have found that men are more apt to help out in Canada, many are still burdened with arduous weekday schedules that include an extensive day of work followed by an evening of household chores. The salsa dance scene of Montreal might not be truly accessible to many immigrant women of Latin American and Caribbean descent. Their responsibilities at home may give them very little time to embark on a career in teaching salsa. Since most salsa dance classes take place in the evening and on weekends, a dance teacher cannot bear the responsibility of caring for a home and family. A number of the female dance teachers in the city also perform professionally in shows, which further keeps them away from the domestic sphere. The tendency of professional ballroom dancers to delay motherhood could shed some light on the salsa scene. Married ballroom dancers who perform in competitions often postpone having children until they approach the age of forty, a time when they often consider withdrawing from competitions. Rumors that a female dancer is pregnant can hinder her professional reputation (Kornreich, 1998: 126).

The salsa dance business is a public sphere in which concerns of family life do not play a significant role. All the women and most of the men who were actively involved in teaching and promoting the dance in Montreal when I was conducting my ethnographic research do not have children. As well, the majority of female instructors were raised in Quebec, as previously outlined. Why are these women less tied to their motherhood roles than women who have grown up in a Latin American and Caribbean context? Women born in Quebec after the 1960s have been raised in a society that has fostered the "liberation" of women from traditional gender roles. Women from the province are therefore less likely than they were in the past to partake in early childbearing and the care of elderly parents. They may not feel as compelled as certain immigrant women to conform at a young age—or at all—to the conventional model of femininity, which promotes motherhood and women as the primary caretakers of homes and families. Although women in Quebec and Canada are still mainly responsible for domestic chores and the care of children, the sentiment in Quebec, as well as in the rest of Canada, is that men should play a part in the care of children and upkeep of the home.

The majority of Montreal's female dance teachers were born in Quebec and consequently have grown up in a social context marked by radical changes in the lives of women. Prior to the changes associated with the Quiet Revolution, conditions for women in Quebec were exceedingly traditional. The situation in Quebec differs from that in the rest of Canada since this province, which was once more traditional than English Canada, is now on par with or possibly ahead of the other areas of the country in the establishment of equality between men and women. Quebec, which lagged twenty years behind the other provinces in granting women the vote (Lemieux, 1995: 77),[18] is today the only province in Canada that stipulates through legislation, enacted under the leadership of the Parti Québécois, that women keep their family name after marriage in order to further foster equality between men and women. Nonetheless, in comparison to the rest of Canada, Quebec was late in taking steps to liberate women and entrench feminist values in society (Dumont, 1992: 77).

The historical developments of the status of women in Quebec provide insight into why women raised in the province may feel that they have more freedom to define themselves outside of traditional gendered role patterns. This look at the history of Quebec women maps out their movement from the private sphere of the home and family life to the public domains of work and politics. Various events in Quebec between the Second World War and the drastic changes of the Quiet Revolution illustrate how strong political forces were at play to keep Quebecois women within the private domain (Linteau et. al., 1989b: 609).

During the Second World War, institutional and cultural forces sought to maintain women's place within domesticity under the authority of their husbands. Women who worked outside the home during the war were denounced as having abandoned their families and were accused of promoting juvenile delinquency and of jeopardizing the interests of the French Canadian nation (Clio Collective, 1987: 283). One of the main elements of Quebec's collective identity was a family structure in which the mother was in the house, the father was the head of the family, and there were numerous children.

After the Second World War, the government did all it could to get the women who worked during the war years back into the home. They levied a tax on the income of husbands whose wives worked and abolished nurseries (Clio Collective, 1987: 293). After the war, the church established two women's groups, L'Union catholique des femmes rurales and Les Cercles d'économie, both of which maintained the conservative ecclesiastical attitude toward the role of women in society. A woman's vocation was to be a loving and faithful wife, a devoted mother, and an industrious housekeeper (Linteau et al, 1989b: 610). Although many priests, nationalists, and intellectuals were vehemently opposed to women's laboring outside the home, many women in Quebec held jobs because a working-class family could not sustain itself without the employment of both husband and wife (Clio Collective, 1987: 294).

The education of women in Quebec reinforced women's place in the home. In 1943 the liberal government of Adelard Godbout intervened in education by passing the *Compulsory School Attendance Act* and challenged the clergy's absolute control over this institution. Nonetheless, the Catholic Church still had jurisdiction over the content of education. From 1940 to 1950 the clergy's reign over women's schooling was heightened. It increased the number of domestic science schools that stressed teaching women how to be feminine and how to take care of a home and family. The academic content of the curriculum in these schools was diminished to such an extent that many female students found it difficult to pass Grade 11 exams (Clio Collective, 1987: 297). The idea that women should be educated differently from men prevailed. While the English-speaking world had begun to choose coeducation by the end of the nineteenth century, until 1965 Quebec had separate educational institutions and curricula for male and female students (Dumont, 1992: 87).

The lives of women underwent radical changes during the rapid modernization of Quebec society in the period of the Quiet Revolution, which officially began with the 1960 provincial election that followed the death of Maurice Duplessis in 1959 (Clio Collective, 1987: 321). After the establishment of the Ministries of Education and Social Affairs in 1964, the massive changes of the Quiet Revolution were set in motion. These changes included the secularization of society, coeducational schools, free access to secondary and collegiate education, mixed institutions and hospitals, bureaucratization, creation of various new professions, extensive entry of women into the workforce, and a massive increase of unionization, particularly in the public sector (Clio Collective, 1987: 325; Dumont, 1992: 86).

In 1964, Bill 16 was adopted, which altered the legal status of married women (Dumont, 1992: 86). Prior to the passing of this bill, the *Civil Code* denied married women rights to the extent that wives, compelled to submit to the control of their husbands, had the legal status of minors. According to Sylvie D'Augerot-Arend, how the *Civil Code* determined the status of women in both Quebec and France has been associated with their shared "Latin" tradition. The *Code* rendered women submissive to male authority (D'Augerot-Arend, 1991: 141). Bill 16 recognized the legal equality of wives and gave them the authority to exercise civil and financial responsibilities, rights that they had previously been denied.

More significant changes occurred in the lives of women in Quebec with the integration of feminist values into the political, economic, and social fabric of the province during the period between 1969 and 1979 (Clio Collective, 1987: 337). The institutionalization of feminist concerns respecting the equality of women became a significant part of union and political action in Quebec, leading to the entrenchment of feminist issues in the structures of society (Lemieux, 1995: 79, 85). Quebec nationalism played a positive role in foregrounding feminists' demands in Quebec and facilitated the rapid transformation of the condition of women in the province (82). This integration of feminist values occurred most strongly during the politically explosive period in the province between 1969 and 1979. In 1970 the question of Quebec nationalism and the October Crisis dominated the political climate (Clio Collective, 1987: 359).

The emergence of the Parti Québécois furthered the dissemination of feminist goals in Quebec (Clio Collective, 1987: 353); when the party came to power, more than half its members were women, who ensured that such issues as child care, abortion, and maternity leave were principal concerns. The Parti Québécois did more than any other party in the history of Quebec to further the equality of women (374), being the first to endorse a specific policy on women (Dumont, 1992: 88). For instance, when elected in 1976, the Parti Québécois commissioned the Conseil du statut de la femme to create a general policy on the status of women in Quebec. The report of the council, entitled *Pour les Québécoises: égalite et indépendance*, was published in 1978 and dealt with a wide range of issues that affected women's lives. The report's mandate was to chart methods by which the government could diminish inequality and establish true independence for women (Clio Collective, 1987: 374). The following year, a permanent ministerial committee was set up to implement the recommendations outlined in the report. The objective of the resulting legislation was to create new reforms that genuinely instilled the principle of equality between the sexes and entrenched these changes in lifestyles and prevailing attitudes. One of these laws, which dealt with the realm of marriage and family, was Bill 89, adopted in 1980. This bill outlines how each member of a couple has the same rights and obligations. Consequently, both husbands and wives keep their last names after marriage, and the last name of the mother can be given to her children. Moreover, Bill 89 puts forward that both spouses must together assure the moral and material well-being of the family, exercise parental authority, and assume the responsibilities that need to be undertaken (Linteau et al., 1989b: 618). The involvement of the Parti Québécois in women's issues illustrates how nationalism is an essential element of the Quebec feminist movement since the question of Quebec sovereignty is a primary concern of this political party (de Sève, 1992: 116).

The status of women in Quebec underwent massive changes during a relatively short period of time. The historians of the Clio Collective nevertheless argue that these transformations did not sufficiently improve the lives of women because the working world did not adequately meet the domestic needs of both men and women (Clio Collective, 1987: 372). The situation in Quebec is far from perfect. Linteau and colleagues argue that negotiating work, maternity, and domestic life is still primarily a woman's responsibility. Women are more often unemployed than men and more often work at part-time employment than men. Even though a small number of women have broken barriers by entering professions that once excluded them, the vast majority of women occupy jobs at the lower end of the pay scale (Linteau et al., 1989b: 619). Despite these disadvantages, the prevailing attitude in Quebec is that there should be a sense of equality between men and women. This balance between the sexes has the potential to extend into the domestic realm. Caring for children and looking after the home are no longer regarded as solely female responsibilities, especially if both members of the couple work. In Quebec, as in the rest of Canada, it is recognized that both men and women have a part to play in the private realm of the home and in the public realm of work. Although this sense of gender equality may not always be realized in practice, it circulates in the mainstream imagination largely as a result of historical changes in the province.

Latin American and Caribbean women may feel the desire to conform to the gender norms of their home country, in which a woman's primary responsibility is to have a family. Since most of the female salsa dance instructors were born and raised in Quebec or elsewhere in Canada, they may feel "freer" to work in the public spaces of clubs and dance studios, employment that involves a schedule and lifestyle that is generally incompatible with family life. Throughout the enormous changes in Quebec, women have fought for equality with men and for active roles in the public sphere. Why not take this stride in dance?

Stepping into a salsa club or class for the first time in Montreal, the novice dancer could easily reduce salsa to a practice that is solely marked by male domination. Men lead women on salsa dance floors. An in-depth exploration of the salsa dance scene shows that despite the male domination inherent in the practice, this scene yields much more complex relationships between the sexes and people of diverse cultures than can be initially ascertained by several jaunts into a club or school. Through this ethnographic investigation of the Montreal scene, male privilege is distilled in order to illustrate how the blanket term "male domination" to describe this Latin cultural sphere does not adequately express what is happening at the level of practice.

A superficial look at the salsa dance scene could also lead to the conclusion that masculine control is solely an expression of the "foreign" Latin culture from which salsa stems. The tendency to promote and sell salsa as a dance with heightened gender differences, in which the male is in command, may reflect more how the dance is sold in the city than how it is performed by those who were raised with this tradition as part of their cultural heritage. According to Ruud Vermay, the narrative of male dominance and female compliance is the most exaggerated in Latin dances influenced by ballroom. When Latin dances are performed in their countries of origin, the relationship between the male and female dancer more often involves a shared transmission of energy than it does control and submission. Vermay's work illustrates how the excessive male dominance that characterizes the salsa vision of some of the Montreal dance schools may be influenced more by European-based ballroom renditions of competitive Latin American dance than by how salsa is performed by people who were raised with this practice as part of their cultural heritage.

Dance instructors may opt to portray gender relationships in salsa in conventional ways because they realize that these stereotypes sell the dance. Many students may enjoy salsa because it allows them to reenact more traditional relationships between men and women in a controlled space that does not necessarily reflect the legal status of men and women within the province. The equation of masculine expression with the male dancer's responsibility for the success of the dance and with his protection of the female dancer—as described by Paolo, for instance—reflects the gender relationships that were produced by the *Civil Code* in Quebec (and France) before they were changed in the province in 1964. The "Latin culture" argument had been used in both France and Quebec to contend that women should not be allowed to vote. Claims were made that these two nations shared a Latin culture. Their Latin nature, rooted in similar civil codes, created an alliance between men and women in which women were entitled to the respect and protection of men and therefore necessarily regarded as inferior (D'Augerot-Arend, 1991: 141). This "Latin culture" argument served to distinguish Quebec from such non-Latin nations as England, the United States, and the Nordic countries, which had a greater tradition of equality between the sexes at the level of legislature (140).

There is no clear link between how a salsa teacher presents the gender dynamic in the dance and whether the instructor is male or female and of Latin origin. Not all Montreal's male salsa dance instructors of Latin descent emphasize male domination in the dance. Not all female dance instructors try to subvert its heightened sense of male privilege, although the majority do. Their tendency to portray salsa as a dance in which the relationship between the sexes is more about complementarities than about domination and submissiveness could stem in part from their desire to play an active role in teaching the dance. The notion that a woman can be a key player in teaching and performing the dance, rather than simply a beautiful object to be displayed and protected by the male, gives female instructors greater authority in a dance scene that is governed by male leadership.

The masculine control of salsa dancing is further complicated by the prominent place that women have in the production and promotion of this dance in the city. Nonetheless, these women are mostly from Quebec (or elsewhere in Canada) and did not emigrate to the province from a Latin nation. Male salsa dance instructors are generally of Latin American or Caribbean descent. The dearth of Latin women who teach and promote the dance reveals how the ability to break through a male-dominated sphere such as the salsa dance world is not shared by all women. A possible explanation for the ethnographic finding that Latin women are not visible in salsa dance teaching and promotion is that gender norms from the countries of origin influence the lives of these immigrant women living in Montreal, making their situation different from that of women raised in Quebec. Nonetheless, considerable historical changes in the province have transformed a once highly patriarchal society into one whose legislation has sought equality between women and men. Whether structural changes promoting equality actually influence how men and women relate to one another in their private domains is open to debate. Still, like the rest of Canada, Quebec acknowledges that women are equally capable in the realms of the private and the public. Research on women and migration reveals that women who have been raised in Latin American and Caribbean nations tend to privilege traditional expressions of womanhood, such as being a mother and raising a family. These gender norms may persist when women migrate to a new nation. Consequently, immigrant females of Latin descent may not feel as "free" as women raised in the province to participate in the salsa dance world. As Daphne points out, teaching salsa dancing is not considered an extremely desirable job for a woman. Not only is it a low-status job, as it does not require professional academic training, but it is also associated with nightclubs and their concomitant lifestyle, which is rarely held in high regard. Nonetheless, Daphne is also the owner and director of a dance school, at which she administers many dance classes. She is an influential figure in the Montreal dance world and performs at many salsa events in the city and around the world. As Daphne herself explains, it is perhaps because she has been raised in Quebec that she is more willing to assert herself as both a dancer and a businesswoman in the male-dominated world of salsa dancing.

Notes

1. Caribe dance school closed in 2004.

2. Une femme peut enseigner a un homme débutant mais pour le developper ca prend un homme. Parce qu'il n' y a pas une femme qui sent qu'est ce que je sens. Meme si elle est un bon professeur, elle ne va jamais developper un homme comme un homme va le developper.

3. The shimmy, a jazz movement that dates back to 1916, comprises isolations of alternating shoulders while the body sways (Malnig, 1992: 111).

4. In the last five years, it has become popular in dance schools in Canada, the United States, Europe, and Australia to teach salsa courses for women that focus specifically on the movements of the female dancers. These courses are called Lady Styling. For instance, in a description of a Lady Styling course advertised on Salsa Site, a website from Oslo, Norway, an extensive list is provided detailing what students will learn in the Lady Styling courses. This list begins, "In the Lady Styling classes with Karina you will learn: How to feel and look feminine in your dance, even doing a basic step" (Salsa Site, 2005). The Lady Styling component of contemporary salsa instruction illustrates how "femininity" in salsa dance is being overtly taught. In salsa courses, men's styling is also taught in salsa schools around the globe. For instance, an advertisement on the Salsa Freak website for a Men's Styling All-Day Bootcamp with Al "Liquid Silver" Espinoza describes what a male student will learn in this intensive lesson, including elements that focus on developing masculinity in the dance, such as "the power of your frame," "masculine body movement," "masculine looking Shimmies," and "spinning techniques with masculine flavor," in addition to spins and partnering techniques to assist the male dancer in taking the lead (Men's Styling All-Day Bootcamp, 2005).

5. Il y toujours quelqu'un qui suit. Cela n'est pas sexiste. Mais parfois, on dit que nous sommes machos et á la maison, c'est l'homme . . . mais si nous le regardons d'un autre point de vue, nous pouvons voir que c'est la femme qui est le spectacle de la danse. C'est l'homme qui fait voir la femme. L'homme fait bouger la femme. Puis, c'est la femme qu'on fait montrer. Et c'est la femme qui suit toujours.

6. Dans la vie, il y a toujours quelqu'un qui mène, même dans une compagnie. Il y toujours une tête. On ne peut pas être deux têtes. Sinon, cela ne marche pas. Dans la danse, comme dans la vie, c'est toujours une personne qui respecte l'autre.

7. La danse est tres sensuelle. Donc, il y a beaucoup de communication. C'est une manière de parler. Quand tu touches quelqu'un, tu la fais tourner et tu la fais danser. Donc la femme sent la masculinité de l'homme dans la danse. Cela nous avons perdu dans l' Amérique du Nord.

8. C'est nous qui conduisons. C'est nous qui décidons quand la fille va tourner dans toute les danse latines. Dans la merengue dans les toutes.

9. Il n'y a aucune différence si c'est un homme ou une femme qui enseigne la salsa. Parce que tant qu'une femme peut apprendre justement à guider et à faire les pas de l'homme, l'homme peut aussi apprendre les pas de filles pour leur montrer les déplacements qu'elles doivent faire. Il y a aucune différence.

10. Nonheterosexual salsa contexts catering to same-sex dance couples include the city's gay and lesbian salsa clubs, Bar Exotica and Bar Exceso Latino.

11. Quand je parle de l'écoute comme je disais tout à l'heure, c'est d'avoir une certaine tension pour être attentif. Et les gars doivent donner la pression nécessaire pour que la fille réussisse à faire ce qu'on veut qu'elle fasse. Quand on dit après qu'il y a un 'feeling' entre les deux, qu'il y a une complicité, on parle justement de 'feeling' et de

complicité, c'est de cette énergie que je parlais tout à l'heure. Pour l'homme et pour la femme, ça donne envie de bouger et ça donne envie de danser. Quand on est deux, on a besoin justement que cette énergie circule entre les deux corps. Pour que cette énergie circule, il doit y avoir une petite résistance pour la fille et la même chose pour le gars. S'il y a un des deux qui a les bras trop durs, trop tendus on le ressent. Il y a l'autre partenaire qui va ressentir que son bras est trop tendu. Et s'il est trop mou on sent aussi comme si on n'était pas en train de danser avec quelqu'un. C'est comme si on était en train de danser tout seul. Alors, justement, on a besoin de cette petite tension des deux pour que cette énergie circule entre les deux corps. Et c'est de là que viennent la communication et la conduite.

12. This situation has changed slightly since I conducted my ethnographic research. A daughter of one male salsa instructor now runs her own dance school in Montreal. She was raised in Quebec.

13. Since I completed my ethnographic research in 2000, the salsa dance instruction scene in Montreal has changed considerably. For instance, many new dance schools have emerged, whereas others have closed down. Nonetheless, women of Latin American or Caribbean background still do not have a prominent place in Montreal's salsa instruction. In 2005 approximately fourteen dance schools are owned and directed by male dancers of Latin American or Caribbean descent. Roughly three dance schools are owned and directed by women who either are Quebecois or were raised in Quebec. Approximately three dance schools are directed by a dancing team consisting of one female dancer of Quebecois background and one or a few male dancers of Latin American or Caribbean origin. Only one dance school in the city is directed by a woman of Latin American background. A male dancer of Quebecois background also directs one of Montreal's salsa schools. These figures are approximate since dance schools readily fold.

14. Les femmes latino-américaines font beaucoup d'enfants, alors elles sortent moins. Les femmes québécoises ont moins d'enfants donc elles sortent plus. Toutefois, les femmes latino-américaines dansent beaucoup. Il y des bonnes danseuses qu'on n'a pas découvertes. Elles ne sont pas dans des clubs Latins.

15. Tu sais, dans le milieu du commerce, il y a beaucoup de façon de faire de l'argent. Mais, si on parle de la réalité. La vérité, c'est la vérité. Donc il y a des filles qui bougent bien mais ça ne veut pas dire qu'elles sont des bonnes professeures ou qu'elles savent danser.

16. It's interesting to note that the local Montreal salsa bands headed by Joé Armando and Papo Ross have included a number of female musicians.

17. Research dealing with how gender patterns in both the country of origin and the host country affect the lives of immigrant women includes, for example, Gmelch and Bohn 1995; Alcalay 1984; Ho 1993; Fincher 1993; Pedraza 1991; Curran 2003; Alicea 1997; Toto-Morn 1995; Pessar 1999a and 1999b; and Morakvasic 1984.

18. Women in Quebec obtained the right to vote at the provincial level in 1940, while women in the rest of Canada received this right in 1918. In English Canada

civil rights for women were changed in 1872, whereas in Quebec they were not modified until 1964. Women in English Canada were permitted to attend university just after 1859; women in Quebec attained the same access in 1907. In Quebec the foundations of the first feminist movement were laid in 1907, while the origins of the first feminist movement in English Canada date back to 1880 (Dumont, 1992: 77).

~

Conclusion

Virtual Migrations

The minds and bodies of travelers and migrants have been the key source of salsa's transmission beyond its sites of "origin." As people move to urban centers or cross community boundaries within cities, they carry their dance cultures with them, diffusing them through physical performance and verbal communication. Written language has typically not had a role in the dissemination of popular dance. The salsa that thrives outside of the ballroom tradition has generally not been recorded or disseminated in textual form. European social dances, on the other hand, have been written down. The elite social dances of Europe that often fused with African traditions in the New World could be transported outside of their "original" contexts through dance manuals. John Charles Chasteen, for example, notes that while manuals describing fashionable high-society European dances were abundant in the United States in the nineteenth century, their usage in Latin America was far less frequent. The dances of Europe were instead diffused in the region through the influx of people arriving or traveling from Europe to the Spanish and Portuguese New World (Chasteen, 2004: 116). Beginning in the twentieth century, Latin social dances from the ballroom tradition were textually recorded, facilitating their transmission to global audiences. Information about dances rooted in popular expression, such as "street" salsa, are predominantly not found in books and manuals but ascertained through actual performance and lived circumstances.

With Internet use rising, popular dance transmission is undergoing a change: it is becoming increasingly textual. There is presently an abundance of written information online about dances that were previously undocumented and consequently unregulated in textual form. While many popular dance sites offer written descriptions as well as various forms of notations, others use video and graphics software to provide audio-visual recordings of dance styles and practices. Salsa is among the myriad popular dance forms disseminated in hypertexts through Internet communication. Salsa websites have become a means to teach dance outside of the context of "real" dance lessons. The transmission of salsa on the Internet has become increasingly pronounced since the beginning of the twenty-first century, further removing this dance from the world of its origins. Salsa dance lessons, which have spread globally since the 1980s, initially uprooted salsa from lived circumstances, a process that is being furthered by the dissemination of dance instruction through Internet communication.

This ethnography of Montreal's salsa schools reveals how movement aesthetics derived from the ballroom tradition have been incorporated into the teaching of street salsa or salsa initially derived from lived Caribbean and Latin American contexts in the city. As salsa is danced both within ballroom circles and lived circumstances, there is an interconnection between these two traditions. In the world of ballroom, salsa is being reconceived in terms of fixed steps, turns, and figures to facilitate its inclusion in the repertoire of Latin American dances performed in competitions and taught at schools. Nevertheless, as salsa has not become completely standardized even within ballroom circles, the ballroom tradition can still be influenced by the multiple interpretations and styles of this dance that continue to flourish in lived circumstances. A dance tradition that thrives in lived circumstances is diffused through collective performance without formal instruction and written rules and regulations. In the United Kingdom the Alliance of Professional Teaching of Dancing, a ballroom dance organization, launched a Club Dance Division in 1998 that codified the Cuban style of salsa by introducing a fixed syllabus (Yeo, 1999). This institution of a Club Dance Division in the United Kingdom more firmly entrenches salsa within the domain of ballroom dance. The ballroom tradition may increasingly transform salsa into a standardized rendition circumscribed by certain written rules much in the same way that Cuban dances such as the *son*, known in ballroom as the rumba, became Latin standards regulated in dance manuals (Moore, 1951: 284). In the contemporary global arena, the commercial versions of salsa dance (ballroom, New York, Los Angeles, Cuban, Puerto Rican, and Colombian) have the potential to become standardized through regulations outlined in texts as well as to resist processes of homogenization by absorbing influences from versions of the dance that continue to thrive in lived oral contexts. The Internet disseminates dance information in textual form, or more specifically in hyper-texts. Despite the textuality that dominates online communication, the Internet also has the potential to disseminate hypertextual information in a manner resembling the mode of communication that characterizes lived oral circumstances. Therefore, due to the renewed orality created by the medium, the textual diffusion of salsa on the Internet may facilitate processes of standardization as well as resistance to concretization.

Having evolved outside of textuality, popular lived dance, defined as a form of collective artistry, could be regarded as oral culture. Oral arts are commonly identified with traditions of the spoken word. Salsa dancers communicate with one another in the couple formation in sensory and kinetic ways, relying on movement and touch and far less frequently on spoken language. Even though speech is but a negligible part of the dancing experience, the use of the term "oral culture" can still be applied to popular dance. Salsa becomes an oral culture in performances of the dance that evolve and flourish within the context of lived circumstances. Communication in such dance contexts intersects with oral traditions, as both take place without the technologies of writing and print. Theorists of orality, moreover, have drawn links between dance and oralist traditions. According to Walter Ong, spoken words often engage body movements that range from hand gestures to dancing, with cultural factors determining the level of gesticulation (Ong, 1982: 67). Eric Havelock regards dance as one of the oral arts, along with songs, chants, epics, and music (Havelock, 1991: 21, 16).

The term "primary orality" is used to describe a condition that existed before the invention of writing (Havelock, 1991: 11, 16). Although this era is long gone, many cultures and subcultures within our current age of high technology perpetuate aspects of primary orality (Ong, 1982: 11). Literacy and orality are therefore not mutually exclusive but intertwine in contemporary society (Havelock, 1991: 11). Salsa dance cultures flourishing in lived contexts retain dimensions of primary orality in how the dance is learned, how it is recorded in memory, and how its performance is shaped by consciousness of the present.

When individuals grow up moving to the rhythms of salsa, this dance is attained in an informal learning context. Acquiring a dance passed on by prior generations takes place without the deliberate study involved in obtaining literary skills. Knowledge is gained through immersion within this dance culture, lived interaction, repeated practice, and actual performance. Pockets of salsa culture in which this dance is learned outside of formal structures exist throughout the Americas. The most prominent are New York, Miami, Los Angeles, Puerto Rico, Colombia, Panama, and Venezuela since these geographic spaces have been key players in salsa's historical develop-ment. Nonetheless, the diffusion of salsa through informal learning mecha-nisms can occur in any geographic location that is home to immigrants of Latin descent whose heritage includes salsa. Within cities and nations not typically associated with Latin culture, informal learning structures are main-tained through dance performance. Salsa can then be disseminated within either the private space of the home or the more public arena of community events and urban dance spaces.

Salsa can pass from previous generations because it is recorded in memory. As part of an oral tradition, this dance is not stored in documents but in the bodies and minds of its dancers. Oral arts need to possess certain qualities that enable them to be memorized and "recorded" for later diffusion without being documented in writing (Denny, 1991: 86). Therefore, oral arts and popular dances unite in their formulaic, patterned, and rhythmic qualities. Salsa is marked by a proliferation of styles named after cities and national origins. These styles rooted in local contexts and histories continue to evolve and transform through their lived performance. Nonetheless, they also con-tain various basic repetitive patterns (i.e., steps and figures) that act as a stor-age vehicle for dance information. Salsa dance styles can be passed on through the repetition of steps, figures, and turns, yet each salsa dance is never reproduced in exactly the same manner. Oral arts are marked by im-provisation created by recombining familiar elements (78).

Oralist traditions thrive within a lived world focused on the present. For instance, in primary oral cultures words do not have meanings that are not relevant to their current use; in literary cultures, dictionaries store the mul-tiple and, at times, archaic meanings for a given word. Similarly, popular dances are constantly changing and renewing themselves as they adapt to present contexts. The contemporary significance of words in oralist modes of communication have of course been shaped by their past uses. Dances that are popular in present circumstances have also evolved from earlier rendi-tions: contemporary salsa, as previously noted, has developed from previous forms. Even though dances may stem from the past, in oral traditions the dances performed are relevant to the present situation and are not out of con-text. A key characteristic of oralism, therefore, is that communication can-not be out of context. Literacy has amplified processes of decontextualization (Denny, 1991: 72).

Keeping alive past traditions that are not necessarily connected to con-temporary lived realities is a process generally associated with cultures of lit-eracy. Typically, a dance that is part of an oral culture is a lived corporeal ex-pression that thrives in present concrete realities and evolves with time; it is not regulated by written rules that resist change and become standardized. Theater dances of the past have been textually recorded with dance notation methods such as Labanotation and Benesch, transforming this ephemeral art into discernible form. Popular dances have also been codified to a limited extent. The Latin dances that are the precursors of today's salsa have become frozen within a tradition that seeks to standardize and contain dances that thrived and evolved in the lived circumstances of previous eras (Thomas and Miller, 1997: 94). The ballroom dance tradition regulated Latin dances through written rules and regulations, creating a syllabus and standards to which dancers are expected to adhere in competitions.

Dance cultures flourishing in lived contexts retain dimensions of primary orality, yet they are not completely removed from the influence of recording technologies that document dance performances. The boundaries between literacy, technology, and orality are porous. For instance, although Cali, Colombia, is a key salsa center that has given rise to a dance learned, performed, and practiced in a lived culture, salsa is not indigenous to the cultural fabric of the city. In her study of the development of salsa in Cali, Lise Waxer points out that the presence of Caribbean music in Colombia dates back to the 1930s, when black Caribbean merchant sailors, called *Chombos*, brought recordings of Cuban and Puerto Rican music to the seaport of Buenaventura. These sailors carried with them a dance tradition that would become the roots of contemporary salsa in Cali (Waxer, 2002a: 56). These Caribbean sailors had learned the dances that they transported to Colombia from their parents in lived oral contexts (Arias Satizábal, 2002: 254). At the same time, films played a role in the diffusion of the Cuban dances of the 1940s and 1950s. Screen dancers such as Tin Tán, Resortes, Antonietta Pons, and Tongolele performed Cuban styles that inspired the dancers of Cali. These dancers featured in films were actually Mexican artists who integrated Cuban forms into their artistry. These cinematic dance representations were crucial in the dissemination of Caribbean dance in Columbia (Waxer, 2002a: 57). Film and television also influence contemporary performances. For instance, *casino* dancers in Cuba, who are primarily from the younger generation, incorporate gestures and expressions of stars from films and soap operas in their dancing (Balbuena, 2003: 99).

Just as speech is transformed from a lived event and utterance into a thing, or manufactured product, through writing processes and, more significantly, print technologies (Ong, 1982: 79), the textual circulation of salsa on the Internet remodels the dance event into a fixed product or commodity. Printing and computers have entrenched writing's bias toward what Walter Ong calls the "reduction of dynamic sound to quiescent space" (82). With the translation of both speech and dance into spatial representations in texts, the essential dynamism of these practices in their lived performance—namely, movement—cannot be captured. Continuous movement underlies spoken language and lived dance. Words in Homer's world are "winged words" (77), marking the consciousness within primary orality that language is a flow of speech and sound. However, writing and, more dramatically, print separate words, creating breaks between them. Like spoken words, the dancers' moves are connected by unbroken motion: even in moments of apparent motionless, the dancing body is not completely rigid. Indeed, by incorporating a philosophy of movement into cultural theory, Brian Massumi has shown the dynamic nature of fixity. Drawing from geological sciences, he describes how the ground is not static but full of dynamism. It is measurement that has stopped the movement (Massumi, 2002: 10). Just as grammar rules and dictionaries try to "freeze" spoken language, which is always changing and evolving, the reduction of salsa to a textual codification attempts to render static that which is in flux in actual performance. The dissemination of salsa on certain Internet websites separates the flow of movement into distinct units. Steps and figures are represented spatially in written descriptions, lists, diagrams, or notation schemes. For instance, on a website entitled "Breaking the 'Breaking' Mystery of the Salsa Timing," a form of notation combining text-based patterns with animated dancing feet is used to depict how dancers can break (or take the first step) on the first, second, and third beats of the music ("Breaking the 'Breaking' Mystery of the Salsa Timing," 12 December 2003). Another site gives a list of moves to be used when *casino* is danced in the *rueda* formation ("Rueda Calls and Descriptions," 12 July 2005).

Dances "frozen" by written regulations or notation resist change, which can facilate processes of standardization. As a result, the Internet may create new forms of standardization. Communications media historians have dealt with the role of technological change in rendering cultural processes more or less uniform. One key focus is Elizabeth Eisenstein's work on the transition from scribal to print culture in fifteenth-century Europe, during which the large-scale production of maps, tables, charts, calendars, dictionaries, grammars, manuals, and other cultural forms altered both the character and dissemination of knowledge (Eisenstein, 1979: 16). The advent of print brought a certain degree of uniformity and homogenization to the processes of textual production, making information more standardized than it had been in scribal culture (80). As a master copy was duplicated by hand in the scribal era, it would eventually become transformed after being repeatedly copied over the course of time. The master copies themselves varied from one to the other. Hence scribal culture was changeable, irregular, and variform (10).

This shift from scribal to print culture influenced how people began to view the world. For example, the creation of maps that contained uniform boundaries and the names of places amplified the awareness of faraway regional borders and locations (Eisenstein, 1979: 83). Processes of standardization had an effect on various facets of everyday life, such as laws, languages, and even dress (83–84). Standardization through print was inextricably linked to the production of diversity since the mechanisms that created uniformity could potentially produce a multiple of standard forms. For instance, fashion publications in the sixteenth century not only rendered dress uniform, but also stimulated the development of an assortment of standard trends. As Eisenstein writes, "Books illustrating diverse costumes, worn throughout the world, were studied by artists and engravers and duplicated in so many contexts that stereotypes of regional dress styles were developed. They acquired a paper life for all eternity and may be recognized even now on dolls, in operas, or at costume balls" (84). The graphic and textual renderings of dance forms on the Internet might be expected to bring about similar processes of standardization: the circulation of salsa styles in hypertexts, for instance, may transform dance trends that have the potential to evolve in oral contexts into standard renditions that become bounded and fixed.

The "space" in which these recordings of dance circulate might also have a role in concretizing culture: the potential for culture to become standardized on the Internet is linked to its status as a world-space. David Holmes theorizes about world-spaces, building upon Roland Robertson's work on agents of cultural globalization. These agents, of which the most significant include migration, commodity exchange, global media, tourism, and telecommunications, have created a "consciousness of the world as a whole" (Robertson, 1992: 8). Cultural globalization could be viewed as a means to promote diversity by uniting the world's cultures, but Holmes asserts that, positioned from another vantage point, this process dislodges cultures from their ethnic, regional, and national significances. These agents of cultural globalization are not only modes of exchange, but also cultures that have a hand in standardizing and homogenizing world-spaces. Thus the uniformity of airports, shopping malls, freeways, tourist resorts, modern cities, and television and computer screens throughout the world is both a representation and product of cultural globalization. The Internet, along with other world-spaces, forms an abstract culture of homogeneity that spans the globe (Holmes, 2001: 3).

Although the Internet is really a collection of computers communicating via the TCP/IP protocol (Hine, 2000: 27), the spatial metaphors that have been used to comprehend it have transformed this assembly of computers into a space. Metaphors can have real effects: Mark Stefik argues that the metaphors that are used to describe the Internet have played a crucial role in influencing its development (Stefik, 1997), and theorists have imagined cyberspace as a global city (Nunes, 2001: 64), a metaphor that has contributed to the Internet's transformation into a world-space. Drawing on the work of Michael Sorkin, Jennifer S. Light suggests that since actual cities are being imagined as increasingly dematerialized, it has become easier to draw a comparison between cities and cyberspaces, "mediated places without physical structure" (Light, 1999: 121). As Sorkin himself writes, "Indeed, recent years have seen the emergence of a wholly new kind of city, a city without a place attached to it" (Sorkin, 1992: xi). Although cities obviously need an actual physical site, the dematerialization of cities today is created through the declining connection that many of them have to their local geographies (Light, 1999: 120–21). Moreover, Barry Wellman and Milena Gulia depict virtual life as city life, or more precisely as life "in the heart of densely populated, heterogeneous, physically safe, big cities" (Wellman and Gulia, 1999: 172).

Just as actual urban centers market the cultures of cities and nations, cyberspace absorbs urban and national expressions that circulate as global commodities. When disseminated on webpages, cultural practices such as popular dance styles are disconnected from their historical and contemporary developments in real-world locations. This cultural globalization created through the exchange of information in the world-space of the Internet has the potential to further standardize dance practices that are already being concretized via their circulation as texts.

How the Internet becomes a global city can be illustrated through this online circulation of salsa dance. Descriptions of all commercial styles of salsa that originate in actual cities or nations can be found on the web. Salsa styles circulate in metropolitan areas throughout the globe, yet it is rare to find a city in which all the styles flourish. The popularity of one particular style or various styles within a given city depends on several factors, such as migration, travel, and commerce. For instance, as this ethnography of the Montreal salsa scene shows, New York salsa dominated dance instruction in the latter half of the 1990s. Nonetheless, various other dancing styles, namely the Colombian, could be seen in Latin clubs in the 1990s. With the rise of Cuban immigrants to the city and increased travel to Cuba, Cuban salsa became popular in the late 1990s and early 2000s. Today, information about all the commercial styles of salsa can be found on the Internet. Some websites are devoted to a particular rendition, and others provide information about various styles. Often specific instructors and schools promote their teaching and dancing expertise on these websites.

The Internet mirrors a "real-life" city through its heterogeneity and absorption of global culture. Yet I would add that the Internet is a city in miniature. With "real-life" cities, particularly American ones, becoming increasingly dangerous—which has caused people to flee urban centers and led to fortressing (Sardar, 2000)—the Internet is viewed as a safer, more controllable city. The miniaturization of the Internet space is related to its diminutive size and its potential for manipulation, which stand in contrast to the out-of-control real-life global city.

Susan Stewart claims that miniature objects, such as toys and dollhouses, typically the stuff of childhood, are cultural products that both attend to and manipulate the physical world (Stewart, 1993: 55). Miniatures offer domesticated and controllable copies of real-world artifacts. Hence the online miniature city becomes more manageable than its real-life counterpart. The miniature also produces a world unto itself with its own logic of time and space. For instance, according to Stewart, miniaturizations of the physical world, such as historical reconstructions and amusement parks, transcend historical time and the possibility of understanding through time by bringing historical events "to life," or into the immediate present (60). In these small worlds, historical events become removed from the past circumstances of their origins because they unfold in tableau-like forms whose structure marks a break with historical narration. In a similar vein, Christine M. Boyer shows how the reconstructions of the old parts of some cities in the United States are transformed into "historic tableaux" designed for commercial purposes. These tableaux become severed both historically and geographically from the cities in which they are situated. Boyer writes, "But in fact these tableaux are the true nonplaces, hollowed out urban remnants, without connection to the rest of the city or the past, waiting to be filled with contemporary fantasies, colonized by wishful projections and turned into spectacles of consumption" (Boyer, 1992: 191). There is an analogy between these miniaturized versions of the past, presented as historical tableaux in real cities, and dance styles circulating on the Internet as webpages that assume the form of tableaux. Although the styles transmitted on the Internet have developed over time in specific real-world locations, their dissemination online not only dissolves the distinction between local and global culture, but also erases their historical evolution, presenting all these styles in a single space, the global metropolis of cyberspace, and at a single historical time, the present.

How can the Internet be viewed as a miniaturized space when it provides the user with such an expanse of information? The seemingly infinite potential of the Internet does not render it any less miniature. Immensity, according to Gaston Bachelard, is contained with the sphere of the miniature. He writes in the *Poetics of Space*, "The cleverer I am at miniaturizing the world, the better I possess it. But in doing this, it must be understood that values become condensed and enriched in miniature. Platonic dialectics of large and small do not suffice for us to become cognizant of the dynamic virtues of miniature thinking. One must go beyond logic in order to experience what is large in what is small" (Bachelard, 1958: 150). To illustrate how tiny and immense are compatible in thought, Bachelard offers a simple yet poignant example: when one looks toward the horizon, distance creates miniatures (172). The miniatures on the horizon are not in reality diminutive but become small through the mind's eye. Space, in Bachelard's poetic interpretation, is not an objective construct but is produced through the workings of the imagination: memory and daydream. The boundaries of a given concrete space, such as a childhood home, can transform with imagination. Imagination is localized in this space, and we envision it in our daydreams, which remain lodged in memory. Memory in turn changes our perception of space. The virtual space of the Internet lends itself well to the philosophy of Bachelard: virtual spaces, as David Holmes suggests, are phenomenological realms created out of perception (Holmes, 2001: 15). Although the Internet has been imagined as space, this medium is, as already mentioned, merely a way of transmitting information and a tool of communication. Yet, fantasy and imagination are deployed by net users who transform the Internet into a space. In order for the users, who are isolated in their homes or offices, to envision themselves connected to a vast city, they need to create this space by filling it in with images that transform it into a virtual sphere. The single page that the user is looking at is extended into a gigantic realm. Virtuality, then, to paraphrase Daniel Miller and Don Slater, is not an assumed feature of the Internet but a social accomplishment (Miller and Slater, 2000: 6).

This discussion of the miniature leads to the question: does the removal of salsa from its historical and concrete lived realities through its circulation as hypertexts within this miniaturized and thus controllable virtual global city facilitate processes of standardization? The codification of performance practices on the Internet allows for a heightened globalization of culture, compared to the circulation of dance commodities such as videos, books, and manuals in lived circumstances. Roland Robertson's definition of globalization as a concept that "refers both to the compression of the world and the intensification of consciousness of the world as a whole" (Robertson, 1992: 8) can be applied to this worldwide online circulation of dance. Connectivity produced at a global level provides people with a cultural resource, namely an awareness of the global. Consequently, the technological connectivity of the Internet provides a means to virtually bring local cultures together in one global space, which in turn fosters in its users a consciousness of global unicity. This absorption of local cultures in one miniaturized global sphere and the concomitant consciousness of the "world as a whole" that is generated could perhaps already have contributed to the concretization of salsa into various recognized global styles.

The classification of salsa into six commercial styles (ballroom, New York, Puerto Rican, Colombian, Cuban, and Los Angeles) has possibly been facilitated by Internet communication. The grouping of the dance into various styles is relatively recent and did not always characterize how salsa was presented. For instance, when this Latin dance was becoming fashionable in Montreal during the late 1980s and early 1990s, salsa dancers and instructors simply referred to the dance as "salsa." They rarely verbally differentiated it in terms of particular styles. This categorization of the dance into six styles can be regarded as a form of standardization in itself: it has reduced a practice that has the potential to be highly diverse into a finite set of stylistic distinctions. In lived local circumstances, salsa dancing has been marked by a proliferation of styles that greatly exceeds the six styles now used to market the dance for global audiences. Lise Waxer, for instance, points out that in Venezuela from the mid 1970s to early 1980s, salsa was so varied that each working-class barrio had a different style of dancing (Waxer, 2002b: 230).

The effect of salsa's dissemination via the Internet might be to further the standardization process beyond a classification scheme. The Internet may amplify the establishment of fixed distinctions, or "standards," that differentiate each style. These distinctions may take the form of guidelines or even rules and regulations, echoing how Latin American dances in ballroom have become regulated. The possibility of establishing standards is surfacing on websites. For instance, in a discussion forum entitled "Salsa Syllabus/Standards," there has been ongoing debate since 22 January 2001 about whether the commercial styles of salsa should be standardized for, in part, teaching purposes ("Salsa Syllabus/Standards," 2003). Another salsa webpage illustrates the desire among some ballroom dancers to standardize salsa within this tradition. In the article "What Is Salsa: Is It *Mambo* in Disguise?" an online writer, Armando, reveals his dismay that unlike with *mambo* there is no standard for salsa, meaning that anything goes in dance competitions. He writes, "Are we who have a passion for Salsa ready to organize ourselves and establish a standard? Will Salsa finally be given its deserving place among the other established dances recognized by the worldwide dance community?" (Armando, 2003). The globalizing potential of Internet communication may perhaps serve to hasten the mechanisms of standardization.

It is also possible that the commercial versions of salsa are today evolving into a single standard club dance form. For instance, one style of dance, the New York style, is becoming predominant in Montreal. According to Montreal salsa instructor Charlot, whom I re-interviewed in July 2005, the New York style is dominating the club scene in the city today. Other styles, such as the Colombian and Cuban, are being danced far less in clubs. In the summer of 2005, I returned to the clubs where I had danced and saw that this was indeed the case. The clubs that had formed the core of my ethnographic study in the 1990s were once marked by a proliferation of dancing styles: Colombian, New York, and Cuban. In 2005 the New York style is almost the only style to be seen on Montreal dance floors. This domination of the New York style is not surprising: my ethnographic research showed that the majority of the dance instructors were teaching the New York style in the late 1990s. Many of the city's dancers from Central America who initially taught the Colombian style, or what some referred to as the classical style, eventually adopted the New York version. Furthermore, as noted by Montreal music promoter Alvaro in chapter 2, there was a rising trend in the 1990s to promote New York–style music and dance in Montreal despite the variety that had been thriving in the city during this period. The New York style, as it is performed in Montreal, is marked by ballroom as opposed to Latin-Caribbean aesthetics. These differences have been extensively documented throughout this book, yet their distinctions can be briefly summarized. A dancer displaying a Latin Caribbean aesthetic, for instance, lowers her or his center of gravity, bends the joints slightly, exhibits subtle body isolations, moves with smaller steps, and puts more emphasis on feeling the rhythm of the music with the body than on turning and spinning. The ballroom-influenced aesthetic stresses straighter joints, bigger steps, and a higher center of gravity, while emphasizing turning and spinning. In the 1990s a large percentage of the Montreal club audience were of Latin America and Caribbean background, yet by the summer of 2005 this Latin American and Caribbean presence had considerably diminished.

Norman Urquía has observed a transformation in the London scene that is similar to the change that has occurred in Montreal. Colombians are credited with bringing salsa to London in the 1990s. At this time, Colombians and other Latin Americans were the dominant audience for salsa music and dance in London salsa clubs (Urquía, 2004: 109). The Colombian style of dancing therefore predominated in the city. As described in chapter 1, the Colombian style that developed outside Cali is characterized by small compact steps, a close embrace, attention to rhythm, and few spins and turns. In the early 1990s being able to dance salsa was associated with Latin American culture and identity. Some Latin American salsa teachers even conveyed the idea that only those who were of their background could ever in actuality gain mastery of the dance since it was inherently linked to culture (109). Gradually, local audiences began to enter salsa clubs, and their participation in the scene transformed the London dance style. The belief that only people of Latin American descent could ever really dance salsa was viewed by the local audience as a form of discrimination. Rather than learning a dance style that they could never fully master, namely the Latin American–derived Colombian version, these local salsa dancers adopted the New York style, which in their view located the source of salsa outside the Latin American context (109–10). In keeping with England's history of integrating products of American popular culture into English culture, this adoption of the New York style has become a way for the local English club patrons to make salsa their own. In his ethnographic work, Urquía documents how for some London salsa dancers the New York style has become the English style (102). Knowledge of salsa in contemporary contexts lies not with those Latin Americans who initially brought salsa to London but with the local dance instructors who teach the New York style. According to Urquía, the Colombian style is denigrated by the local audiences and seen as an impoverished version of the dance. Dance instruction in London has become highly elaborate and formalized: salsa schools offer examinations and certificates at the various levels (110). The predominance of the New York style in both London and Montreal, two cities that are geographically distant from one another, raises the question of whether the New York style will predominate in other cities in Europe, Australia, and North America.

According to Charlot, the establishment of the New York style as a standard version of the dance today is being mobilized primarily by the dissemination of dance videos on the Internet. Charlot would not consider the dominance of the New York style in Montreal or in London to be an original characteristic of these specific locations. He argues that eventually the New York style will be the way salsa is danced in global commercial venues (i.e., clubs and schools) around the world. The ability of users to download free videos of the New York style is a key reason for the New York style's reign (MamBostOn2Online Salsa Congress, 7 August 2005). For instance, there are hardly any websites where videos of Cuban dance can be downloaded for free. The New York style, according to Charlot, is also the key style performed at salsa dance congresses, where dancers from around the world meet in numerous cities in North America, Australia, and Europe as well as the Caribbean, the Philippines, Hong Kong, and South Africa to attend workshops and perform ("Dance Forums: Annual Salsa Congresses and Events,"

2005). Given the globalizing potential of the Internet, Charlot envisions the New York style predominating throughout the world salsa market and becoming *the* standard style in the not-too-distant future.

The circulation of hypertext salsa information is perhaps contributing to the standardization of this dance form in offline circumstances. This online dissemination may at the same time work against processes of standardization. The homogenizing possibility of the medium is both maintained and challenged through the production of Internet spaces. Downloading or uploading videos, reading and writing texts, and creating and viewing images are ways for users to forge Internet spaces. Therefore, the generation of space on the Internet is not only phenomenological and fashioned by perception (Holmes, 2001: 15), but also produced by lived embodied practices. Net users, for instance, can defy the potential uniformity of culture by actively providing alternative perspectives that form new spaces.

The recording of salsa information in online texts and videos has the potential to standardize popular dance in ways not possible through lived oral transmission. However, the renewed orality of the Internet may challenge the very processes of standardization that Internet communication creates. The printed word places speech and sound within the rigid confines of space, yet online hypertexts circulate within a net that is in flux, interconnected, and changeable. At the simplest level, if a hypertext is defined as a space of possible readings, the reader (or navigator) helps to write the hypertext by manipulating how nodes, such as written texts and images, are combined. At a more profound level, readers/navigators can also add or modify written texts and images. Pierre Lévy has shown how cyberspace blends the function of reading and writing (Lévy, 2001: 38). This production of online space creates a communication potential among its users that resembles the context of oral cultures: interactive, fluid, evolving, and never out of context. Cyberspace returns the user to a preliterate situation, despite its reliance upon written language. The technological potential of the Internet lies in the interconnection between machines, people, and information within a vast network. As users are immersed in the same expansive interconnected "space," there are no messages, so to speak, that are "out of context." The Internet is distinct from forms of media that, since the advent of writing and print, have decontextualized communication (98–99).

An example of a specific salsa website illustrates how the play of textuality and orality on the Internet facilitates both cultural fluidity and concretization in the salsa dance world. In a discussion forum on dance styles, the issue of whether the North American salsa styles (Los Angeles and New York) are less authentic than those of Cuba and Colombia has been debated since 21 January 2002 ("Salsa Dance Styles," 2003). I heard and recorded very similar conversations in my ethnographic research in Montreal. The Internet is currently concretizing in textual form debates that had traditionally been produced in salsa dance settings through verbal communication. Nevertheless, this transference of popular oral discourse could perhaps further fix salsa styles by recording their distinctions. Since the differences between styles, until the advent of the Internet, had been delineated only through spoken language and performance in oral contexts, they remain unregulated and hence open to debate. On the other hand, the dissemination of a discourse concerning styles on the Internet could lead to the opposite result: a resistance to fixity. For instance, whenever respondents in this online forum argue, based on their experience, knowledge, and lived context, that one style is either more authentic than another or that a given style can be characterized by an essential quality or various traits, these claims are often challenged by users from around the world who are of both Latin and non-Latin backgrounds. The speed and interactivity of the Internet enables the changeable and diverse nature of salsa styles to be transmitted. The widespread accessibility of the Internet facilitates communication resembling that of lived oral circumstances by placing users in a single yet expansive context. Multiple voices, experiences, and opinions are given room on the Internet, defying the fixing of cultural forms and facilitating the fluidity of practices.

This potential of the Internet to disseminate cultural diversity positions new technology and its relation to the transmission of dance practices in a positive light. Despite this optimism concerning the diffusion of dance on the Internet, it seems that in the case of salsa, this technology may eventually serve only to transform the commercial versions of salsa into a cultural form derived from North American and western European practices and aesthetic ideals. Although Latin cultural expressions such as salsa originate with Spanish-speaking people from various nations in the Caribbean and Latin America, most of the websites featuring salsa dance as a codified practice are in the English language and based in cities in North America, Australia, and Europe. The effect of the rising dissemination of salsa through textual or video dance instruction and information may eventually transform salsa into a social dance that resembles the standardized Latin dances of the North American— and British-based commercial industry of ballroom dancing. The dance styles that stem and evolve from the lived realities of people of Latin descent in the Americas may have less and less of an impact on the development of the salsa styles that are being marketed worldwide. Embedded within this exploration of salsa, there perhaps lies an implicit desire on my part to celebrate a lived dance culture that began in the 1960s with salsa's golden age and was rooted in the international migration of Cuban dance in previous decades.

This sense of nostalgia is not without a certain irony. As I did not grow up with the salsa of the 1960s and 1970s, I do not have a historical memory of this epoch. Nonetheless, I am not alone in my nostalgic sentiments for cultures of the past. The desire to reclaim cultures that one has never lost is characteristic of this era of globalization (Appadurai, 1996: 30). This nostalgia holds on to a vision of a salsa dance that cannot be completely standardized, always recreated, fashioned, and formed through the changing circumstances of lived practice. Salsa's potential to resist fixity emanates from its inherent potential for improvisation, derived from the African influence in Caribbean dance. With ornate prose, Fernando Ortiz[1] depicts this resistance to standardization that is at the heart of Cuban dance inspired by African culture. He refers to "the dance where the mulatto[2] always incorporates improvisation, expressive mimesis, social dialogue, exhibitionism in figuration, flourishes, 'rebellious democracy against excessive internal and external order, against uniformity, against *geometrization*,[3] against standardization,' curves of sensuality, fluidity, and seductive grace. And in that cultural mixture lies its secret and its diabolism" (Ortiz, 1951: 266, my translation).[4] This opposition to standardization and control envisioned by Fernando Ortiz in African-inspired dances of Cuba more than a half-century ago resonates in contemporary versions of salsa rooted in a Caribbean-influenced dance heritage and thriving in lived circumstances. Despite the global commodification of salsa that is potentially transforming its commercial forms into fixed standard styles (or perhaps even a singular style), the versions of salsa that endure in lived contexts from which the commercial forms initially stemmed will perhaps continue to resist being concretized by remaining always rooted in lived dance experience.

Notes

1. As a researcher of the African influences in Cuban culture, Fernando Ortiz is a controversial figure. For instance, in an early work, *Hampa afro-cubana: Los negros brujos*, Ortiz saw the black subject and his or her culture as a negative force in Cuban society. He claimed that blacks brought cultural elements, such as superstition and dialects, that fragmented Cuban society (Ortiz, 1906). In the second edition of this text (1917), he changed his perspective. The black subject, whom he had described as a disturbing feature of Cuban society, was repositioned within historical and social circumstances. Blacks were no longer essentially corrupt in themselves; rather, the dominant group relegated them to the margins in order to control their way of life, which not only differed from that of the majority, but also could eventually challenge dominant norms (Catoira, 2005: 184). Fernando Ortiz countered the racialist discourse of the nineteenth century and the intellectual thought that grew from it—

particularly, Nazism—by seeking a discourse that would unify Cubans in an all-embracing concept of Cuban culture (184). Ortiz's concept of transculturaltion, first introduced in *Contrapunteo cubano del tabaco y el azúcar* (1940), enabled him to resist the racialist discourse that prevailed at the time (Catoira, 2005: 185). "Transculturation," a term coined by Ortiz, describes the phenomenon whereby cultures merge and converge. Patricia Catoira argues that in his discussion of the transculturation process, Ortiz did not addresss how exchanges between the various sectors of Cuban society were embedded within a context of unequal power dynamics between groups. For instance, he did not consider that enslaved Africans may have had to adopt the dominant Hispanic culture, such as by learning Spanish in order to improve their working conditions (187). Ortiz focused on the transculturation between blacks and whites because he believed that only through their interconnection could a single modern, unified Cuban nation be built. He elaborates on the merging of black and white cultures in "Por la integracíon cubana de blancos y negros" (1943), which Patricia Catoira regards as a problematic essay because Ortiz focuses primarily on the whites and blacks in Cuba while ignoring other cultures affected by the processes of transculturation, such as the Chinese. Furthermore, Ortiz's analysis of the phenomenon of transculturation as it occurs between blacks and whites serves primarily to illustrate how blacks would eventually become assimilated into the culture of white society. The phases of transculturation—hostility, accommodation, adaptation, self-affirmation, and integration—whiten black culture rather than fusing the two groups (Catoira, 2005: 188).

2. Prior to this citation, Fernando Ortiz refers to the work of Gilberto Freyre (1945), who wrote that to be Brazilian was to be mulatto (Ortiz, 1951: 265). Ortiz does not believe that the term "mulatto" can be used to describe all Cubans, as Freyre claims is the case for Brazilians. Fernando Ortiz states instead that the African influences from Cuban blacks have seeped into sectors of the national culture, such as music and dance, as well as into many aspects of everyday life (265). Ortiz uses the term "mulatto" in this context in a metaphorical sense—that is, not too describe all Cubans but to refer to the African influences that have informed the national Cuban culture.

3. "Geometrization" is a made-up term to describe in English the meaning of the Spanish word *geometrizacíon*.

4. Como en el baile donde el mulato pone siempre improvisacíon, mimesis expresiva, diálogo social, exhibiocionismo o *figurao*, *floreos,* "democracia rebelde a la excesiva ordenacíon, interna y externa, a la uniformidad, a la geometrizacíon, a la estandardizacíon," curvas de sensualidad, morbidez, *sandunga*. Y en esa mixtura cultural están su secreto y su diabolismo.

References

Acosta-Belén, Edna, and Christine E. Bose, eds. 1993. *Researching Women in Latin America and the Caribbbean*. Boulder, CO: Westview.

Adorno, Theodor W., and Max Horkheimer. 1972. "The Culture Industry: Enlightenment as Mass Deception." In *Dialectic of Enlightenment*, trans. J. Cumming, 120–67. New York: Herder and Herder.

Agar, Michael H. 1985. *Speaking of Ethnography*. Vol. 2 in Sage University Paper Series on Qualitative Research Methods. Beverley Hills, CA: Sage.

Aggar, Ben. 1992. *Cultural Studies as Critical Theory*. London: Falmer Press.

Alcalay, Rina. 1984. "Hispanic Women in the United States: Family and Work Relationship." *Migration Today* 12, 3: 13–20.

Aldrich, Elizabeth. 1991. *From the Ballroom to Hell: Grace and Folly in Nineteenth-Century Dance*. Evanston, IL: Northwestern University Press.

Alicea, Marixsa. 1997. "A Chambered Nautilus: The Contradictory Nature of Puerto Rican Women's Role in the Social Construction of a Transnational Community." *Gender and Society* 11 (October): 597–626.

Anderson, Benedict. 1983. *Imagined Communities: Reflections on the Origin and Spread of Nationalism*. London: Verso.

Angeloro, Al. 1992. "Back to Africa: The 'Reverse' Transculturation of Salsa/Cuban Popular Music." In *Salsiology: Afro-Cuban Music and the Evolution of Salsa in New York City*, ed. Vernon Boggs, 301–6. Westport, CT: Greenwood.

Aparicio, Frances. 1998. *Listening to Salsa: Gender, Latin Popular Music and Puerto Rican Cultures*. Hanover, NH: Wesleyan University Press.

———, and Cándida F. Jáquez. 2003. "Introduction." In *Musical Migrations: Transnationalism and Cultural Hybridity in Latin/o America*, vol. 1, ed. Frances R. Aparicio and Cándida F. Jáquez, with Mariá Elena Cepeda, 1–10. New York: Palgrave Macmillan.

Appadurai, Arjan. 1992. "Putting Hierarchy in Its Place." In *Rereading Cultural Anthropology*, ed. George Marcus, 35–47. Durham, NC: Duke University Press.

———. 1996. *Modernity at Large: Cultural Dimensions of Globalization*. Minneapolis: University of Minnesota Press.

Arias Satizábal, Medardo. 2002. "Se Prohíbe Escuchar 'Salsa y Control:' When Salsa Arrived in Buenaventura, Colombia." Trans. Lise Waxer. In *Situating Salsa: Global Markets and Local Meaning in Latin Popular Music*, ed. Lise Waxer, 247–58. New York and London: Routledge.

Armando. 2003. "What Is Salsa?: Is It Mambo in Disguise?" *The World's Largest Latin Entertainment Magazine*, 30 June, http://www.dancefreak.com/stories/mamsals.htm.

Arteaga Rodriguez, José. 1988. "Salsa y Violencia: Una Aproximación Sonora Histórica." *Revista Musical Puertorriqueña* 4: 16–33.

Aschenbrenner, Joyce. 1981. *Katherine Dunham: Reflections on the Social and Political Context of Afro-American Dance*. New York: Cord.

Austerlitz, Paul. 1997. *Merengue: Dominican Music and Dominican Identity*. Philadelphia: Temple University Press.

———. 1998. "From Transplant to Transnational Circuit: Merengue in New York." In *Island Sounds in the Global City: Caribbean Popular Music and Identity in New York*, ed. Ray Allen and Lois Wilcken, 44–60. New York: New York Folklore Society and the Institute for Studies in American Music, Brooklyn College.

Bachelard, Gaston. 1958. *The Poetics of Space*. Trans. Maria Jolas. Reprint, Boston: Beacon, 1994.

Bakhtin, M. M. 1981. *The Dialogic Imagination*. Trans. Caryl Emerson and Michael Holquist. Ed. Michael Holquist. Austin, TX: University of Texas Press.

Balbuena, Bárbara. 2003. *El Casino y La Salsa en Cuba*. La Habana, Cuba: Editorial Letras Cubanas.

Bauman, Zygmunt. 1998. *Globalization: The Human Consequences*. New York: Columbia University Press.

Beal, Frances. 1970. "Double Jeopardy: To Be Black and Female." In *Sisterhood Is Powerful*, ed. Robin Morgan, 382–96. New York: Vintage Books.

Beaulieu, Agnes, and Maria Elena Concha. 1988. *Les Latino-Américains au Québec: Portrait des Familles de Côte-des-Neiges*. Montreal: CLSC Côte-des-Neiges, Association des Immigrants Latino-Américains.

Becker, Howard. 1982. *Art Worlds*. Berkeley, CA: University of California Press.

Berríos-Miranda, Marisol. 2002. "Is Salsa a Musical Genre?" In *Situating Salsa: Global Markets and Local Meaning in Latin Popular Music*, ed. Lise Waxer, 23–50. New York and London: Routledge.

Berry, J. W., and J. A. Laponce. 1994. "Evaluating Research on Canada's Multiethnic and Multicultural Society: An Introduction." In *Ethnicity and Culture in Canada: The Research Landscape*, ed. J. W. Berry and J. A. Laponce, 3–16. Toronto: University of Toronto Press.

bhabha, homi k. 1994. *The Location of Culture*. London: Routledge.

Birnbaum, Pierre. 1996. "From Multiculturalism to Nationalism." *Political Theory* 24, 1 (February): 33–45.

Blacking, John. 1977. *The Anthropology of the Body*. London: Academic Press.

———. 1985. "Movement, Dance, Music and the Venda Girls' Initiation Cycle." In *Society and the Dance: The Social Anthropology of Process and Performance*, ed. Paul Spencer, 64–91. Cambridge, UK: Cambridge University Press.

Boggs, Vernon. 1992a. "Founding Fathers and Changes in Cuban Music Called Salsa." In *Salsiology: Afro-Cuban Music and the Evolution of Salsa in New York City*, ed. Vernon Boggs, 97–105. Westport, CT: Greenwood.

———. 1992b. "Latin Ladies and Afro-Hispanic Music: On the Periphery but Not Forgotten." In *Salsiology: Afro-Cuban Music and the Evolution of Salsa in New York City*, ed. Vernon Boggs, 107–19. Westport, CT: Greenwood.

———. 1992c. "The Palladium Ballroom and Other Venues: Showcases for Latin Music in N.Y.C." In *Salsiology: Afro-Cuban Music and the Evolution of Salsa in New York City*, ed. Vernon Boggs, 125–32. Westport, CT: Greenwood.

———, ed. 1992d. *Salsiology: Afro-Cuban Music and the Evolution of Salsa in New York City*. Westport, CT: Greenwood.

Boothroyd, Jim. 1995. "Steamy Salsa: Six of the City's Hottest Latin Dance Clubs." *Montreal Gazette*, 16 July.

Bottomer, Paul. 1996. *Salsa Dance Crazy*. London: Lorenz Books.

Bourdieu, Pierre. 1977. *Outline of a Theory of Practice*. Trans. Richard Nice. Cambridge, UK: Cambridge University Press.

———. 1984. *Distinction: A Social Critique of the Judgment of Taste*. Trans. Richard Nice. Cambridge, MA: Harvard University Press.

———. 1990. *The Logic of Practice*. Trans. Richard Nice. Cambridge, UK: Polity Press.

———. 1991. "Sport and Social Class." In *Rethinking Popular Culture: Contemporary Perspectives in Cultural Studies*, ed. Chandra Mukerji and Michael Schudson, 357–73. Berkeley, CA: University of California Press.

Boyer, Christine M. 1992. "Cities for Sale: Merchandising History at South Street Seaport." In *Variations on a Theme Park: The New American City and the End of Public Space*, ed. Michael Sorkin, 181–204. New York: Hill and Wang.

"Breaking the 'Breaking' Mystery of Salsa Timing." 12 December 2003. http://www.dancefreak.com/stories/steps.htm.

Brinson, Peter. 1985. "Epilogue: Anthropology and the Study of Dance." In *Society and the Dance: The Social Anthropology of Process and Performance*, ed. Paul Spencer, 206–14. Cambridge, UK: Cambridge University Press.

Browning, Barbara. 1995. *Samba: Resistance in Motion*. Bloomington, IN: Indiana University Press.

Bryson, Norman. 1997. "Cultural Studies and Dance History." In *Meaning in Motion: New Cultural Studies of Dance*, ed. Jane C. Desmond, 55–80. Durham, NC: Duke University Press.

Buckman, Peter. 1978. *Let's Dance: Social, Ballroom and Folk Dancing*. New York: Paddington Press.

Bulmer, Martin, and John Solomos. 1998. "Introduction: Re-thinking Ethnic and Racial Studies." *Ethnic and Racial Studies* 21, 5 (September): 819–37.

Burton, Kim. 1994. "Cumbia! Cumbia! Colombia's Gold Includes Hot Cumbia and Crazed Vallenato Accordions." In *World Music: Rough Guide*, ed. Simon Broughton et al., 549–56. London: Rough Guide.

Butler, Judith. 1988. "Performative Acts and Gender Constitution: An Essay in Phenomenology and Feminist Theory." *Theatre Journal* 20, 3: 519–31.

———. 1990. *Gender Trouble: Feminism and the Subversion of Identity*. New York: Routledge.

Calzado, David. 1994. *Hey, You, Loca! David Calzado and La Charanga Habanera*. Magic Music compact disc. Barcelona, Spain: Cosmopolitan Caribbean Music.

Canadian Statistics. 2001. *Visible Minority Population by Census Metropolitan Areas (2001 Census)*. http://www40.statcan.ca/l01/cst01/demo53b.htm.

Carey, James W. 1992. *Communication as Culture: Essays on Media and Society*. London: Routledge.

Carino, Marites. 1999. "Flirty Dancing: Lookin' for Love in All the Latin Places." *Montreal Hour*, 11–19 February, 41.

Catapano, Peter. 2001. "Salsa: Made in New York." *New York Times on the Web*, 17 February. http://www.nytimes.com/library/music/102400salsa-intro.html.

Catoira, Patricia. 2005. "Transculturation à la *Ajiaco*: A Recipe for Modernity." In *Cuban Counterpoints: The Legacy of Fernando Ortiz*, ed. Mauricio A. Font and Alfonso W. Quiroz, 181–91. Lanham, MD: Rowman and Littlefield.

Chambers, Ian. 1985. *Urban Rhythms: Pop Music and Popular Culture*. London: Macmillan.

Chao Carbonero, Graciela. 1996. "De la contradanza al casino." *Toda la danza, la danza toda*, no. 2 (July–December): n.p.

Chasteen, Charles John. 2004. *National Rhythms, African Roots: The Deep History of Latin American Popular Dance*. Albuquerque, NM: University of New Mexico Press.

Clifford, James. 1988. *The Predicament of Culture: Twentieth-Century Ethnography, Literature, and Art*. Cambridge, MA: Harvard University Press.

———. 1994. "Diasporas." *Cultural Anthropology* 9, 3: 302–38.

———. 1997. *Routes: Travel and Translation in the Late Twentieth Century*. Cambridge, MA, and London: Harvard University Press.

———, and George E. Marcus, eds. 1986. *Writing Culture: The Poetics and Politics of Ethnography*. Berkeley, CA: University of California Press.

Clifford, Paul F. 2001. "Background to Mambo, Salsa and Cha Cha." *StreetDance: Australia's Dance Survival Guide*. 26 March. http://www.geocities.com/sd_au/mambo/sdhmambo.htm.

Clio Collective. 1987. *Quebec Women: A History*. Toronto: Women's Press.

Combahee River Collective. 1983. "A Black Feminist Statement." In *This Bridge Called My Back: Writings by Radical Women of Color*, ed. Cherrie Moraga and Gloria Anzaldria, 210–18. New York: Kitchen Table, Women of Color Press.

Cooper Albright, Ann. 1997a. *Choreographing Difference: The Body and Identity in Contemporary Dance*. Hanover, NH: University Press of New England.

———. 1997b. "Feminist Theory and Contemporary Dance." In *Dancing Female: Lives and Issues of Women in Contemporary Dance*, ed. Sharon E. Friedler and Susan B. Glazer, 139–52. Amsterdam: Harwood Academic Publishers.

Copeland, Roger. 1993. "Dance, Feminism and the Critique of the Visual." In *Dance, Gender and Culture*, ed. Helen Thomas, 139–50. Reprint, New York: St. Martin's Press, 1995.

———. 1997. "Sexual Politics." In *Dancing Female: Lives and Issues of Women in Contemporary Dance*, ed. Sharon E. Friedler and Susan B. Glazer, 123–38. Amsterdam: Harwood Academic Publishers.

Corchado, Serafin (Vicente). 2005. "Rhythms of Salsa." *InScenes Magazine*, 3 August. http://www.inscenes.com/salsart.htm.

Cousins, Mark, and Athar Hussain. 1984. "Sexuality and Power." In *Michel Foucault*, 202–52. New York: St. Martin's Press.

Cowan, Jane K. 1990. *Dance and the Body Politic in Northern Greece*. Princeton, NJ: Princeton University Press.

Crapanzano, Vincent. 1986. "Hermes' Dilemma: The Masking of Subversion in Ethnographic Description." In *Writing Culture: The Poetics and Politics of Ethnography*, ed. James Clifford and George E. Marcus, 51–76. Berkeley, CA: University of California Press.

Crook, Larry. 1992. "The Form and the Formation of the Rumba in Cuba." In *Salsiology: Afro-Cuban Music and the Evolution of Salsa in New York City*, ed. Vernon Boggs, 29–43. Westport, CT: Greenwood.

"Cross-Body Lead: Overview." 18 July 2005. http://salsa_club.tripod.com/basics/id7.html.

Curran, Sara R. 2003. "Engendering Migrant Networks: The Case of Mexican Migration." *Demography* 40, 2: 289–307.

Daly, Ann. 1987. "The Balanchine Woman: Of Humming Birds and Channel Swimmers." *Drama Review* 31, 1 (Spring): 8–21.

———. 1997. "Classical Ballet: A Discourse of Difference." In *Meaning in Motion: New Cultural Studies of Dance*, ed. Jane C. Desmond, 111–19. Durham, NC: Duke University Press.

"Dance Forums: Annual Salsa Congresses and Events." 2005. http://www.danceforums.com/viewtopic.php?topic=4135.

The Dance Store Online: Your Source for Ballroom and Latin dance Instruction. 2005. "Dancer's Dictionary." http://www.thedancestoreonline.com/dancer-dictionary/dictionary-s.htm; and http://www.thedancestoreonline.com/dancer-dictionary/dictionary-q.htm.

Daniel, Yvonne. 1995. *Rumba: Dance and Social Change in Contemporary Cuba*. Bloomington, IN: Indiana University Press.

——. 2002. "Cuban Dance: An Orchard of Caribbean Creativity." In *Caribbean Dance from Abakuá to Zouk: How Movement Shapes Identity*, ed. Susanna Sloat, 23–55. Gainesville, Florida: University Press of Florida.

d'Augerot-Arend, Sylvie. 1991. "Why So Late? Cultural and Institutional Factors in the Granting of Quebec and French Women's Political Rights." *Journal of Canadian Studies* 26, 1 (Spring): 138–65.

Davidson, Boaz, director. 1988. *Salsa: The Motion Picture*. Cannon Films.

Dávila, Arlene. 2001. *Latinos Inc.: The Marketing and Making of a People*. Berkeley, CA, and London: University of California Press.

Dawson, Jim. 1995. *The Twist: The Story of the Song and Dance That Changed the World*. Boston: Faber and Faber.

DeGarmo, William B. 1875. *The Dance of Society*. New York: William A. Pond.

Deleuze, Gilles, and Felix Guattari. 1987. *A Thousand Plateaus*. Minneapolis MN: University of Minnesota Press.

Delgado, Celeste Fraser, and Paolo Esteban Munoz, eds. 1997. *Every-night Life: Culture and Dance in Latin/o America*. Durham, NC: Duke University Press.

Dempster, Elizabeth. 1998. "Women Writing the Body: Let's Watch a Little How She Dances." In *The Routledge Dance Studies Reader*, ed. Alexandra Carter, 223–29. London: Routledge.

Denny, Peter J. 1991. "Rational Thought in Oral Culture and Literate Decontextualization." In *Literacy and Orality*, ed. David R. Olson and Nancy Torrance, 66–89. Cambridge, UK: Cambridge University Press.

de Sève, Micheline. 1992. "The Perspectives of Quebec Feminists." In *Challenging Times: The Women's Movement in Canada and the United States*, ed. Constance Backhouse and David H. Flaherty, 110–16. Montreal and Kingston: McGill-Queen's University Press.

Desmond, Jane C. 1993–1994. "Embodying Difference: Issues in Dance and Cultural Studies." *Cultural Critique* (Winter): 32–63.

Dixon Gottschild, Brenda. 1995. "Stripping the Emperor: The Africanist Presence in American Concert Dance." In *Looking Out: Perspectives on Dance and Criticism in a Multicultural World*, ed. Marcus Gere et al., 95–121. New York: Schirmer Books.

——. 2002. "Crossroads, Continuities and Contradictions: The Afro-Euro-Caribbean Triangle." In *Caribbean Dance from Abakuá to Zouk: How Movement Shapes Identity*, ed. Susanna Sloat, 3–10. Gainesville, FL: University Press of Florida.

Doane, Mary Ann. 1982. "Film and the Masquerade: Theorizing the Female Spectator." *Screen* 23: 3–4.

Dodworth, Allen. 1900. "Chapter IV: Positions and Motions." In *Dancing and Its Relation to Education and Social Life*. Compiled in *An American Ballroom Companion: Dance Instruction Manuals Ca.1490–1920*. Music Division, Library of Congress. http://www.memory.loc.gov/cgi-bin/ampage?collId=musdi&fileName=186/ musdi186.db&recNum=49.

Driedger, Leo. 1996. *Multi-Ethnic Canada: Identities and Inequalities.* Toronto: Oxford University Press.

Duany, Jorge. 1992. "Popular Music in Puerto Rico: Toward an Anthropology of Salsa." In *Salsiology: Afro-Cuban Music and the Evolution of Salsa in New York,* ed. Vernon Boggs, 72–85. Westport CT: Greenwood.

———. 2000. "Nation on the Move: The Construction of Cultural Identities in Puerto Rico and the Diaspora." *American Ethnologist* 27, 1: 5–30.

Dumont, Micheline. 1992. "The Origins of the Women's Movement in Quebec." In *Challenging Times: The Women's Movement in Canada and the United States,* ed. Constance Backhouse and David H. Flaherty, 72–89. Montreal and Kingston: McGill-Queen's University Press.

During, Simon. 1993. "Introduction." In *The Cultural Studies Reader,* ed. Simon During, 1–29. London: Routledge.

Dyer, Richard. 1990. "In Defense of Disco." In *On Record: Rock, Pop, and the Written Word,* ed. Simon Frith and Andrew Goodwin, 410–18. New York: Pantheon.

———. 1993. "'I Seem to Find the Happiness I Seek': Heterosexuality and Dance in the Musical." In *Dance, Gender and Culture,* ed. Helen Thomas, 16–33. Reprint, New York: St. Martin's Press, 1995.

Ebuchi, Kazukimi. 1986. "Ukrainian Identity and Boundary Maintenance in the Context of Canadian Multiculturalism: The Case of Edmonton." In *Ethnicity and Multiculturalism in Canada: An Anthropological Study (1984),* ed. Tsuneo Ayabe, 115–70. Ibaraki, Japan: Institute of History and Anthropology, University of Tsukuba.

Eco, Umberto. 1984. *The Role of the Reader: Explorations in the Semiotics of Texts.* Bloomington, IN: Indiana University Press.

Edie (The Salsa Freak). 1999. "Salsa Dance Styles of the World." *The World's Largest Latin Entertainment Online Magazine,* 15 January. http://www.dancefreak.com/stories/dance_styles.htm.

Eisenstein, Elizabeth L. 1979. *The Printing Press as an Agent of Change: Communications and Cultural Transformations in Early-Modern Europe.* Vol 1. Cambridge, UK, and New York: Cambridge University Press.

Erenberg, Lewis A. 1981. *Steppin' Out: New York Nightlife and the Transformation of American Culture, 1890–1930.* Westport, CT: Greenwood.

Fairley, Jan. 2000. "Cuba: Son and Afro-Cuban Music: Que rico baila yo!" *World Music,* vol. 2, *Latin and North America, Caribbean, India, Asia and Pacific: Rough Guide,* ed. Simon Broughton and Mark Ellingham, 386–407. London: Penguin.

Fang, Irving. 1997. *History of Mass Communication: Six Information Revolutions.* Boston: Focal Press.

Farley, Christopher John. 1999. "Latin Music Pops." *Time,* 24 May, 40–45.

Fernández, María Antonia. 1974. *Bailes populares cubanos.* La Habana, Cuba: Editorial Pueblo y Educacíon.

Fincher, Ruth. 1993. "Gender Relationships and the Geography of Migration." *Environment and Planning* A, 25 (December): 1703–705.

Firmat, Gustavo Perez. 1994. *Life on the Hyphen: The Cuban-America Way*. Austin, TX: University of Texas.

Flores, Juan. 1997. "The Latino Imaginary: Dimensions of Community and Identity." In *Tropicalizations: Transcultural Representations of Latinidad*, ed. Frances R. Aparicio and Susana Chavez-Silverman, 183–93. Hanover, NH: University Press of New England.

Foner, Nancy. 1998. "Benefits and Burdens: Immigrant Women and Work in New York City." *Gender Issues* 16, 4 (Fall): 5–24.

———. 1999. "Immigrant Women and Work in New York City, Then and Now." *Journal of American Ethnic History* (Spring): 95–113.

Fontaine, Louise. 1995. "Immigration and Cultural Policies: A Bone of Contention between the Province of Quebec and the Canadian Federal Government." *International Migration Review* 29 (Winter): 1041–48.

Foucault, Michel. 1978. *The History of Sexuality*. Vol. 1, *An Introduction*. Trans. Robert Hurley. New York: Random Books.

———. 1980. "Body/Power." In *Power/Knowledge: Selected Interviews and Other Writings, 1972–1977*, ed. Colin Gordon, trans. Colin Gordon et al., 53–63. New York: Pantheon.

Fraleigh, Sondra Horton. 1987. *Dance and the Lived Body: A Descriptive Aesthetics*. Pittsburgh: University of Pittsburgh Press.

Franks, A. H. 1963. *Social Dance: A Short History*. London: Routledge and Kegan Paul.

Friede, Eva. 1999. "Swing Time." *Montreal Gazette*, 7 September, C1, C4.

Friedler, Marla. 2000. "How to Dance New York Style Mambo." *Salsa Web*, 3 April. http://www.salsaweb.com/features/ny2.htm.

Friedman, Jonathan. 1994. *Cultural Identity and Global Process*. London: Sage.

Frith, Simon. 1978. *The Sociology of Rock*. London: Constable.

Frye, Marilyn. 1983. *The Politics of Reality: Essays in Feminist Theory*. Freedman, CA: Crossing Press.

Fuss, Diana. 1989. *Essentially Speaking: Feminism, Nature and Difference*. New York: Routledge Press.

Garnham, Nicholas, and Raymond Williams. 1986. "Pierre Bourdieu and Sociology of Culture: An Introduction." In *Media, Culture and Society: A Critical Reader*, ed. Richard Collins et al., 116–30. London: Sage.

Geertz, Clifford. 1973. *The Interpretation of Culture*. New York: Basic Books.

———. 1991. "Deep Play: Notes on the Balinese Cockfight." In *Rethinking Popular Culture: Contemporary Perspectives in Cultural Studies*, ed. Chandra Mukerji and Michael Schudson, 239–77. Berkeley, CA: University of California Press.

Gere, Marcus, et al., eds. 1995. *Looking Out: Perspectives on Dance and Criticism in a Multicultural World*. New York: Schirmer Books.

Giddens, Anthony. 1984. *The Constitution of Society: Outline of a Theory of Structuralism*. Cambridge, UK: Polity Press.

———. 1987. *Social Theory and Modern Sociology*. Oxford, UK: Polity Press.

——. 1990. *The Consequences of Modernity.* Stanford, CA: Stanford University Press.

——. 1991. *Modernity and Self-Identity: Self and Society in the Late Modern Age.* Cambridge, UK: Polity Press.

——. 1994. "Living in a Post-Traditional Society." In *Reflexive Modernization: Politics, Tradition and Aesthetics in the Modern Social Order,* ed. Ulrich Beck, Anthony Giddens, and Scott Lash, 57–109. Cambridge, UK: Polity Press.

Gilroy, Paul. 1987. *There Ain't No Black in the Union Jack: The Cultural Politics of Race and Nation.* London: Hutchinson.

——. 1993. *The Black Atlantic: Modernity and Double Consciousness.* Cambridge, MA: Harvard University Press.

Glasser, Ruth. 1998. "Buscando Ambiente: Puerto Rican Musicians in New York City, 1917–1940." In *Island Sounds in the Global City: Caribbean and Popular Music and Identity in New York,* ed. Ray Allen and Lois Wilcken, 7–22. New York: New York Folklore Society and the Institute for Studies in American Music, Brooklyn College.

Gmelch, George, and Sharon Bohn. 1995. "Gender and Migration: The Readjustment of Women Migrants in Barbados, Ireland and Newfoundland." *Human Organization* 54 (Winter): 470–73.

Goellner, Ellen W., and Jacqueline Shea Murphy, eds. 1995. *Bodies of the Text: Dance as Theory, Literature as Dance.* New Brunswick, NJ: Rutgers University Press.

Goldberg, David Theo, ed. 1994. *Multiculturalism: A Critical Reader.* Oxford and Cambridge, MA: Blackwell.

Gomez, Mayte. 1995. "Healing the Border Wound: *Fronteras Americanas* and the Future of Canadian Multiculturalism." *Theatre Research in Canada* 16, 1–2: 26–39.

Gotfrit, Leslie. 1991. "Women Dancing Back: Disruption and the Politics of Pleasure." In *Postmodernism, Feminism, and Cultural Politics,* ed. Henry A. Giroux, 174–95. Albany, NY: State University of New York Press.

Gottlieb, William. 1992. "What Makes Rhumba?" In *Salsiology: Afro-Cuban Music and the Evolution of Salsa in New York,* ed. Vernon Boggs, 23–28. Westport CT: Greenwood.

Government of Quebec. 1978. *La politique québécoise du développement culturel.* 2 vols. Quebec: Editeur official.

——. 1981. *Autant de façons d'être Québécois: Plan d'action de gouvernement du Québec a l'intention des communautés culturelles.* 1st ed. Quebec: Ministère des Communautés culturelles et de l'Immigration.

——. 2000. Le goupe-conseil sur la Politique du patrimoine culturel du Québec. "Onzième Orientation: Des Communautés Ethnoculturelles." In *Notre patrimoine, un présent du passé: Proposition pour une politique du patrimoine culturel.* http://www.politique-patrimoine.org/html/Rapport/Chap3/Or11.html.

Gramsci, Antonio. 1971. *Selections from the Prison Notebooks.* Ed. Q. Hoare and G. Nowell. London: Lawrence and Wishart.

Grenier, Line, and Jocelyn Guilbault. 1990. "'Authority' Revisited: The 'Other' in Anthropology and Popular Music Studies." *Ethnomusicology* 34, 3: 381–97.

Grosz, Elizabeth. 1994. *Volatile Bodies: Toward a Corporeal Feminism*. Bloomington: Indiana University Press.

Guatemala. 1987. Ministerio de Cultura y Deporte, Direccion General de Bellas Artes, Folklore. *Musica de Guatemala*. Ciudad de Guatemala: Ministerio de Cultura y Deporte.

Guerra, Ramiro. 1993. *Calibán danzante: Procesos socioculturales de la danza en América Latina y en la zona del Caribe*. Reprint, Caracas: Monte Avile Editores Latinoamericana, 1998.

Guilbault, Jocelyne. 1997. "Interpreting World Music: A Challenge in Theory and Practice." *Popular Music* 16, 1: 31–44.

Guillot, Genevieve, and Germaine Prudhommeau. 1976. *The Book of Ballet*. Trans. Katherine Carson. Englewood Cliffs, NJ: Prentice-Hall.

Gutman, Amy. 1993. "The Challenge of Multiculturalism in Political Ethics." *Philosophy and Public Affairs* 22, 3: 171–206.

——— , ed. 1994. "Introduction." In *Multiculturalism: Examining the Politics of Recognition*, ed. Charles Taylor et al., 3–24. Princeton: Princeton University Press.

Hamilton Crowell, Nathaniel, Jr. 2002. "What Is Congolese in Caribbean Dance." In *Caribbean Dance from Abakuá to Zouk: How Movement Shapes Identity*, ed. Susanna Sloat, 11–20. Gainesville, FL: University Press of Florida.

Hanna, Judith Lynne. 1979a. *To Dance Is Human: A Theory of Nonverbal Communication*. Austin, TX: University of Texas Press.

——— . 1979b. "Toward a Cross-Cultural Conceptualization of Dance and Some Correlate Considerations." In *The Performing Arts: Music and Dance*, ed. John Blacking and Joann Kealiinohomoku, 17–47. The Hague: Mouton.

——— . 1987. "The Anthropology of Dance." In *Dance: Current Selected Research*, vol. 1, ed. Lynnette Y. Overby and James H. Humphrey, 219–37. New York: AMS Press.

——— . 1988. *Dance, Sex and Gender: Signs of Identity, Dominance, Defiance and Desire*. Chicago: University of Chicago Press.

Harvey, David. 1989. *The Condition of Postmodernity*. Oxford: Blackwell.

Havelock, Eric. 1991. "The Oral-Literate Equation: A Formula for the Modern Mind." In *Literacy and Orality*, ed. David R. Olson and Nancy Torrance, 11–27. Cambridge, UK: Cambridge University Press.

Hazzard-Gordon, Katrina. 1985. "African-American Vernacular Dance: Core Cultures and Meaning Operatives." *Journal of Black Studies* 15, 4: 427–45.

——— . 1990. *Jookin': The Rise of Social Dance Formations in African-American Culture*. Philadelphia: Temple University Press.

Hebdige, Dick. 1979. *Subculture: The Meaning of Style*. London: Methuen.

Hiebert, Daniel. 1999. "Local Geographies of Labour Market Segmentations: Montreal, Toronto and Vancouver, 1991." *Economic Geography* 75, 4 (October): 339–69.

Hine, Christine. 2000. *Virtual Ethnographies*. London: Sage.

Hirsh, Paul. 1972. "Processing Fads and Fashions: An Organization Set Analysis of Cultural Industry Systems." *American Journal of Sociology* 77: 639–59.

Ho, Cristine G. T. 1993. "The Internalization of Kinship and the Feminization of Caribbean Migration: The Case of Afro-Trinidadian Immigrants in Los Angeles." *Human Organization* 52 (Spring): 32–40.

Holmes, David. 2001. "Virtual Globalisation: Introduction." In *Virtual Globalization: Virtual Spaces/Tourist Spaces,* ed. David Holmes, 1–53. London and New York: Routledge.

hooks, bell. 1984. *Feminist Theory: From Margin to Center.* Boston: South End Press.

Hryniuk, Stella, ed. 1992. *Twenty Years of Multiculturalism: Success and Failures.* Winnipeg: St. John's College Press.

Jessop, Bob. 2005. "Interview with Bob Jessop." Department of Sociology, Lancaster University. http://www.lancs.ac.uk/fss/sociology/papers/jessop-interview.pdf.

Joppke, Christian. 1996. "Multiculturalism and Immigration: A Comparison of the United States, Germany, and Great Britain." *Theory and Society* 25: 449–500.

Jordan, Stephanie, and Helen Thomas. 1998. "Dance and Gender: Formalism and Semiotics Reconsidered." In *The Routledge Dance Studies Reader,* ed. Alexandra Carter, 241–49. London: Routledge.

Kaeppler, Adrienne. 1978. "Dance in Anthropological Perspective." *Annual Review of Anthropology* 7: 31–49.

———. 1985. "Structured Movement Systems in Tonga." In *Society and the Dance: The Social Anthropoiogy of Process and Performance,* ed. Paul Spencer, 92–114. Cambridge, UK: Cambridge University Press.

Kalin, Rudolf, and J. W. Berry. 1994. "Ethnic and Multicultural Attitudes." In *Ethnicity and Culture in Canada: The Research Landscape,* ed. J. W. Berry and J. A. Laponce, 293–321. Toronto: University of Toronto Press.

Kaplan, Cora. 1986. *Sea Changes: Essays on Culture and Feminism.* London: Verso.

Kaplan, David, and Robert A. Manners. 1972. *Culture Theory.* Englewood Cliffs, NJ: Prentice-Hall.

Kaplan, Jay. 1996–1997. "New York, New York: Cultural Life and Civic Experience in the Global City." *World Policy Journal* 13, 4 (Winter): 53–60.

Kealiinohomoku, Joann. 1979a. "Cultural Change: Functional and Dysfunctional Expressions of Dance, a Form of Affective Culture." In *The Performing Arts: Music and Dance,* ed. John Blacking and Joann W. Kealiinohomoku, 47–67. The Hague: Mouton.

———. 1979b. "You Dance What You Wear, and You Wear Your Cultural Values." In *The Fabrics of Culture: The Anthropology of Clothing and Adornment,* ed. J. M. Cordwell and R. A. Schwarz, 77–83. The Hague: Mouton.

———. 1983. "An Anthropologist Looks at Ballet As a Form of Ethnic Dance." In *What Is Dance?,* ed. Roger Copeland and Marshall Cohen, 533–49. Oxford, UK: Oxford University Press.

Kern, Stephen. 1975. *Anatomy and Destiny: A Cultural History of the Human Body.* New York: Bobbs-Merrill.

Kornreich, Jennifer. 1998. "Ballroom Blitz." *Detour Magazine*, September, 124–28.

Kostash, Myrna. 1995. "Ethnic Adventures of the Third Generation." *Journal of Canadian Studies* 30, 2 (Summer): 124–29.

Kubik, Gerhard. 1979. "Pattern Perception and Recognition in African Music." In *The Performing Arts: Music and Dance*, ed. John Blacking and Joann Kealiinohomoku, 221–51. The Hague: Mouton.

Labelle, Micheline, et al. 1987. *Histoires d'immigreés: Itinéraires d'ouvrières colombiennes, grecques, haïtiennes et portugaises de Montreal*. Montreal: Boréal.

"Lady Styling: Move Like a Diva with Karina." 2005. http://www.salsasite.com/classes/lady-styling.htm.

LaForest, Guy. 1993. "Introduction." In Charles Taylor, *Reconciling the Solitudes: Essays on Canadian Federalism and Nationalism*, ed. Guy LaForest, ix-xv. Montreal and Kingston: McGill-Queen's University Press, 1993.

Lefebvre, Henri. 1991. *Production of Space*. Oxford: Blackwell.

———. 1996. *Writings on Cities*. Oxford: Blackwell.

Lemieux, Denise. 1995. "Movements sociaux et culture: Le movement feministe au Québec." *Journal of Canadian Studies* (Spring): 75–89.

León, Argeliers. 1974. "De la Contradanza al Danzón." In *Bailes populares cubanos*, by María Antonia Fernández, 7–18. La Habana, Cuba: Editorial Pueblo y Educacíon.

Lévy, Pierre. 2001. *Cyberculture*. Trans. Robert Bononno. Minneapolis, MN: University of Minnesota Press.

Leymaire, Isabelle. 1993. *La Salsa et le Latin Jazz*. Paris: Presses Universitaires de France.

———. 1995. "Mambo Mania." *UNESCO Courier* 48, 1 (January): 40, http://www.laventure.net/tourist/mambo.htm.

Li, Peter S. 1994. "A World Apart: The Multicultural World of Visible Minorities and the Art World of Canada." *Canadian Review of Sociology and Anthropology* 31, 4: 365–91.

———, ed. 1990. *Race and Ethnic Relations in Canada*. Toronto: Oxford University Press.

Light, Jennifer S. 1999. "From City Space to Cyberspace." In *Virtual Geographies: Bodies, Spaces and Relations*, ed. Mike Crang, Phil Crang, and Jon May, 109–30. London and New York: Routledge.

Linares, María Teresa. 1974. *La musíca y el pueblo*. La Habana, Cuba: Editorial Pueblo y Educacíon.

Linteau, Paul André, et al. 1989a. *Histoire du Québec Contemporain*. Vol. 1, *De la Confédération à la crise, 1867–1929*. Montreal: Boréal.

———, et al. 1989b. *Histoire du Québec Contemporain*. Vol. 2, *Le Québec depuis 1930*. Montreal: Boréal.

Lipsitz, George. 1994. *Dangerous Crossroads: Popular Music, Postmodernism and the Poetics of Place*. London: Verso.

Lorde, Audre. 1984. *Sister Outside: Essays and Speeches*. Trumansburg, NY: Crossing Press.

Lubiano, Wahneema. 1996. "Like Being Mugged by a Metaphor." *Mapping Multiculturalism*, ed. Avery F. Gordon and Christopher Newfield, 64–75. Minneapolis: University of Minnesota Press.

Mahar, Cheleen, Richard Harker, and Chris Wilkes. 1990. "The Basic Theoretical Position." In *An Introduction to the Work of Pierre Bourdieu: The Practice of Theory*, ed. Cheleen Mahar, Richard Harker, and Chris Wilkes, 1–26. New York: St. Martin's Press.

Malnig, Julie. 1992. *Dancing 'Till Dawn: A Century of Exhibition Ballroom Dance*. Westport, CT: Greenwood.

———. 2001. "Two-Stepping to Glory: Social Dance and the Rhetoric of Social Mobility." In *Moving History/Dancing Cultures: A Dance History Reader*, ed. Ann Dills and Ann Cooper Albright, 271–87. Middletown, CT: Wesleyan University Press.

Malone, Jacqui. 1996. *Stepping on the Blues: The Visible Rhythms of African-American Dance*. Urbana, IL: University of Illinois Press.

MamBostOn2Online Salsa Congress. 7 August 2005. Video Gallery. http://www.mamboston2.com/Congress/vclips.php.

Manègre, Jean-Francois. 1994. *Statistiques: Demographie, Immigration et Communautés culturelles au Québec depuis 1871*. Montreal: Conseil des communautés culturelles et de l'Immigration.

Manuel, Peter. 1994a. "Puerto Rican Music and Cultural Identity: Creative Appropriation of Cuban Sources from Danza to Salsa." *Ethnomusicology* 38, 2: 249–80.

———. 1994b. "The Soul of the Barrio: 30 Years of Salsa." *NACLA Report on the Americas* 28, 2 (September): 22–25, http://www.kcsalsa.com/articles/Soul_of_the_Barrio.html.

———. 1995. *Caribbean Currents: Caribbean Music from Rumba to Reggae*. Philadelphia: Temple University Press.

———. 1998. "Representations of New York City in Latin Music." In *Island Sounds in the Global City: Caribbean Popular Music and Identity in New York*, ed. Ray Allen and Lois Wilcken, 23–43. New York: New York Folklore Society and the Institute for Studies in American Music, Brooklyn College.

Marcus, George, and Michael M. J. Fischer. 1986. *Anthropology As Cultural Critique: An Experimental Moment in Human Sciences*. Chicago: University of Chicago Press.

Marre, Jeremy, and Hannah Charleton. 1985. *Beats of the Heart: Popular Music of the World*. New York: Pantheon.

Martin, John. 1965. *The Dance in Theory*. Princeton, NY: Dance Horizons.

Martin, Michèle. 1997. *Communication and Mass Media: Culture, Domination and Opposition*. Trans. Benoît Ouellette. Scarborough, ON: Prentice-Hall.

Martínez Furé, Rogelio. 1974. "Las Comparsas." In *Bailes populares cubanos*, by María Antonia Fernández, 87–89. La Habana, Cuba: Editorial Pueblo y Educacíon.

Marx, Karl. 1844. "Alienated Labour." In *Karl Marx: Selected Writings*, ed. David McLellan, 77–87. Oxford: Oxford University Press, 1977.

Massumi, Brian. 2002. *Parables for the Virtual: Movement, Affect and Sensation*. Durham, NC, and London: Duke University Press.

Mattelart, Armand, and Michèle Mattelart. 1998. *Theories of Communication: A Short Introduction*. Trans. Susan Gruenbeck Taponier and James A. Cohen. London: Sage.

McDonagh, Don. 1979. *Dance Fever*. New York: Random House.

McMains, Juliet. 2000. "Brownface: A New Performance of Minstrelsy in Competitive Latin American Dancing?" Paper presented at the international conference "Dancing in the Millennium," Washington Marriot Hotel, George Washington University, Kennedy Center, Washington, DC, 19–23 July.

———. 2001/02. "Brownface: Representations of Latin-ness in Dancesport." *Dance Research Journal* 33, 2 (Winter): 54–71.

McRobbie, Angela. 1984. "Dance and Social Fantasy." In *Gender and Generation*, ed. Angela McRobbie and Mica Niva, 130–61. London: Macmillan.

———. 1991. *Feminism and Youth Culture: From "Jackie" to "Just Seventeen."* Houndmills, Basingstoke, Hampshire: Macmillan.

———. 1993. "Shut Up and Dance: Youth Culture and Changing Modes of Femininity." *Cultural Studies* 7, 3: 406–27.

———. 1997. "Second-Hand Dresses and the Ragmarket." In *The Subcultures Reader*, ed. Ken Gelder and Sarah Thornton, 191–99. London: Routledge.

Meintel, Deirdre, et al. 1987. "The New Double Workday of Immigrant Women Workers in Québec." *Women's Studies* 13: 273–93.

Mendieta, Eduardo. 2000. "The Making of New Peoples: Hispanizing Race." In *Hispanics/Latinos in the United States: Ethnicity, Race and Rights*, ed. Jorge J. E. Gracia and Pablo de Greiff, 45–60. New York: Routledge.

Men's Styling All-Day Bootcamp with Al "Liquid Silver" Espinoza. 2005. http://www.dancefreak.com/bootcamp/mens_bootcamp.htm.

Mercer, John. 1995. "Canadian Cities and Their Immigrants: New Realities." *Annals of the American Academy*, AAPSS 538 (March): 169–98.

Miège, Bernard. 1989. *The Capitalization of Cultural Production*. Trans. Josiane Hay and Nicolas Garnham. New York: International General Publishers.

Miller, Daniel, and Don Slater. 2000. *The Internet: An Ethnographic Approach*. Oxford: International Publishers.

Mitchell, Alanna. "Face of Big Cities Changing." *Globe and Mail*, 18 February 1998, A1, A3.

Mitra, Ananda. 2000. "Virtual Commonality: Looking for India on the Internet." In *The Cybercultures Reader*, ed. David Bell and Barbara M. Kennedy, 676–94. London and New York: Routledge.

———. 2004. "Voices of the Marginalized on the Internet: Examples from a Website for Women of South Asia." *Journal of Communication* (September): 492–510.

Moghaddam, Fathali M., et al. 1994. "The Warped Looking Glass: How Minorities Perceive Themselves, Believe They Are Perceived and Are Actually Perceived by Majority Group Members in Quebec, Canada." *Canadian Ethnic Studies* 26, 2: 112–23.

Moore, Alex. 1951. *Ballroom Dancing*. 6th ed. London: Sir Isaac Pitman and Sons.

Moore, Robin. 2002. "Salsa and Socialism: Dance Music in Cuba, 1959–99." In *Situating Salsa: Global Markets and Local Meaning in Latin Popular Music*, ed. Lise Waxer, 51–74. New York and London: Routledge.

Morakvasic, Mirjana. 1984. "Birds of Passage Are Also Women." *International Migration Review* 18 (Winter): 886–907.

Morley, David. 1986. *Family Television: Cultural Power and Domestic Leisure*. London: Routledge.

Mukerji, Chandra, and Michael Schudson. 1991a. "Introduction." In *Rethinking Popular Culture: Contemporary Perspectives in Cultural Studies*, ed. Chandra Mukerji and Michael Schudson, 1–61. Berkeley, CA: University of California Press.

———, and Michael Schudson, eds. 1991b. *Rethinking Popular Culture: Contemporary Perspectives in Cultural Studies*. Berkeley, CA: University of California Press.

Mulvey, Laura. 1975. "Visual Pleasure and Narrative Cinema." *Screen* 16, 3: 6–18.

Mulvey, Mina. 1991. "Forward." In *From the Ballroom to Hell: Grace and Folly in Nineteenth-Century Dance*, by Elizabeth Aldrich, 75–76. Evanston, IL: Northwestern University Press.

Narasimhan, R. 1991. "Literacy: Its Characterization and Implications." In *Literacy and Orality*, ed. David R. Olson and Nancy Torrance, 177–97. Cambridge, UK: Cambridge University Press.

Nederveen Pieterse, Jan. 1995. "Globalization As Hybridization." In *Global Modernities*, ed. Mike Featherstone, Scott Lash, and Roland Robertson, 45–68. London and Thousand Oaks, CA: Sage.

Negus, Keith. 1999. *Music Genres and Corporate Cultures*. London and New York: Routledge.

Ness, Sally Ann. 1996. "The Contribution of Kealiinohomoku's 'An Anthropologist Looks at Ballet as a Form of Ethnic Dance' to Anthropologist Research in Dance." Paper presented to the CORD Annual Meeting, Greensboro, NC, 9 November.

Nijman, Jan. 1997. "Globalization to a Latin Beat: The Miami Growth Machine." *Annals of the American Academy*, AAPSS 551 (May): 165–77.

Ninja, Willy. 1994. "Not a Mutant Turtle." In *Microphone Friends: Youth Music/Youth Culture*, ed. Andrew Ross and Tricia Rose, 160–62. New York and London: Routledge.

Novack, Cynthia J. 1990. *Sharing the Dance: Contact Improvisation and American Culture*. Madison: University of Wisconsin Press.

———. 1993. "Ballet, Gender and Cultural Power." In *Dance, Gender and Culture*, ed. Helen Thomas, 34–48. Reprint, New York: St. Martin's Press, 1995.

Nunes, Mark. 2001. "Ephemeral Cities: Postmodern Urbanism and the Production of Online Space." In *Virtual Globalization: Virtual Spaces/Tourist Spaces*, ed. David Holmes, 57–76. London and New York: Routledge.

Ong, Walter J. 1982. *Orality and Literacy: The Technologizing of the Word*. London and New York: Methuen.

Ortiz, Fernando. 1906. *Hampa afro-cubana: Los negros brujos (apuntes para un estudio de etnología criminal)*. Madrid, Spain: Librería de Fernando Fe.

———. 1940. *Contrapunteo cubano del tabaco y el azúcar: Advertencia de sus contrastes agrarios, económomicos, históricos y sociales, su etnografía y su transculturacíon.* Havana, Cuba: Jesús Montero.

———. 1943. "Por la integracíon cubana de blancos y negros." *Revista Bimestre Cubana* 51, 2: 256–72.

———. 1951. *Los bailes y el teatro de los negros en el folklore de Cuba.* 2nd ed. Reprint, La Habana, Cuba: Editorial Letras Cubanas, 1981.

Ortner, Sherry B. 1984. "Theory in Anthropology since the Sixties." *Comparative Studies in Society and History* 26: 126–66.

"Our Mag in Havana." 1 April 1999. http://www.salsaworld.co.uk/ngeneral.htm.

Pacini Hernández, Deborah. 1998. "Dancing with the Enemy: Cuban Popular Music, Race, Authenticity, and the World-Music Landscape." *Latin American Perspectives* 25, 3 (May): 110–25.

———. 2003. "Amalgamating Musics: Popular Music and Cultural Hybridity in the Americas." In *Musical Migrations: Transnationalism and Cultural Hybridity in Latin/o America,* vol. 1, ed. Frances R. Aparicio and Cándida F. Jáquez, with Mariá Elena Cepeda, 13–31. New York: Palgrave Macmillan.

Padilla, Felix M. 1989. "Salsa Music as Cultural Expression of Latino Consciousness and Unity." *Hispanic Journal of Behavioural Sciences* 11, 1 (February): 28–45.

Paquet, Gilles. 1994. "Political Philosophy of Multiculturalism." In *Ethnicity and Culture in Canada: The Research of Landscape,* ed. J. W. Berry and J. A. Laponce, 60–80. Toronto: University of Toronto Press.

Pedraza, Silvia. 1991. "Women and Migration: The Social Consequences of Gender." *Annual Review of Sociology* 17: 303–25.

Pessar, Patricia R. 1984. "The Linkage between the Household and Workplace of Dominican Women in the U.S." *International Migration Review* 18, 4 (Winter): 1188–1211.

———. 1995. "On the Homefront and in the Workplace: Integrating Immigrant Women into Feminist Discourse." *Anthropological Quarterly* 68: 37–47.

———. 1999a. "Engendering Migration Studies: The Case of New Immigrants in the United States." *American Behavioral Scientist* 42, 4 (January): 577–600.

———. 1999b. "The Role of Gender, Households and Social Networks in the Migration Process: A Review and Reappraisal." In *The Handbook of International Migration: The American Experience,* ed. Charles Hirschman, Philip Kasinitz, and Josh DeWind, 53–70. New York: Russell Sage Foundation.

Piedra, José. 1991. "Poetics for the Hip." *New Literary History* 22: 633–75.

Pietrobruno, Sheenagh. 2001. "Salsa and Its Transnational Moves: The Commodification of Latin Dance in Montréal." Ph.D. dissertation, Department of Art History and Communications Studies, McGill University.

———. 2002. "Embodying Canadian Multiculturalism: The Case of Salsa Dancing in Montreal." *Revista mexicana de estudios canadienses,* 3: n.p.

———. 2004a. "Dancing in Cyberspace: A Return to Orality through Hypertexts." Paper presented at the symposium "Body, Dance and Performance Practices," Interdisciplinary Centre on the Body and Performance, Goldsmiths College, London, UK, 31 January.

———. 2004b. "From Local Performances to Global Web Pages: Technologizing Movement." Paper presented at "Critical World: First International Conference," Centre culturel Georges-Vanier, Montreal, 13 November.

Pini, Maria. 1997. "Cyborg, Nomads and the Raving Feminine." In *Dance in the City*, ed. Helen Thomas, 111–29. New York: St. Martin's Press.

Pizanias, Caterina. 1996. "(Re)-thinking the Ethnic Body: Performing 'Greekness' in Canada." *Journal of the Hellenic Diaspora* 22, 1: 7–60.

Polhemus, Ted. 1993. "Dance, Gender and Culture." In *Dance, Gender and Culture*, ed. Helen Thomas, 3–15. Reprint, New York: St. Martin's Press, 1995.

Price, Janet, and Margrit Shildrick, eds. 1999. *Feminist Theory and the Body: A Reader*. New York: Routledge.

Radway, Janice A. 1993. "The Institutional Matrix of Romance." In *The Cultural Studies Reader*, ed. Simon During, 438–54. London: Routledge.

Richardson, P. J. S. 1948. *A History of English Ballroom Dancing, 1910–1945: The Story of the Development of the English Style*. London: Herbert Jenkins.

Ritzer, George. 2004. *The Globalization of Nothing*. Thousand Oaks, CA, and London: Sage and Pine Forge Press.

Robbins, James. 1989. "Practical and Abstract Taxonomy in Cuban Music." *Ethnomusicology* 33, 3: 379–89.

Robertson, Roland. 1992. *Globalization: Social Theory and Global Culture*. London: Sage.

———. 1995. "Glocalization: Time–Space and Homogeneity-Heterogeneity." In *Global Modernities*, ed. Mike Featherstone, Scott Lash, and Roland Robertson, 25–44. London: Sage.

Roman-Velazquez, Patria. 1999. "The Embodiment of Salsa: Musicians, Instruments and the Performance of a Latin Style and Identity." *Popular Music* 18, 1: 115–31.

———. 1999. *The Making of Latin London: Salsa Music, Place and Identity*. Aldershot: Ashgate.

Rondón, Cesar Miguel. 1980. *El libro de la salsa: Crónica de la música del caribe urbano*. Caracas, Venezuela: Editorial Arte.

Roy, Patricia E. 1995. "The Fifth Force: Multiculturalism and the English Canadian Identity." *Annals of the American Academy*, AAPSS 538 (March): 199–209.

Royce, Anya Peterson. 1977. *The Anthropology of Dance*. Bloomington, IN: Indiana University Press.

"Rueda Calls and Descriptions." 12 July 2005. http://www.salsarueda.com/rueda/rueda_calls.html.

Rust, Frances. 1969. *Dance in Society*. London: Routledge and Kegan Paul.

Safran, William. 1991. "Diasporas in Modern Societies: Myths of Homeland and Return." *Diasporas* 1, 1: 83–99.

"Salsa Dance Styles: North American Salsa Dancing versus Cuban or Latin style." 2003. Discussion forum, 5 December. http://www.tosalsa.com/DearTOsalsa/dto_dancestyles6.htm.

"Salsa and Mambo Dance History." 9 November 2000. http://homepages.ihug.co.nz/ ~nealchch/Salsa-History.htm.

Salsa Site. 2005. http://www.salsasite.com/classes/lady-styling.htm.

"Salsa Syllabus/Standards." 2003. Discussion forum, 15 December. http://www .tosalsa.com/DearTOsalsa/dto111salsastands.htm.

Sánchez González, Lisa. 1999. "Reclaiming Salsa." *Cultural Studies* 13, 2: 237–50.

Sánchez Vignot, Roberto. 2004. Director of the Cutumba Folkloric Ensemble, 9 July. http://www.qbania.com/rsv_2.htm.

Santos Gracia, Caridad, and Nieves Armas Rigal. 2002. *Danzas Populares Tradicionales Cubanas*. La Habana, Cuba: Centro de Investigacíon y Desarrollo de la Cultura Cubana Juan Marinello.

Sardar, Ziauddin. 2000. "Alt.Civilization.Faq: Cyberspace As the Darker Side of the West." In *The Cybercultures Reader*, ed. David Bell and Barbara M. Kennedy, 732–52. London and New York: Routledge.

Savagliano, Marta E. 1995a. *Tango and the Political Economy of Passion*. Boulder, CO: Westview Press.

———. 1995b. "Whiny Ruffians and Rebellious Broads: Tango As a Spectacle of Eroticized Social Tension." *Theatre Journal* 47: 83–104.

———. 1996. "Fragments for a Story of Tango Bodies: On Choreocritics and the Memory of Power." In *Corporealities: Dancing Knowledge, Culture and Power*, ed. Susan Leigh Foster, 199–232. London: Routledge.

Sawicki, Jana. 1991. *Disciplining Foucault: Feminism, Power and Body*. New York and London: Routledge.

Schilling, Chris. 1993. *The Body and Social Theory*. London: Sage.

Senghor, Léopold Sédar. 1956. "African-Negro Aesthetics." *Diogenes* 16 (Winter): 23–38

Shaw, Peter. 1998. "Clean Dancing." *Commentary* 86 (October): 53–54.

Shildrick, Margrit, with Janet Price. 1999. "Openings on the Body: A Critical Introduction." In *Feminist Theory and the Body: A Reader*, ed. Janet Price and Margrit Shildrick, 1–31. New York: Routledge.

Smith, Allen. 1970. "Metaphor and Nationality in North America." *Canadian Historical Review* 51, 3 (September): 247–75.

Smith, Barbara. 1988. *The Truth That Never Hurts: Writings on Race, Gender and Freedom*. New Brunswick, NJ, and London: Rutger's University Press.

Smith, Marc A., and Peter Kollock, eds. 1999. *Communities in Cyberspace*. London and New York: Routledge.

Sommer, Sally. 1996. "Check Your Body at the Door." Video and discussion, the CORD Annual Meeting, Greensboro, NC, 9 November.

"Sonny Watson's Dance History: The Hustle." 2001. *Dance History Archive*, 9 March. http://www.streetswing.com/histmain/z3hustl1.htm.

Sorkin, Michael. 1992. "Introduction: Variations on a Theme Park." In *Variations on a Theme Park: The New American City and the End of Public Space*, ed. Michael Sorkin, xi–xv. New York: Hill and Wang.

Spencer, Paul. 1985. *Society and Dance: The Social Anthropology of Process and Performance*. Cambridge, UK: Cambridge University Press.

Stanton, Gareth. 1996. "Ethnography, Anthropology and Cultural Studies: Links and Connections." In *Cultural Studies and Communications*, ed. James Curran, David Morley, and Valerie Walkerdine, 334–58. London and New York: E. Arnold.

Stearns, Marshall, and Jean Stearns. 1968. *Jazz Dance: The Story of American Vernacular Dance*. Reprint, New York: Da Capo, 1994.

Stefik, Mark. 1997. *Internet Dreams: Archetypes, Myths and Metaphors*. Cambridge, MA: MIT Press.

Stephens, Mitchell. 1998. "Which Communication Revolution Is It, Anyway?" *Journalism and Mass Communications Quarterly* 75, 1 (Spring): 9–13.

Stephenson, Richard M., and Joseph Iaccarino. 1980. *The Complete Book of Ballroom Dancing*. New York: Doubleday.

Steward, Sue. 1994. "Dancing with the Saints: The International Sound of Salsa." In *World Music: Rough Guide*, ed. Simon Broughton et al., 485–95. London: Penguin.

———. 2000. "Salsa: Cubans, Nuyoricans and the Global Sound." In *World Music*, vol. 2, *Latin and North America, Caribbean, India, Asia and Pacific: Rough Guide*, ed. Simon Broughton and Mark Ellingham, 488–506. London: Penguin.

Stewart, Susan. 1993. *On Longing: Narratives of the Miniature, the Gigantic, the Souvenir, the Collection*. Durham, NC, and London: Duke University Press.

Storm Roberts, John. 1999. *The Latin Tinge: The Impact of Latin American Music on the United States*. 2nd ed. 1979. New York: Oxford University Press.

Straw, Will. 1991. "Systems of Articulation, Logics of Change: Communities and Scenes in Popular Music." *Cultural Studies* 5, 3: 368–88.

———. 1993. "The Booth, the Floor and the Wall: Dance Music and the Fear of Falling." *Public* 8: 169–82.

———. 2001. "Dance Music." In *The Cambridge Companion to Rock and Pop*, ed. Simon Frith, Will Straw, and John Street, 158–75. Cambridge, UK: Cambridge University Press.

Studlar, Gaylyn. 1993. "Valentino, 'Optic Intoxication' and Dance Madness." In *Screening the Male: Exploring Masculinities in Hollywood Cinema*, ed. Stevan Cohan and Ina Rae Hark, 23–46. London: Routledge.

Szwed, John F., and Morton Marks. 1988. "The Afro-American Transformation of European Set Dances and Dance Suites." *Dance Research Journal* 20, 1: 29–36.

Tambiah, Stanley J. 2000. "Transnational Movements, Diaspora and Multiple Modernities." *Daedalus* 129, 1 (Winter): 163–94.

Taylor, Charles. 1986. "Foucault on Freedom and Truth." In *Foucault: A Critical Reader*, ed. Marcus Couzens Hoy, 69–103. Oxford: Basil Blackwell.

———. 1994. "The Politics of Recognition." In *Multiculturalism: Examining the Politics of Recognition*, ed. Amy Gutman, 25–73. Princeton, NJ: Princeton University Press.

Therborn, Göran. 1995. "Routes to/through Modernity." In *Global Modernities*, ed. Mike Featherstone, Scott Lash, and Roland Robertson, 108–39. London: Sage.

Thomas, Helen. 1995. *Dance, Modernity and Culture*. London: Routledge.

———. 1996. "Do You Want to Join the Dance? Postmodernism/Poststructuralism, the Body and Dance." In *Moving Words: Re-Writing Dance*, ed. Gay Morris, 63–87. London: Routledge.

———, and Nicola Miller. 1997. "Ballroom Blitz." *Dance in the City*, ed. Helen Thomas, 89–110. New York: St. Martin's Press.

Thompson, John Herd, and Morton Weinfeld. 1995. "Entry and Exit: Canadian Immigration Policy in Context." *Annals of the American Academy*, AAPSS 538 (March): 185–98.

Thompson, Robert Farris. 2002. "Teaching the People to Triumph Over Time: Notes from the World of Mambo." In *Caribbean Dance from Abakuá to Zouk: How Movement Shapes Identity*, ed. Susanna Sloat, 336–44. Gainesville, FL: University Press of Florida.

Thornton, Robert J. 1992. "The Rhetoric of Ethnographic Holism." In *Rereading Cultural Anthropology*, ed. George Marcus, 15–33. Durham NC: Duke University Press.

Thornton, Sarah. 1994. "Moral Panic, the Media and British Rave Culture." In *Microphone Friends: Youth Music/Youth Culture*, ed. Andrew Ross and Tricia Rose, 176–93. London: Routledge.

———. 1995. *Club Cultures: Music, Media and Subcultural Capital*. Hanover, NH: University Press of New England.

Tomlinson, John. 1999. *Globalization and Culture*. Cambridge, UK: Polity Press.

Toto-Morn, Maura I. 1995. "Gender, Class, Family and Migration: Puerto Rican Women in Chicago." *Gender and Society* 9 (December): 712–26.

Turner, Bryan. 1984. *The Body and Society*. Oxford: Basil Blackwell.

Turow, Joseph. 1997. *Media Systems in Society: Understanding Industries, Strategies and Power*. 2nd ed. New York: Longman.

Urfé, Odilio. 1974. "Del Mambo Y El Cha-Cha-Chá." In *Bailes populares cubanos*, by María Antonia Fernández, 71–72. La Habana, Cuba: Editorial Pueblo y Educacíon.

Urquía, Norman. 2004. "'Doin' It Right': Contested Authority in London's Salsa Scene." In *Music Scenes: Local, Translocal, and Virtual*, ed. Andy Bennett and Richard A. Peterson, 96–112. Nashville, TN: Vanderbilt University Press.

Valenzuela, Lidice. 2005. "Music with the Values of the American People: An Interview with Maria Teresa Linares." *CubaNow.net: The Digital Magazine of Cuban Arts and Culture*, 20 June. http://www.cubanow.info/global/loader.php?secc=1&cont=feature/num13/index.htm.

Vermay, Ruud. 1994. *Latin: Thinking, Sensing and Doing in Latin American Dancing*. Munich: Kasterl Verlag.

Virilio, Paul. 2000. *Polar Inertia*. Trans. Patrick Camiller. London: Sage.

Walsh, David. 1993. "Saturday Night Fever: An Ethnography of Disco Dancing." In *Dance, Gender and Culture*, ed. Helen Thomas, 112–18. Reprint, New York: St. Martin's Press, 1995.

Ward, Andrew. 1993. "Dancing in the Dark: Rationalism and the Neglect of Social Dance." In *Dance, Gender and Culture*, ed. Helen Thomas, 16–34. Reprint, New York: St. Martin's Press, 1995.

Washburne, Christopher. 2002. "Salsa Romántica: An Analysis of Style." In *Situating Salsa: Global Markets and Local Meaning in Latin Popular Music*, ed. Lise Waxer, 101–21. New York and London: Routledge.

Waxer, Lise. 2002a. *The City of Musical Memory: Salsa, Record Grooves, and Popular Culture in Cali, Colombia*. Middletown, CT: Wesleyan University Press.

——. 2002b. "*Llegó la Salsa*: The Rise of Salsa in Venezuela and Colombia." In *Situating Salsa: Global Markets and Local Meaning in Latin Popular Music*, ed. Lise Waxer, 219–45. New York: Routledge.

——. 2002c. "Situating Salsa: Latin Music at the Crossroads." In *Situating Salsa: Global Markets and Local Meaning in Latin Popular Music*, ed. Lise Waxer, 3–22. New York: Routledge.

——. 2002d. *Situating Salsa: Global Markets and Local Meaning in Latin Popular Music*. New York: Routledge.

Weinfeld, Morton. 1988. "Ethnic and Race Relations." In *Understanding Canadian Society*, ed. J. Curtis and L. Tepperman, 587–618. Toronto: McGraw-Hill Ryerson.

"Welcome to Streethustle." 9 March 2001. http://www.thedancekings.com/page1.html.

Wellman, Barry, and Milena Gulia, 1999. "Virtual Communities As Communities: Net Surfers Don't Ride Alone." In *Communities in Cyberspace*, ed. Mark A. Smith and Peter Kollock, 167–94. London and New York: Routledge.

Werbner, Pnina. 1997. "Introduction: The Dialectics of Cultural Hybridity." In *Debating Cultural Hybridity: Multi-Cultural Identities and the Politics of Anti-Racisim*, ed. Pnina Werbner and Tariq Modood, 1–26. London: Zed Books.

Wieviorka, Michel. 1998. "Is Multiculturalism the Solution?" *Ethnic and Racial Studies* 21, 5 (September): 881–910.

Williams, Drid. 1978. "Deep Structures of the Dance." *Yearbook of Symbolic Anthropology* 1: 211–30.

Willis, Paul. 1975. "The Expressive Style of a Motor Bike Culture." In *The Body as Medium of Expression*, ed. J. Benthall and T. Polhemus. London: Allen, Lane.

Wolff, Janet. 1975. *Hermeneutic Philosophy and the Sociology of Art*. London: Routledge and Kegan Paul.

——. 1997. "Reinstating Corporeality: Feminism and Body Politics." In *Meaning in Motion: New Cultural Studies of Dance*, ed. Jane C. Desmond, 81–99. Durham, NC, and London: Duke University Press.

Wright, Gwendolyn. 1998. "On Modern Vernaculars and J.B. Jackson." *The Geographical Review* 88, 4 (October): 474–82.

Yeo, Loo Yen. 1999. "A History of Salsa." Part 7, "Salsa in the U.K." Salsa and Merengue Society. http://www.salsa-merengue.co.uk/revealit/histsal/part7.html.

~

About the Author

Sheenagh Pietrobruno is Assistant Professor of English at Fatih University in Istanbul. Previously, she was a Postdoctoral Research Fellow at Gold-smiths College, University of London. She also holds a doctoral degree in communication studies from McGill University in Montreal.